DEAREST VICKY, DARLING FRITZ

❖ ❖ ❖ ❖ ❖

The Tragic Love Story of
Queen Victoria's Eldest Daughter
and the German Emperor

JOHN VAN DER KISTE

SUTTON PUBLISHING

First published in 2001 by
Sutton Publishing Limited · Phoenix Mill
Thrupp · Stroud · Gloucestershire · GL5 2BU

British Library Cataloguing in Publication Data
A catalogue record for this book is available from the British
Library.

ISBN 0 7509 2583 3

Typeset in 11/14.5 pt Sabon.
Typesetting and origination by
Sutton Publishing Limited.
Printed and bound in England by
J.H. Haynes & Co. Ltd, Sparkford.

Contents

Sources and Acknowledgements

Vicky has attracted several biographers, from the anonymous writer (believed to be Marie Belloc Lowndes) of the authoritative *The Empress Frederick: a Memoir* (1913), her friend Princess Catherine Radziwill (1934), and a rather emotional, unsympathetic account by E.E.P. Tisdall (1940), to more recent studies by Richard Barkeley (1956), Egon Conte Caesar Corti (1957), Daphne Bennett (1971), Andrew Sinclair (1981) and Hannah Pakula (1996).

Fritz has fared less well. Within three years there were two biographies, a short volume by Rennell Rodd (1888) and a more extensive one by Lucy Taylor (1891). Apart from a few titles published only in Germany, there were no works in English between a one-volume English translation of Margaretha von Poschinger's three-volume life edited by Sidney Whitman (1901) and one by the present author (1981). A more recent study by Patricia Kollander (1995), a political rather than personal life, has necessitated a re-evaluation of his liberal principles, which in her view have been rather exaggerated. To these may be added a dual biography of both published during their lifetime, by Dorothea Roberts (1887), which is naturally incomplete but still useful within its limitations.

These have been supplemented by a valuable series of correspondence and diaries. The Empress's letters to and from Queen Victoria have been edited successively by Roger Fulford and Agatha Ramm in six volumes, supplementing two earlier works, the controversial, largely political *Letters of the Empress Frederick*, edited by her godson Sir Frederick Ponsonby (1928) and the more personal *The Empress Frederick writes to Sophie*, edited by Arthur Gould Lee (1955). Selections from the Emperor's diaries have been published in English translation, notably his 'war diary' kept during the Franco-Prussian campaign, and those describing his travels to the east and to Spain.

Sources and Acknowledgements

I wish to acknowledge the gracious permission of Her Majesty The Queen to publish certain letters of which she owns the copyright, and others which are held in the Royal Archives, Windsor. For permission to publish the latter I wish to acknowledge the gracious permission of Prince Moritz, Landgraf von Hessen, as representative of the owners of copyright in the Empress Frederick's letters. I am also indebted to the India Office Library, British Museum, for permission to publish extracts from correspondence between the Emperor, Empress, and Count Seckendorff with Baron Napier of Magdala.

I am grateful to the following publishers for permission to quote from printed sources: Cambridge University Press (*Young Wilhelm*, by John Röhl, © 1998; *The Holstein Papers*, edited by Norman Rich & M.H. Fisher, © 1955–63); Cassell Ltd (*The English Empress*, Conte Egon Caesar Corti, © 1957); and Greenwood Press (*Frederick III, Germany's liberal Emperor*, by Patricia Kollander, © 1995).

As ever I am eternally grateful to various friends for their moral support, advice and loan of various materials while writing this book, especially Karen Roth, Sue Woolmans, Theo Aronson, Dale Headington, and Robin Piguet; to the staff of Kensington and Chelsea Public Libraries, for ready access to their reserve collection; to my editors, Jaqueline Mitchell and Paul Ingrams. Last but not least, my mother, Kate Van der Kiste, has as always been a tower of strength in discussions on the subject and in reading through the draft manuscript.

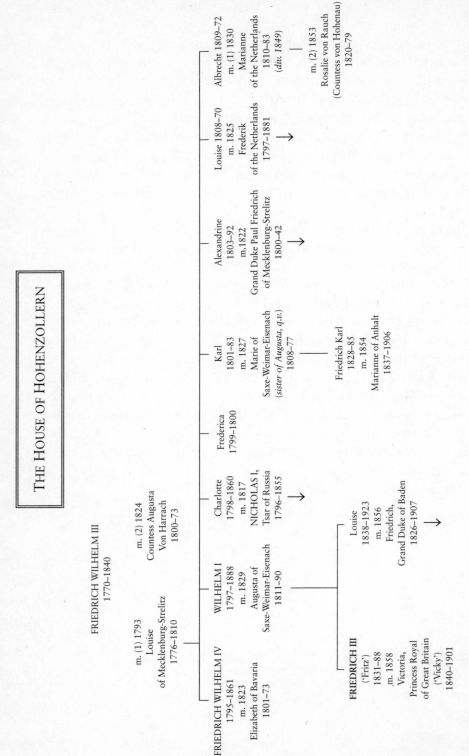

THE HOUSE OF HOHENZOLLERN

FRIEDRICH WILHELM III
1770–1840

m. (1) 1793
Louise
of Mecklenburg-Strelitz
1776–1810

m. (2) 1824
Countess Augusta
Von Harrach
1800–73

FRIEDRICH WILHELM IV
1795–1861
m. 1823
Elizabeth of Bavaria
1801–73

WILHELM I
1797–1888
m. 1829
Augusta of
Saxe-Weimar-Eisenach
1811–90

Charlotte
1798–1860
m. 1817
NICHOLAS I,
Tsar of Russia
1796–1855
→

Frederica
1799–1800

Karl
1801–83
m. 1827
Marie of
Saxe-Weimar-Eisenach
(*sister of Augusta, q.v.*)
1808–77

Friedrich Karl
1828–85
m. 1854
Marianne of Anhalt
1837–1906

Alexandrine
1803–92
m.1822
Grand Duke Paul Friedrich
of Mecklenburg-Strelitz
1800–42
→

Louise 1808–70
m. 1825
Frederik
of the Netherlands
1797–1881
→

Albrecht 1809–72
m. (1) 1830
Marianne
of the Netherlands
1810–83
(*div. 1849*)

m. (2) 1853
Rosalie von Rauch
(Countess von Hohenau)
1820–79

FRIEDRICH III
('Fritz')
1831–88
m. 1858
Victoria,
Princess Royal
of Great Britain
('Vicky')
1840–1901

Louise
1838–1923
m. 1856
Friedrich,
Grand Duke of Baden
1826–1907
→

for descendants see next table

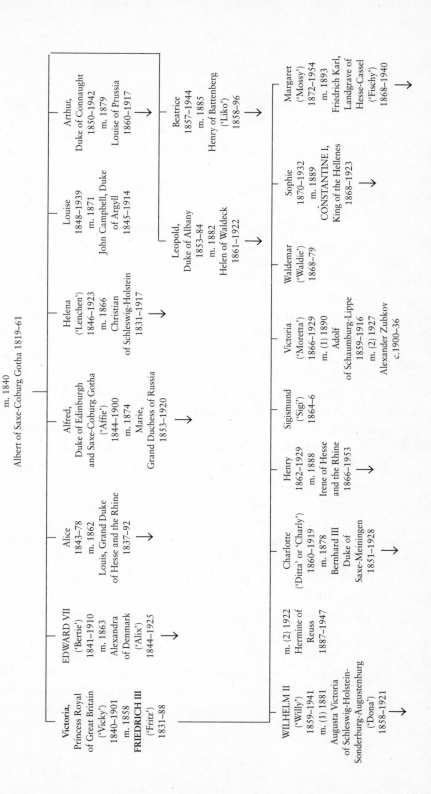

THE HOUSE OF SAXE-COBURG GOTHA

VICTORIA
1819–1901
m. 1840
Albert of Saxe-Coburg Gotha 1819–61

Victoria,
Princess Royal
of Great Britain
('Vicky')
1840–1901
m. 1858
FRIEDRICH III
('Fritz')
1831–88

EDWARD VII
('Bertie')
1841–1910
m. 1863
Alexandra
of Denmark
('Alix')
1844–1925

Alice
1843–78
m. 1862
Louis, Grand Duke
of Hesse and the Rhine
1837–92

Alfred,
Duke of Edinburgh
and Saxe-Coburg Gotha
('Affie')
1844–1900
m. 1874
Marie,
Grand Duchess of Russia
1853–1920

Helena
('Lenchen')
1846–1923
m. 1866
Christian
of Schleswig-Holstein
1831–1917

Louise
1848–1939
m. 1871
John Campbell, Duke
of Argyll
1845–1914

Arthur,
Duke of Connaught
1850–1942
m. 1879
Louise of Prussia
1860–1917

Leopold,
Duke of Albany
1853–84
m. 1882
Helen of Waldeck
1861–1922

Beatrice
1857–1944
m. 1885
Henry of Battenberg
('Liko')
1858–96

WILHELM II
('Willy')
1859–1941
m. (1) 1881
Augusta Victoria
of Schleswig-Holstein-
Sonderburg-Augustenburg
('Dona')
1858–1921

m. (2) 1922
Hermine of
Reuss
1887–1947

Charlotte
('Ditta' or 'Charly')
1860–1919
m. 1878
Bernhard III
Duke of
Saxe-Meiningen
1851–1928

Henry
1862–1929
m. 1888
Irene of Hesse
and the Rhine
1866–1953

Sigismund
('Sigi')
1864–6

Victoria
('Moretta')
1866–1929
m. (1) 1890
Adolf
of Schaumburg-Lippe
1859–1916
m. (2) 1927
Alexander Zubkov
c.1900–36

Waldemar
('Waldie')
1868–79

Sophie
1870–1932
m. 1889
CONSTANTINE I,
King of the Hellenes
1868–1923

Margaret
('Mossy')
1872–1954
m. 1893
Friedrich Karl,
Landgrave of
Hesse-Cassel
('Fischy')
1868–1940

Introduction

On 25 January 1858 'Vicky', Princess Royal, eldest daughter of Queen Victoria and Albert, Prince Consort, of England married 'Fritz', Prince Friedrich Wilhelm, second in succession to the throne of Prussia. London sparkled with illuminations in her public buildings and firework displays in her grand parks. The festivities spread far beyond the centre of the capital as the whole nation went *en fête* for 'England's Daughter' and her husband, with gifts and public dinners for the needy in cities up and down the country.

Having made their responses 'very *plainly*', in Queen Victoria's words, at the altar in the chapel of St James's, Vicky and Fritz walked hand in hand to the vestry to join the rest of the family for the signing of the marriage register, full of confidence and beaming at the assembled guests. Before the wedding breakfast they stepped out on to the balcony at Buckingham Palace, to be cheered by the crowds in Pall Mall who had braved the winter cold for a glimpse of the Royal couple. They may have been overwhelmed by this reception, conscious of the fact that they were carrying the hopes of a generation; but they were deliriously happy nonetheless. When bride and groom reached Windsor later that day they were met by yet more fireworks, a guard of honour, and a crowd of boys from Eton College who pulled their carriage from the railway station uphill to the castle. It was a heady start to one of the great love matches of its time.

Historians and biographers have never doubted that it was, in personal terms, an extremely successful marriage. Thirteen years later, a political union was achieved; but it was neither the united constitutional or liberal power that they and their elders had envisaged. Within less than five years of the wedding, two events occurred which were to shake the destiny of the young couple to its very core: firstly, the unexpected death of their mentor, Vicky's father, Prince Albert; and secondly, the appointment of Count Otto von Bismarck as Minister-President of Prussia. Ultimately, Vicky and Fritz were to be eclipsed by the ambitions of their eldest son, Wilhelm, and by the eventual failure of the hoped-for alliance which would later disintegrate into the carnage and confusion of the First World War.

Personal factors apart, the marriage had begun with high hopes. It was a truly grand dynastic alliance between the Hohenzollerns of Prussia and Queen Victoria's family of Saxe-Coburg and Gotha, later the House of Windsor, intended to bring to fruition the vision of Prince Albert and his mentors, King Leopold of the Belgians and Baron Christian von Stockmar, of a united, liberal and constitutional Germany. This was to be led by Prussia, with King Friedrich Wilhelm and his consort, a 'second' Queen Victoria, at the helm. At the same time as it was intended to fulfil this high-minded ambition, however, theirs was undeniably a genuine love match. For, in the annals of nineteenth century history, Vicky and Fritz were almost uniquely well-suited. She was a charming, bubbly, naïve child of seventeen; he a handsome, chivalrous, yet somewhat withdrawn and self-effacing young man of twenty-six. They had been besotted with one another since their betrothal a little over two years before, and were to remain passionately in love for thirty more years.

Most royal matrimonial unions of the age were marriages of convenience for which the parents, usually in consultation with their senior ministers and ambassadors at court, arranged betrothals between more-or-less eligible parties for reasons of state, sometimes when the princes and princesses concerned were little more than children. Certainly, they may never even have met. If such a marriage turned out to be a personal success, as it did in the case of King William IV and the much younger Queen Adelaide of England, all well and good. In many cases, for example that of Fritz's ill-matched parents, Wilhelm and Augusta, husband and wife were totally incompatible and remained thus for almost sixty years during which they lived more happily apart.

Sadly, Vicky and Fritz's eldest son and heir Willy, later Kaiser Wilhelm II, did not personify the peaceful or liberal instincts of his parents, but came under the darker influence of his own 'mentor', the nationalist hard-liner, Bismarck. It was one of the tragedies of modern history that this enlightened couple were denied the chance to play the role for which they had been so well prepared, of helping to create the political climate for a more liberal united Germany, which would take its place as one of the leading nations of Europe in an era of unprecedented peace and stability.

On 25 January 1858, it had all seemed so well within their grasp. But, by the time Fritz ascended the throne a little over thirty years later as Emperor, he was already mortally ill. Ironically, the man who had struggled all his life to find a voice in the affairs of his nation died voiceless, robbed of speech by cancer of the larynx. His reign lasted a mere three months, whereupon such political import-ance as his wife ever possessed ceased abruptly; and, for her remaining thirteen years, she was reluctantly tolerated and often abused by a son under whose rule she found no political satisfaction and only a degree of personal contentment.

Was Vicky a courageous, grossly maligned woman determined to do the best for her adopted Prussia – and later Germany – without regard to the personal consequences for herself; or was she the tactless, domineering Englishwoman, a pampered Princess who remained a slavish disciple of her long-dead father, refusing to accept that there was any other way than the English one? Was Fritz an enlightened Prince who realized that the political mood in Germany was changing, and that the royal house had to change with it; or was he a dreamy, weak-willed depressive who allowed his wife to dominate him? As *The Times* of London had noted presciently when discussing their betrothal back in 1855, these two complex, ultimately tragic characters surely deserved 'a better fate'.

ONE

'She seemed almost too perfect'

On 18 October 1831, Prince Friedrich Wilhelm Niklaus Karl of Prussia was born at the Neue Palais, Potsdam, the first child and only son of Prince Wilhelm and Princess Augusta. Within the family he was always known as Fritz, and more formally as Prince Friedrich, until the age of eight. At his birth he was third in succession to the throne.

Prince Wilhelm, second son of Crown Prince Friedrich Wilhelm and his wife, the former Princess Louise of Mecklenburg-Strelitz, was born on 22 March 1797. Almost eight months later, on 16 November, his grandfather King Friedrich Wilhelm II died after a reign of eleven years. According to his great-great-grandson, the last King of Prussia and German Emperor, he had been 'indolent, good-humoured, vain, a server of women, incapable of wide vision and lofty flights of mind'.[1] The Crown Prince succeeded him as King Friedrich Wilhelm III and reigned for forty-two years.

As the marriage of the King's eldest son and namesake to Elizabeth of Bavaria was childless, it was Wilhelm's responsibility to marry and produce an heir. Much to the misfortune of all involved, the only woman whom he ever really loved was Elise Radziwill, a member of the Polish nobility who were considered inferior in rank to the Hohenzollerns of Prussia. He wished to marry her, and in order to facilitate betrothal it was suggested that his brother-in-law, Tsar Nicholas I of Russia, who had married his sister Charlotte, should be asked to adopt Elise as his daughter. Nothing came of this, or of a scheme for one of the other Hohenzollern princes to do likewise. In his heart no princess could ever take the place of his beloved Elise, who died in 1834 of consumption, or a broken heart, as contemporary gossips would have it. All the same, he was ordered to look to the other reigning families of Germany for a more eligible bride.

1

On 11 June 1829 he married Augusta of Saxe-Weimar Eisenach, one of the most politically advanced states in the German Confederation. She deserved better than this dour, reactionary Prussian soldier prince, who was fourteen years her senior. A vivacious young woman in whom her tutor the poet Goethe had inculcated a keen appreciation of literature, she was a free-thinker with liberal sympathies and a sense of religious toleration at odds with the bigotry, anti-Semitism, anti-Catholicism and generally narrow outlook of the philistine Berlin court. Many a true word is spoken in jest, and her brother-in-law Crown Prince Friedrich Wilhelm said it all when he commented wryly that if he and his brothers had been born sons of a petty official he would have become an architect, Wilhelm a sergeant-major, Karl would have gone to prison, and Albrecht would have been a ne'er-do-well.[2]

In nearly sixty years of marriage Wilhelm and Augusta would eventually develop a grudging mutual respect, but they were happier under separate roofs. It did not take her long to find he was seeking his pleasures elsewhere, and she naïvely appealed to her father-in-law who told her patronizingly that if she expected a model of virtue in her husband, she should not have married a Hohenzollern.[3] This loveless union turned her into a disagreeable woman with what Catherine Radziwill, Elise's distant relative, called 'an almost insane need of flattery', noting that 'only those who told her that she was perfection itself ever obtained her favour or enjoyed her confidence.'[4] Nevertheless conjugal relations had to be maintained long enough for husband and wife to do their duty to the state, and two years after the wedding Fritz was born. Seven years later, with the birth of a daughter Louise on 3 December 1838, the family was complete.

Wilhelm was an unimaginative, remote father who took little interest in his son. Fritz was brought up by nurses and governesses until he was seven, when Colonel von Unruh, his father's aide-de-camp, was appointed his military governor while Friedrich Godet, a Swiss theologian, and Dr Ernst Curtius, a professor of classics, became his tutors. Learning was considered less important than introducing the boy to military routine, which included drill, the study of artillery, and practical aspects such as shoeing, harnessing, grooming cavalry horses, and cleaning their tack. His father insisted that he should grow up to be a good soldier, turning out punctually and smartly on parade regardless of the weather. One wet day a palace servant watched him on his exercises while soaked to the skin, and dashed out to the parade ground with an umbrella to hold over him. The little prince refused to take advantage of such shelter, asking the well-intentioned man indignantly if he had 'ever seen a Prussian helmet under a *thing like that*?'[5]

Off the parade ground, Godet and Curtius supervised his learning languages, music, dancing, gymnastics, book-binding, carpentry, and the rudiments of typesetting, and when he was twelve the proprietor of a Berlin printing firm presented him with a small hand-printing press. Though he neither liked nor understood mathematics and science he acquired a taste for reading, and spent much of his spare time in the royal library. As a boy he rarely attended the theatre or concert hall. His father declared that music gave him a headache, and he once walked out of a Wagner opera to go on manoeuvres.

On 7 June 1840 King Friedrich Wilhelm III died. His eldest son, now King Friedrich Wilhelm IV, a bald, ugly man with a high-pitched voice and a taste for the bottle, was a contradictory character who wanted to be remembered as a progressive monarch. His accession was marked with an amnesty for political prisoners, concessions to the Roman Catholic church, and a relaxation in press censorship. He enjoyed planning and building castles in mock-Renaissance style, and he was one of the few Hohenzollerns who really appreciated the fine arts. Nonetheless his horror of the French revolution had given him an almost medieval view of his position, and the idea of becoming a constitutional monarch in the British sense was anathema to him. Politically he was a reactionary at heart, agreeing with his contemporaries that only soldiers were any help against democrats. His brother Wilhelm, now heir apparent, was styled Prince of Prussia, and at the age of eight Fritz, henceforth known formally as Prince Friedrich Wilhelm, became heir presumptive.

Three days after the accession of King Friedrich Wilhelm IV, Queen Victoria and Prince Albert of England were leaving Buckingham

3

Palace for a drive up Constitution Hill in an open carriage, when a youth fired his pistol at them and narrowly missed. Thankfully they were unhurt, for the Queen was some three months pregnant with her first child. On 21 November she went into labour, and when the doctor announced almost apologetically that the baby was a princess, she answered defiantly that 'the next will be a Prince'.[6] Referred to as 'the child' until her christening in February 1841, the infant was named Victoria Adelaide Mary Louisa, and styled Princess Royal as the sovereign's eldest daughter. Called Puss or Pussy at first by her parents, she later became Vicky and remained thus *en famille* for the rest of her life.

Prince Albert was delighted with her winning ways and agile mind, and she always remained his favourite child. The Queen's elder half-sister Feodora of Hohenlohe-Langenburg also idolised her. On a visit to their uncle King Leopold of the Belgians and his family at Brussels, she could not help comparing three-year-old Vicky favourably with her second cousin and contemporary, Charlotte, who was a few months older and 'a great beauty but I must say that she does not outshine dear Puss in my eyes, she may be more beautiful, but she has not that vivacity and animation in her countenance and manners which make her so irresistible in my eyes, she is a *treasure*!'[7]

The proud father never appreciated that the constant praise he gave and the self-confidence which he was at pains to inculcate in Vicky, added to the opportunities he took of showing her off to relations, nursemaids and courtiers, risked creating in her a sense of superiority and the belief that she was never wrong. Queen Victoria, who was not particularly maternal by nature and always ready to criticize her offspring, had earlier made a subconscious effort to counteract this unalloyed adulation when writing to King Leopold of their eldest child, who at little more than a year of age was 'quite a dear little companion', but 'sadly backward'. The woman soon to be appointed senior governess, Sarah, Baroness Lyttelton, might find her young charge mischievous and liable to answer back, but never backward. Even before her seventh birthday, she noted, the Princess 'might pass (if not seen, but only overheard) for a lady of seventeen in whichever of her three languages she chose to entertain the company'.[8]

From an early age she learnt French verses by heart and enjoyed working them into normal conversation. When she was three, Queen Victoria wrote to King Leopold of 'our fat Vic or Pussette' learning lines by Lamartine with her governess Mademoiselle Charrier, ending with 'le tableau se déroule à mes pieds'.* Riding on her pony, looking at the cows and sheep, she turned to the governess, gestured with her hand, and said: '*Voilà* le tableau se déroule à mes pieds'. 'Is this not extraordinary for a little child of three years old? It is more like what a person of twenty would say. You have no notion *what* a knowing, and I am sorry to say *sly*, little rogue she is, and *so obstinate*.'[9]

Vicky had inherited her mother's obstinacy, and also tended to behave like a little autocrat, again following the Queen's example. When a junior governess on a carriage drive refused to stop and get out to pick her a sprig of heather, she muttered indignantly that of course the governess could not, then she glanced at two young ladies-in-waiting, 'but those girls might get out and fetch me some.' Easily bored with routine, and often frustrated, she often gave her mother cause to complain of her 'difficult and rebellious' character. Scolded for misbehaving by Lady Lyttelton, whom she called 'Laddle', she answered nonchalantly, 'I am very sorry, Laddle, but I mean to be just as naughty next time.'[10]

For the first few years of Queen Victoria's marriage the main royal residences were Buckingham Palace, where Vicky was born, and Windsor Castle. During her childhood they acquired two rural retreats further afield. At Osborne on the Isle of Wight, an existing mansion was demolished and rebuilt to Albert's directions as a home far away from London where the children could be brought up as simply as possible. The mild climate, the sea where they learnt to swim, the gardens where they had their own tools, and grounds for riding made it an island paradise for them all. They had their own playhouse, a Swiss Cottage in the garden, where Vicky and her sisters learned to cook and bake cakes. A few years later Albert

---

* The picture unfolds beneath my feet.

purchased another estate at Balmoral, in the heart of a wooded valley in the Scottish Highlands, where they built another imposing mansion which they visited every year. In the surrounding countryside they could enjoy pony expeditions and picnics, deer-stalking, shooting, fishing by day, and Scottish dancing to the sound of bagpipes in the evening.

From childhood the handsome, red-haired Fritz was generous, unselfish, even-tempered, and like his father he was quiet and serious-minded. After his eighth birthday party when the guests had all gone, Unruh found him deep in concentration at his desk and left him alone, returning later to discover him asleep with his head on his hands. A servant carried the boy to bed and on looking at what lay on the desk, the tutor saw a list of presents that Fritz planned to buy for other people, using money given him by his uncle, 'with reference to the estimated merits of each case, as well as their separate circumstances and conditions.'[11] Even though he knew Fritz so well, he was most impressed by his pupil's kindness of heart.

On another occasion Fritz had a trivial argument with his father, and wanted an impartial opinion as to which of them was wrong. Unruh was asked to arbitrate, and after listening carefully to both sides of the dispute said he believed the Prince of Prussia was in the wrong and his son in the right. Everyone, he continued, was liable to err, and the tutor wanted to tell him not to boast about it, but was forestalled when the boy threw himself on the floor, sobbing, 'Now everything is lost!' He had desperately hoped that his father would have been judged right, and was not comforted until Wilhelm took him in his arms and told him gently, 'You are wrong, Fritz, but you are also right, and so you shall carry your point.'[12]

Another time Fritz complained to Unruh about one of his teachers, who had puzzled him by referring to the fact that one day he would be King. Pressing the teacher for an explanation, the man told him that on the death of His Majesty, the Prince of Prussia would be King, and in due course he too would die. Here Fritz angrily interrupted him; 'I know nothing about this; I have never thought of it, and I do not wish my father's death to be referred to.'[13] On 18 October 1841, his tenth birthday, in accordance with family tradition he received his commission as Second Lieutenant in the First Infantry Regiment of Guards, and was invested with the Order of the Black Eagle.

While his tutors found him kind and obedient, they thought he was not particularly intelligent. Augusta was disappointed if not surprised to find her son apparently growing up as a typical Prussian prince, with no early evidence of interest in her progressive political views, but instead a typical Hohenzollern sense of devotion to the army and Prussian monarchy inherited from the father whom he admired but feared. Though it was an age when sons were expected to be in awe of their fathers, Augusta once told a friend that she was alarmed to see how much her son was 'agitated and nervous' in his father's presence.[14]

In the spring of 1848 Germany, like much of Europe, was shaken by unrest; street fighting broke out in Berlin, and the temporarily unnerved King promised immediate reforms in consultation with the *Landtag* (Prussian Parliament). Fritz and Louise could see shots being fired between guards and revolutionaries from the palace, and with a sense of shame on behalf of his family the Prince of sixteen also watched the King being forced by demonstrators to salute the bodies of dead revolutionaries in the palace square at Berlin. After a few days Augusta decided that the capital was no place for her children and she took them to Babelsberg, their summer retreat three miles from Potsdam. Here Otto von Bismarck, one of the most reactionary members of the United Diet in Germany, approached Augusta with a plan to persuade the King to abdicate, ask Wilhelm to renounce his right to the succession and place Friedrich, young, innocent, untarnished by any connection with the past, and therefore more acceptable to the rebels than any other Hohen-zollern, on the throne. It had been suggested by Karl, the King's arch-conservative younger brother, who intended that he himself should be the power behind the throne. By coincidence a similar manoeuvre later that year brought the young Habsburg Franz Josef to the imperial Austrian throne in succession to his uncle, the epileptic Emperor Ferdinand. However Augusta's loyalty to her husband and brother-in-law, or more possibly the desire to see herself as a Queen Consort in waiting, rather than as Queen Mother, overruled her. She refused to contemplate the idea, and never forgave Bismarck.

Meanwhile mobs demanded the blood of Prince Wilhelm, regarded by the Prussian conservatives as their champion at court, after he had summoned troops into the Berlin streets to put down rioting, thus earning himself the epithet of 'the Grapeshot Prince'. Significantly his was the only royal palace in Berlin to be attacked by revolutionaries, who painted slogans on the walls and smashed the windows. The King sent him a letter advising him 'to repair to the friendly Court of England',[15] and he trimmed his whiskers with a pair of scissors in order to avoid recognition. Making for the safety of the Prussian Embassy at Carlton House Terrace in London, he was invited to Windsor by Prince Albert who lectured him on his schemes for a united liberal Germany, and the lessons that could be learnt from England's acceptance of parliamentary government without any adverse effect on national loyalty to the crown. Wilhelm listened in silence, more out of good manners than agreement. Interpreting his acquiescence partly as depression and partly agreement, Albert wrote approvingly to King Leopold that Germany could 'ill spare people like him.'[16] While he was in exile his name was removed from the church prayers until reinstated by order of the government. In May he left England to return home, and was appointed commander of forces in Prussia and Hesse who were charged with putting down the last remnants of rebellion, ordering summary executions with a vengeance that shocked the other German states and secured the order of *Pour le Mérite* from the King.

Fritz regarded the popular agitation for constitutional reform with distaste, and was shocked to learn that the King had ridden through the streets of Berlin wearing a revolutionary tricolour armband, the symbol of revolutionaries calling for German unification. He told his cousin Friedrich Karl that he would never fall so low; 'I intend to keep my Prussian cockade on my cap and will not wear the

German one.' Those weeks of March, April and May 1848, he noted in his diary, were 'the most tragic spring of my life', and democratic reformers were 'the unruly mob' who had 'trampled the majesty of the crown under their feet.'[17]

In adolescence Fritz gradually came to see the virtues of his mother's more liberal political views, as well as noting the lessons of the previous year. At a banquet at Potsdam in May 1849 he was seated next to the conservative Leopold von Gerlach, the King's Adjutant-General. The latter said he envied the prince his youth, as he would doubtless 'survive the end of the absurd constitutionalism.' Fritz shocked him by replying that he believed some form of representation of the people would become a necessity.[18] There had to be a parliament, he believed, implying that the integrity of such an assembly provided by the monarchy had to be respected.[19]

In the summer of 1849, after Unruh's retirement, he began full-time military service with his regiment and was promoted to the rank of First Lieutenant; that autumn he commanded the regiment for the first time during seasonal routine manoeuvres. In October he celebrated his eighteenth birthday in the traditional Hohenzollern manner with a reception attended by family and various officials including Prussian state ministers, military commanders, and deputations from town magistrates, all in full dress. He received their congratulations, the Mayor of Berlin, Herr Naumyn, read out addresses from the town officials, and made several short speeches of thanks in return.

Three weeks later he made a break with tradition by becoming the first Hohenzollern prince to receive a university education. Until then military training had been considered adequate for the heirs to the Prussian throne and their kin, but Augusta had used her influence to have her nephew Friedrich Karl, son of the scheming Prince Karl, enrolled at the University of Bonn. In doing so she set a precedent for sending her son there; and in November 1849 he settled in Bonn, on the first floor of the university building, the former Elector's castle, to study literature, history and law. In his third term he wrote a long essay on his educational experiences, acknowledging that 'no true picture of the life and doings of man' could be gleaned at court; one had to meet and exchange views regularly with people from all social classes. 'At Court one is surrounded by people who invariably meet royalty with politeness, with the observance of ancient traditional forms, and only too frequently with deceitful flatteries, so that habit gradually leads one to think of life in no other way, and to estimate all men with whom one comes in contact by the same standard.'[20] It met with qualified approval from his mother who remarked with asperity that, while his knowledge of human nature had certainly improved, 'his intellectual development does not equal that of his peers.'[21]

Life in the palaces surrounded by fawning courtiers and servants was stifling, and he found it a refreshing change to get together with royal fellow-students and others in his rooms at Bonn for a 'social round table'. Though he worked hard, studying into the small hours rather than joining in the all-night drinking and singing parties enjoyed by other students, he was never priggish; he mixed freely with his contemporaries and the people of Bonn, and was accepted by them as 'one of the crowd'. While he kept his distance from political discussions, knowing that in his position it was politic not to take sides, he had a sense of humour and relished a joke as well as anyone. Only those who failed to treat him with respect due to a prince of the blood royal risked incurring his displeasure, for while he had 'the common touch', he insisted on the appropriate deference to his rank.

When not at Bonn he was happiest visiting his mother and sister at Koblenz, their rural retreat in West Prussia. Despite the seven years in age between them, the childhood lack of intimacy between Fritz and Louise had lessened by the time of his early manhood. They were a familiar sight together strolling along the banks of the Elbe, shopping in nearby towns, or visiting local fairs, with a small pug dog scampering at their heels.

His English tutor Copland Perry gave him three lessons in English language and literature a week, and was struck by his sincere affection for the country, for the Queen and her family, and also for her political and social way of life. As Fritz had not yet been to England or met Queen Victoria, such Anglophile sentiments were presumably inspired by his mother, who was too impatient or transparent by nature to try and hide her dislike of reactionary Berlin and her preference for English ways from him. At the end of each formal study session, tutor and student amused themselves 'by writing imaginary letters to ministers and leaders of society'.[22] At that time Bonn had a small English-speaking colony which used to celebrate Divine Service each Sunday according to the rites of the Church of England. Fritz and Perry often attended these services, sharing a pew and a copy of the Book of Common Prayer together. Fritz enjoyed the service so much that his tutor allowed him to keep the book, which he carried about with him for years afterwards.

Although it was not yet taken for granted that Prince Friedrich Wilhelm would eventually marry the Princess Royal, some of the elder generation clearly had this very much in mind. The idea may have originally been proposed by King Leopold, who had been instrumental in encouraging the marriage of Victoria and Albert themselves and was always keen to extend Coburg influence, partly for reasons of family ambition and partly as a means of safe-guarding and strengthening the guarantee of Belgian independence. He encouraged the Queen to cultivate her friendship with Princess Augusta, though the latter was equally keen to make the most of the friendship with Queen Victoria herself, hoping to convert her son to liberalism and nationalism through a marriage to the eldest daughter of the new generation of Coburgs at Windsor Castle.[23] Alternatively the *eminence grise* might have been Baron Stockmar, King Leopold's physician and unofficial family counsellor who supported anything that would bring together 'the two great Protestant dynasties in Europe'[24] and who had first spoken of the issue when Vicky was only six. Finally there was Albert himself, who may not have been the architect but was certainly the catalyst in the match between his daughter and the eventual heir to the Prussian throne.

His vision of a progressive Germany, with the Hohenzollerns of Prussia at the helm, living under constitutional law, and allied to England, seemed well within the bounds of possibility. King Friedrich Wilhelm of Prussia had begun to suffer from a series of increasingly debilitating strokes, and he was not expected to live for much longer. As his eldest brother and heir Wilhelm was already in his fifties, his reign was unlikely to be long. He would be succeeded by his only son, now a young man of almost twenty, trained in the liberal tradition by his mother, and open to good English influences. With another Queen Victoria as the consort of King Frederick, the royal houses of Britain and Prussia, and therefore both nations, would be united.

According to another theory, Augusta was anxious to bring such a marriage to fruition as she wanted to forestall her husband's scheme for their son to wed a Russian Grand Duchess. Political and family ties between Romanovs and Hohenzollerns had been cemented by their membership of the Holy Alliance since 1815, and the King of Prussia's sister Charlotte's marriage to Tsar Nicholas I. Not wanting yet another autocratic Russian in the family, Augusta was suspected of using her friendship with Victoria to further the marriage of her only son to Victoria's eldest daughter. Augusta and Wilhelm had first met the Queen and Albert briefly when the latter couple visited Coburg in 1845, and in September the following year Augusta was invited to stay at Windsor for a week. After her departure the Queen wrote to King Leopold that she found her 'so clever, so amiable, so well informed, and so good . . . *I believe* that she is a friend to us and to our family, and I do believe that *I* have a friend in her, who may be most useful to us.'[25]

Impressed with her liberal ideas and belief in constitutional government, as well as her criticisms of backward, autocratic Russia and weak France, Albert began to convince himself that this was the person through whom he could bring some influence to bear by furthering the unification of Germany under Prussia.

In the spring of 1851 Queen Victoria and Prince Albert invited Wilhelm, Augusta and their two children to England for the opening of the Great Exhibition in London in May so they could meet Fritz, and introduce him to Vicky. She was a well-educated, well-read child, familiar with the plays of Shakespeare and the histories of Gibbon and Macaulay. Queen Victoria, who was skilled at drawing and painting in watercolour, encouraged her daughter to work with her and the latter soon revealed even greater gifts as an artist. Prince Albert fostered her interest in music, and she loved sitting beside him on the organ stool and listen to him playing, though with her impatience she had to be persuaded to make an effort with the drudgery of endless scales and five-finger exercises.

Fritz was nineteen and Vicky only ten, and it was too early to raise the subject of marriage. Nevertheless, to disguise any suspicions of matchmaking other European monarchs were also invited. Mindful of the upheavals of 1848 and reluctant to leave their kingdoms or empires unless really necessary, they all refused to come. London, a byword for its toleration of political refugees and dethroned exiles, was regarded by other European monarchs as a hotbed of underground socialism and anarchy. The Crystal Palace in Hyde Park, purpose-built for the exhibition, was seen less by observers as the triumph of nineteenth century engineering its creators intended it to be, than a potential disaster. Merchants of doom prophesied that the enormous glass structure would surely collapse from the weight of bird droppings, or else shatter from the salvo of the guns at the opening ceremony.

Even the Prince of Prussia and his family had to be persuaded to attend. A few days before their departure from Germany, King Ernest Augustus of Hanover (Queen Victoria's sole surviving uncle, though there was no love lost between either) warned King Friedrich Wilhelm IV that London was full of potential republican assassins who would undoubtedly seize the chance to make an attempt on his brother's life. King Friedrich Wilhelm's subsequent letter to Albert, asserting that a mob was on its way to London for the very purpose, drew a sarcastic reply assuring him that all guests would receive the same degree of protection as Queen Victoria and Albert himself, as they were presumably also on the list of potential victims. To this there was no answer, the King withdrew his objections, and on 29 April Prince Wilhelm, Princess Augusta and their two children arrived together at Buckingham Palace.

Queen Victoria's initial verdict in her journal on Fritz was remarkably restrained; 'The young Prince, who is 19, is not handsome, but has a most amiable, attractive countenance & fine blue eyes.'[26]

Vicky and Fritz came face to face for the first time in the magnificent setting of the Chinese Drawing Room at Buckingham Palace. She had been allowed to join the adults ostensibly as company for Louise, who was barely two years older than her. True to her upbringing as a good submissive Prussian princess, Louise hardly said a word all the time and looked thoroughly bored. Chattering in fluent German and English with a remarkable lack of self-consciousness, Vicky could hardly have failed to make an impression. She had already had a private visit to the exhibition, and thanks to her father she knew much about the items on display. When the royal party went for a drive to the exhibition she rose to the occasion magnificently and astounded Fritz with her knowledge as she took him on a conducted tour around the Crystal Palace, full of energy despite the heat and dust which gave him a headache, answering the questions he asked in faltering English. She could see that he was rather taken with her, and the added fact that he was puzzled by the exhibits, which gave her a chance to flaunt her superior knowledge, brought out the best in her. Like her father, she could never resist an opportunity to instruct others or give them the benefit of her superior education, a trait which would have seemed priggish in a child with less charm. With a sense of tact well in advance of her tender years, she swiftly led him by the arm to show him something different every time his parents began to argue, in order to spare them embarrassment.

When they were at Crystal Palace the Queen's mother, the Duchess of Kent, became accidentally separated from their party. At once Fritz was quite concerned, only to find with astonishment that all of them went into peals of laughter at the thought that any harm could possibly come to her in a place like London.[27] To the prince who had stood at the palace window in Berlin and seen the first shots fired in the disturbances of 1848, this was a revelation.

Inclined to be shy and tongue-tied with people his own age, Fritz was amazed by this girl who was obviously flattered by his attention, and eagerness to be guided around the exhibition by a child half his age. She too was normally shy in the presence of strangers, but there was no trace of timidity in her manner as she played the part of hostess to him with a poise well beyond her years. She only spoilt things, understandably in view of her age, when her parents told her afterwards that she was too young to be allowed to stay up late and attend the opera. With a display of petulance which showed how much she was her mother's daughter, she stumped off to bed in a sulk, refusing to say goodnight. Even paragons had their human side.

Over the next two weeks Vicky and Fritz were allowed to spend several hours in each other's company, something her parents would never have allowed had she been a few years older. During their conversations they learnt much about each other, though Vicky was the more forthcoming. She told him plenty about the family and about England, and when he mentioned that he was attending the university at Bonn where her father had studied, she warmed to him even more.

Any theories in hindsight that Vicky and Fritz fell in love with each other on this first meeting are palpably nonsense. She was still an undeveloped, plump child of only ten, but it was obvious that she made a vivid impression on him. Some thirty years later he told Catherine Radziwill, who had become a close friend of them both, how taken he had been with her from the start. 'She seemed almost too perfect; so perfect, indeed, that often I caught myself wondering whether she was really a human being.'[28]

It might be more accurate to say that in 1851 he fell in love with England. He had already learnt something about the country's renowned technological superiority, respectability, and tolerant political outlook from his tutors at Bonn; but seeing it at first hand was a different matter entirely. Above all, he was totally captivated by the royal family. Queen Victoria was already the mother of seven children (with two more to come) who were affectionate, healthy, well-mannered, and devoted to their parents, and the leader of this group of children was the Princess Royal, full of interest in everything around her, blessed with high spirits and a well-developed sense of humour. In the French phrase of the day, she was encouraged to 'produce herself' and be seen to her best advantage. To Fritz the contrast between these young hosts at Windsor, and the royal children of German courts, overwhelmed by etiquette and with individuality fiercely suppressed if not drummed out of them altogether by a conventional upbringing, could hardly have been greater. The difference between Windsor and his forbidding home life at Berlin, presided over by a profoundly disunited and unhappy family, was equally pronounced.

As for Vicky, she had led a very sheltered life with only her younger siblings and parents, plus the usual courtiers and servants, for company. Fritz was a handsome, dashing young man with fair, slightly auburn hair and a moustache, holding himself well as befitted a youth with his military upbringing. To her he was more like a distant cousin to whom she naturally looked up, perhaps even regarded as something of a hero. But he had only come to stay with the family for a few days; and when he went back to Prussia, would he remain as such, or would he just be a happy childhood memory?

Within a few days, the Queen was coming to like their young guest more and more. On 8 May she noted: 'Am extremely pleased with Fritz, who I find so right & liberal minded, quite under-standing the poor King's character & well aware, that when he joins his Regiment at Potsdam, he will be exposed to every kind of intrigue & attempt to imbue him with the old traditionary [*sic*] doctrines. But he said there was no fear whatever of his listening to, or being influenced by, these people'.[29]

Fritz stayed briefly with the family at Osborne before returning home, having asked Albert if he would help him with the occasional letter or memorandum in future. This was the man who would henceforth be his mentor, he had decided, rather than the distant military tutor demanding total unquestioning obedience, who happened to be his father. Albert was more than happy to oblige, intent on giving him much the same advice that he had offered his father during his temporary exile, on the merits of constitutionalism and a modern monarchy for the modern age. All that he had seen in England confirmed Fritz in this belief. In contrast to fighting in the streets of Berlin in 1848, English revolutionary fervour had amounted to no more than a few half-hearted Chartist riots and broken windows at Buckingham Palace. Augusta's visions of liberalism and German unification did not look nearly so remote in the light of Prince Albert's words on the subject. His mother's liberal views, he began to find for himself, were being applied successfully in the most powerful industrial country in the world.

After the visit Fritz and Vicky began to correspond regularly, while the Queen had at last gained some insight into the unhappiness of her guests' family life. She was in a good position to sympathize, for after the marriage of her half-sister Feodora her own childhood had been lonely, dominated by her ambitious widowed mother and a grasping comptroller, with only a middle-aged governess for a friend. She begged Augusta to show confidence in her son, so that he would likewise have a little more confidence in himself. She wrote a few weeks later: 'I am always afraid in his case of the consequences of a moral clash, should his father strongly recommend something and his mother warn him against it. He will wish to please both, and the fear of not succeeding will make him uncertain and hesitating.'[30]

Soon after his return to Bonn, Fritz was at a dance with several other students. He struck up a conversation with their host, Eberhard von Claer, and told him how much he had loved England. Suddenly becoming very grave, he lowered his voice and said to him, 'If you will give me your word of honour that you will not repeat anything, I will show you something.' Claer assured him that His Royal Highness could rely on his discretion. Ensuring that nobody was eavesdropping on them, Fritz pulled out a large gold locket which had been near his heart, pressed the spring, and showed him what was inside – a charming portrait of a young girl, little more than a child. After letting Claer look at it for some time he gazed at it himself clearly moved, kissed it fervently, and placed it again near his heart. He then put his finger to his lips in order to request silence on the matter, and went back to join the other guests.[31]

For a while his university studies were interrupted by further military activities. He was commissioned to take command of the castle guard at the public unveiling of a statue to Friedrich the Great in Berlin, and then accompanied his father to observe Russian manoeuvres at Warsaw, where he was appointed Commander of a Russian regiment. After spending the autumn on duty with the First Regiment of Infantry Guards, he was promoted to the rank of Captain. In October he went back to Bonn for the final session of his studies, which came to an end in March 1852. On leaving the university he was presented with a testimonial and various gifts, and the other students staged a torchlight procession in his honour.

University life may have been an unusual move for a Hohenzollern prince, but for Fritz there was to be no respite from the Prussian military tradition, and it is unlikely that he would have wished it otherwise. At camp near Potsdam he celebrated his twenty-first birthday with a supper and dance for the officers of his regiment, followed by manoeuvres and the study of theory. In the spring of 1853 he became indisposed with a chill which developed into a severe inflammation of the lungs. On medical advice he went to recuperate at Ems, a holiday and health resort in Hanover, and thence to Switzerland, to spend a few months on the shores of Lake Geneva, within sight of a perpetual mantle of snow on the Alpine slopes, and the picturesque castle of Chillon.

This period of absence and ill-health was to have disagreeable consequences at home. Not a man to be trusted, Prince Karl took it upon himself to suggest that his nephew might be too delicate to ascend the throne; it would surely be more practical, he argued, to have an heir apparent who was 'healthy and capable of work', namely his own son Friedrich Karl. Wilhelm and Augusta insisted that the succession could not be tampered with in this way, but this defence of their son could not prevent the gathering of supporters in both camps among the army officers, one party upholding Fritz's rights, the other those of his cousin. The affair went no further, but Fritz never trusted either his uncle nor his cousin again.

Once he was pronounced fit and well he returned to resume his duties, taking part in an inspection of the Austrian contingent in the German Federal Army at Olmutz with the Tsar and Emperor Franz Josef, who awarded him a Colonelcy-in-Chief of an Austrian regiment. In December 1853 he went on his travels again, visiting classical Italy. Just before Christmas he met Pope Pius IX, who held out his hand for the ring to be kissed; but Fritz, either not realising the significance of the gesture or else deciding that Protestants should do otherwise, grasped it and shook it heartily. On their subsequent meetings the Pope kept both hands carefully behind his back. During the next few months Fritz's interest in art and archaeology, already fostered by his classics tutor Professor Ernst Curtius, came to life; he was fascinated by Roman ruins, churches, palaces and art treasures, which till then had been little more than names in a book to him. He stayed in Rome until March, visiting Naples, Vesuvius, Pompeii and Sicily among other places, returning to the papal capital for Easter, and attending the Good Friday service in the Sistine Chapel. After leaving Rome for a second time he returned home via Florence and Venice with various treasures, including an exact model of the triumphal arch of Titus made from marble, two vases, and several copperplate engravings of paintings hanging in the Vatican.

Meanwhile Queen Victoria continued her correspondence with Augusta, rarely letting an opportunity slip of singing Vicky's praises. Her eldest daughter, the Queen wrote of the twelve-year-old child in the spring of 1853, 'has made much progress with her music, and has a great deal of talent for drawing; she has a genuine love of art and expresses opinions about it like a grown-up person, with rare good sense.'[32] The Queen's own 'rare good sense' was questionable in writing with such honesty, for Augusta cannot have been too favourably inclined towards hearing about this old head on young shoulders whom, she knew, was regarded by both mothers as a possible wife for the future King of Prussia. One story which was doubtless kept from Augusta was Vicky's mischievous effort at coquetry. On a drive she dropped her handkerchief over the side so that one of the equerries could recover it for her. Seeing through her daughter's motives, Queen Victoria ordered the coachman to stop the carriage and let down the steps, then she told the smirking girl to get out and fetch it herself.[33]

Theatricals and *tableaux vivants* were regularly staged by Queen Victoria's children, partly for the amusement of their parents, household and invited guests, and partly as an extension of their lessons, particularly in French and German. Prince Albert generally supervised their efforts, while the French governess Madame Rolande took an active role as *metteur-en-scène*. As the eldest child Vicky was always given one of the leading parts. One of their favourite plays was Racine's *Athalie*, in which she was cast as the murderous Queen, and their first performance was staged at Windsor on 10 February 1852, the Queen and Albert's twelfth wedding anniversary. Vicky, her mother wrote, 'looked very well and spoke and acted her long and difficult part . . . really admirably, with immense expression and dignity and with the true French emphasis'.[34] It was such a success that the children staged three more performances in January 1853 with Vicky 'very grand and tragic' in her role, especially at 'the scene of fury, where she rushes out in a rage, extremely well' at the dress rehearsal and first performance. However the last night was not such a success, with 'divers mishaps', especially when she 'entirely forgot her part.'[35]

By this time there was a threat to the Anglo-Prussian unity so carefully nurtured by both royal families. It had long been a maxim of European diplomacy that peace would be maintained throughout Europe as long as the four powers, England, France, Austria and Prussia, were broadly united in their foreign policy. But when England and France fell out with Russia over the Turkish question and the Crimean war broke out in March 1854, Prussia stood aloof. Queen Victoria and Prince Albert were extremely disappointed, and the Queen sent Augusta a copy of the formal declaration, a gesture which the Prince of Prussia found rather tactless as he thought it should have been sent to him, adding that 'We had hoped to proceed hand in hand'.[36] King Friedrich Wilhelm IV, inclined to bow towards the demands and views of his more forceful brother-in-law, Tsar Nicholas of Russia, considered the Anglo-French alliance 'shameful', and in April he concluded an offensive and defensive alliance with Austria. Henceforth Prussia's policy during the conflict was to be one of 'ostentatious neutrality'.[37] Wilhelm supported the Anglo-French alliance, believing that if Prussia was to side with both nations, Russia would be more amenable to reason.[38] He protested to his brother that ministers and ambassadors sympathetic to both powers were being ostracized and dismissed without consultation, and for his pains he was temporarily relieved of his duties at Berlin and banished to Koblenz.

Queen Victoria had faith that Anglo-Prussian relations would soon mend, while Albert knew that the 'Prussian marriage' had to be kept in mind. Prince Friedrich Wilhelm, they believed, would soon ascend the throne, and therefore be in an excellent position to help save the continent of Europe from the twin evils of French intrigue and Russian reaction. Moreover this handsome, intelligent young man would surely be sought by some other European state's unmarried princesses if they delayed too long.

In the spring of 1855 Napoleon III and Eugenie, Emperor and Empress of the French, came to Windsor for a state visit, largely as a demonstration of solidarity between both countries during the Crimean war. Vicky was very shy of the Emperor on their first meeting, and the Queen noted in her journal, the fourteen-year-old girl 'with very alarmed eyes making very low curtsies'.[39] At a ball later that week she 'danced with the Emperor, which frightened her very much',[40] but the Empress went out of her way to make friends with her and soon put her at her ease.

A reciprocal visit was paid to Paris four months later, and Vicky and Bertie Prince of Wales, her eldest brother, were allowed to accompany their parents to the Palace of St Cloud. For Vicky it was the height of luxury; at home she had to share a bedroom with her sister Alice, but for a few days in Paris she had her own, amidst pictures and furniture that were the epitome of elegance and sophistication. She was dressed in style as well, for the Emperor knew that beside Empress Eugenie the dowdy Queen and her daughter might make a poor impression. Having found out that the Princess Royal had a lifesize doll, he obtained the measurements and had a number of dresses made and sent to London, addressed to Her Royal Highness's doll. The subterfuge was seen through and gratefully accepted, and Vicky easily outshone her mother on their arrival in the French capital.

At first the Queen was reluctant to let her attend the great ball in the Palace des Tuileries, but at the Empress's request the children were allowed to join their hosts at supper. Vicky was equally flattered and embarrassed when the Emperor walked up to her after the meal, bowed, and asked her for a dance. Blushing deeply, she allowed him to escort her through the Salle des Glaces. It was a rite of passage which she would always remember with pleasure if a touch of embarrassment as well.

She was spared a meeting with the Prussian ambassador to Paris, Otto von Bismarck, who was presented to her parents. Queen Victoria greeted him with civility if coldness, while Prince Albert, Bismarck later recalled, gave him the impression of 'a certain ill-disposed curiosity' when they spoke together. It was the only time both men, who figured so strongly in the ultimate destiny of Vicky's life, ever came face to face. Albert was well aware of the ambassador's pro-Russian stance and anti-western Europe influence on the indecisive King Friedrich Wilhelm IV, and must have found it hard to conceal his displeasure.

As Queen Victoria, Prince Albert and their two eldest children returned from Paris to Osborne in the last days of August 1855, the parents reflected on how their eldest child was maturing fast. As they made plans for their journey north to Balmoral, they also considered the next, and most crucial, stage of her future. Within a month, they knew, she would probably have made the most important decision of her life.

TWO

'Two young, innocent things'

Queen Victoria, Prince Albert and the family arrived at Balmoral on 7 September. A week later a rather nervous Fritz joined them, accompanied by his aide-de-camp, General Helmuth von Moltke. The latter was impressed at once by the homely atmosphere of the British court. It was hard to believe, he wrote to his wife, that the woman whom he called the most powerful monarch in the world could leave court life so much behind; 'it is just plain family life here. . . . Nobody would guess that the Court of one of the most powerful estates resides here, and that from these mountains the fate of the world is decided.' When introduced to the Queen, her husband, and their ladies and gentlemen in attendance, he could 'well imagine that life here, proper family life, must be exceedingly agreeable and I regret having to depart tomorrow.'[1]

To Fritz, the change in the Princess Royal since their first meeting was nothing short of amazing. At the age of fourteen, it was evident that Vicky was maturing into a beautiful woman. The combination of her childish roundness, awakening beauty, mercifully free of her mother's plain looks at the same age, and unforced charm was irresistible. She and Fritz sat next to each other at dinner that first evening, chatting in French and German. It was impossible for her to keep her eyes off this handsome young suitor, still the same gentle unaffected friend she remembered from the first time. Albert and the Queen had already agreed that, had the two young people not given any sign of being attracted to each other, they would do nothing to force the issue. They tried not to look too interested, but they were secretly overjoyed that matters appeared to be turning out as planned.

The next day Albert took Fritz out deer-stalking, got soaked to the skin, and took to his bed with an attack of rheumatism. Fritz was still tense at the thought of what was expected of him, but Vicky had a feeling that he was becoming besotted with her. When they found themselves momentarily alone, she took his hand and squeezed it, and he needed no further signals. After a sleepless night, following breakfast the next day he plucked up courage to ask the Queen and Albert for a quiet word; in the Queen's words, he wanted *'to belong to our* Family; that this had long been his wish, that he had the entire concurrence and *approval* not only of his parents but of the King – and that finding Vicky *so allierliebst*, he could delay *no longer* in making this proposal'.[2]

She agreed at once, on the understanding that Vicky was to know nothing about it until after her confirmation at Easter the next year; he ought to attend the ceremony if possible and propose immediately afterwards. In strict confidence Albert notified the Prime Minister, Lord Palmerston, and his Foreign Secretary, Lord Clarendon. He also wrote to Baron Stockmar that Fritz had 'laid his proposal before us with the permission of his parents, and of the King; we accepted it for ourselves, but requested him to hold it in suspense as regards the other party till after her Confirmation.' It was expected that he would not propose until the following spring, maybe on a visit to Britain with his parents and sister, and the 'seventeenth birthday is to have elapsed before the actual marriage is thought of'.[3]

Yet having taken the first step along the road to betrothal Fritz was unable to wait any longer, and on 25 September he asked the Queen for permission to give Vicky a bracelet. The Queen granted it, adding with a smile that 'something had to be told her and he had better tell her himself'.[4] In a matter-of fact manner which betrayed nothing of her true emotions, she noted in her journal that day that 'we were uncertain, on account of her extreme youth, whether he should speak to her himself, or wait till he came back again. However, we felt it was better he should do so'.[5]

Four days later the family went for a ride up the heather-covered slopes of Craig-na-Ban. Fritz and Vicky lagged behind and he picked her a sprig of white heather, an emblem of good luck, telling her that he hoped she would come to stay with him in Prussia, always. When they reached the carriage where everyone else was waiting, he gave the Queen a meaningful nod to imply that all was well. Back at the castle an agitated, half-remorseful Vicky threw herself into her parents' arms, weeping tears of joy as she told them everything.

Two days later, amid more tears and affectionate embraces from all, Fritz returned to Prussia. Vicky admitted to her parents that she had never been so happy as she was at the moment when he gave her that first kiss. Albert wrote to Fritz that 'From the moment you declared your love and embraced her, the child in her vanished.'[6]

'The description of the rapid development of my dear Vicky's character, in consequence of our mutual declaration, is an extremely joyful piece of news for me', Fritz wrote the next week to Albert. 'I can vividly imagine how the dear child has suddenly moved closer to her parents, and on both sides this development is a very beneficial, amazing one; but it would not be easy for me to say any more, for because I just feel so drawn towards her and discovered so much depth of mind and feeling in her, I really cannot put into words what it was that so specially attracted me.'[7]

Early next month *The Times* remarked acidly on Prince Friedrich Wilhelm's recent arrival at Balmoral, for the sole purpose of 'improving his acquaintance with the Princess Royal'. Emphasizing King Frederick William's tacit pro-Russian attitude during the Crimean war at what had been a critical juncture, it concluded that an alliance with Prussia would be tantamount to one with Russia. If the prince was called up to join the Russian army, his wife would be placed in a situation where loyalty to her husband would be treason to her country; and if Prussia lapsed into the status of a petty power, she would be sent back to England as an exile. 'For our part, we wish for the daughter of our Royal House some better fate.'[8] The criticisms deeply wounded Albert who knew that there was some truth in this view, despite his snort of derision that the newspaper, 'our sulky grandmother [was] deeply offended that its permission was not first asked'.[9] The future, he was sure, belonged to Fritz, who must be destined for a long reign, though he was still only second in line to the throne.

To Augusta, the Queen wrote enthusiastically that, 'now that the bond is tied, nothing can really mar [Fritz's] happiness; he must be fortified by the thought that Vicky truly loves him and that we parents have given them our blessing.' Vicky, she added, 'is still half a child and has to develop herself both physically and morally before their marriage takes place in two years' time'.[10] As part of this development from childhood to adult status, from that time onwards mother, father and daughter dined together *à trois* in the evenings. 'We must look upon her already as a woman, the child is gone forever!'[11] the Queen wrote in her journal on her daughter's fifteenth birthday.

Back at Bonn Fritz called upon Dr Perry, his former tutor, to whom he had already confided his hopes. 'It was not politics, it was not ambition,' he told him, 'it was my heart.'[12] There were two reasons for rejoicing in the family home when he returned, as during his absence Louise, now seventeen, had become betrothed to Friedrich, Prince Regent of Baden.

Whatever may have been his initial doubts about an Anglo-Prussian marriage alliance, King Friedrich Wilhelm IV defended it without hesitation. When Gerlach showed him a copy of the right-wing *Kölnische Zeitung* and complained of the absurd reports that his nephew had gone to England merely to propose to Queen Victoria's daughter, the monarch admitted they were true. Though she had never really liked her brother-in-law, Augusta was keen to give credit where it was due, and thanked the King for his ready support of a family engagement which he had known would not be popular.

Augusta may have had her reservations about the engagement. On a political and personal level she had more in common with Vicky's family than her own. But she was already a little jealous that this girl, so like her in personality and tastes at a similar age, should have had the good fortune to make a love match so unlike her own marriage. It was likely that she, Vicky, would thus be able to have considerable influence over her fond husband when they ascended the throne. The letters Augusta continually received from Queen Victoria praising Vicky did nothing to lessen this feeling of mild resentment. Nearly thirty years of loveless married life had thoroughly embittered her, and she took consolation in the fulfilment of her wishes partly for the prestige that a British princess would bring Prussia, and partly out of satisfaction that her son was not going to marry another haughty Romanov Grand Duchess. Yet she thought Vicky was too clever by half, too full of her own importance to be a suitable daughter-in-law. Relations between both women, who could have been the best of friends, kindred spirits at a hostile court, would rarely be amicable.

None of the other princes and princesses were pleased, Fritz noted ruefully; if any of them were, they seemed afraid to speak their minds. The family evidently did not know what to make of him and his Anglophile ways, 'and one can feel their curiosity, uncertainty, etc.; only they are always letting off random shots in the form of sarcastic, barbed references with pretty unkind content! The unhappy party is seething with anger at not having been informed and consulted in advance, and is now trying to get revenge by incredibly petty cackling that sheds a most revealing light.' Fortunately his friends, particularly from university days, were more gracious in their comments 'expressing joy about the probable purpose of my journey to England [*sic*]. This warms my heart, and without more or much enquiry such indications suffice to give me real happiness.'[13]

That winter Fritz was allowed to see more of contemporary Prussian government and politics. He was unfavourably impressed with his observations of Otto von Manteuffel's reactionary ministry, particularly corruption in the elections to the House of Deputies, which took place as he was returning from Scotland. No efforts were spared, he told his future father-in-law, to secure the return as deputies of provincial councillors who were completely subservient to the government and could be relied on to vote exactly as the ministers instructed.

In Berlin it is incredible what shameless devices the all-powerful police used in order to deliver to people's homes the names of those who were to be elected. And now it has been achieved that completely spineless persons are appearing as deputies, to whom the household gods of popular representation are being offered, and we are probably achieving everything that has long since been intended. Many people are saying that motions will probably be brought forward for abolishing the constitution, and that this is what the party manoeuvring is aiming at. . . . May God protect us, and enlighten our poor most gracious King, who is no longer allowed to see things as they really are.[14]

Prince Albert wholeheartedly agreed, replying prophetically that 'designs such as those contemplated by the reactionaries . . . may result in extreme danger to the monarchy'.[15] It was further reassurance that he had acquired a like-minded future son-in-law.

Vicky wrote Fritz long letters assuring him in her artless way of her love and devotion, although at fourteen they were hardly missives of passion, more conversational messages from an adolescent to a devoted friend. In turn he wrote frequently to her, and sent her a diary in which he had described incidents as an eye-witness during the 1848 revolutions, in order that she should know 'all the secret events of my life'.[16]

The betrothal was officially announced to the European courts in April 1856, a month after Vicky's confirmation, which Fritz could not attend because of his army commitments; it was now discussed openly for the first time. Bismarck was asked by Gerlach for his view of the English marriage and declared that he did not like the English part of it, but the bride-to-be was said to be a lady of intelligence and feeling. If she could 'leave the Englishwoman at home and become a Prussian, then she may be a blessing to the country. If our future Queen on the Prussian throne remains the least bit English, then I see our Court surrounded by English influence,' he observed. 'What will it be like when the first lady in the land is an Englishwoman?'[17]

Writing with hindsight many years later the journalist Charles Lowe, who was a correspondent for *The Times* in Berlin for several years at the height of Bismarck's power, felt that the Princess's remarkable qualities made her ill-equipped for the Prussian capital. 'In truth, if she had been less gifted by nature, and less perfected by education, which had made her the darling and the intellectual image of her father, she would have achieved far greater success at the Court of Berlin.'[18]

Others were less critical, and the Liberal politician Richard Cobden was one who heard nothing but good of the Princess Royal.

Dining with the American minister Mr Buchanan in the spring of 1856, he was told that she was 'All life and spirit, full of frolic and fun, with an excellent head, and a heart as big as a mountain'.[19]

Fritz made a third journey to Britain in the early summer of 1856, to coincide with the Queen's birthday. As the engagement had not yet been formally announced to Parliament, it was again a private visit. Though the Queen insisted on the young couple being chaperoned all the time, she was soon thoroughly bored with having to sit in the next room whenever they wanted to be alone together, while Fritz found it irritating as no such custom existed at home, and he longed to have his future wife to himself if only for a short while. Luckily he had an ally in the Prince of Wales, who was ordered by his mother to keep them company but helped them instead by playing with the younger children in an adjoining room, leaving the door ajar in case she should suddenly return.

While he was in England Vicky had an accident. One evening she was sealing a letter, when the muslin sleeve of her dress caught fire. Fortunately Miss Hildyard and a music teacher were present, and quickly put the fire out with a carpet. Her right arm was severely burned from shoulder to elbow, though she made light of the excruciating pain. Fritz was horrified, telling her that as a result of the accident she had 'really been given to me a second time, but please, please be more careful in future.'[20] For some time afterwards she could not write with her right hand and had to use the left, producing a script which, she said apologetically, looked as if her brother Bertie's parrot had a pen in its hand.

After representing the Hohenzollerns at the coronation of his cousin Tsar Alexander II of Russia at Moscow, Fritz returned to Berlin to help prepare for the wedding of his sister Louise to Prince Friedrich of Baden on 20 September at the Neue Palais Chapel, Potsdam. At the festivities Georgiana, Baroness Bloomfield, wife of the British ambassador, told him that she hoped that the next royal wedding she attended 'would nearly concern him'. He smiled, admitting it seemed a long time to wait, but as the Princess Royal was so young, her mother and also his mother felt they should not marry until the following year, and they hoped that 'by that time party spirit would run less high.'[21]

He returned to England for a month to celebrate Vicky's sixteenth birthday, marred by court mourning for Prince Karl of Leiningen, the Queen's half-brother, who had just died. He had been a wastrel with few redeeming qualities, but the formalities of Victorian mourning demanded that the departed should receive the same attention whether worthy of it or not, and Vicky took to her bed for two days with a 'sick headache'.

Luckily for him, he did not know that the Queen was beginning to be tortured by misgivings at having let her eldest child commit herself to the equivalent of exile so young. Barely four months after the engagement, she had confided to her journal how she dreaded the idea of her daughter 'going to Berlin, more or less the enemy's den!'[22] Only days before Fritz's visit Albert had written critically to his wife taking her to task for being angry with their future son-in-law for preparing to devote his life to their child, of whom she was only too pleased to be rid. Fritz could not help seeing some of this strained atmosphere, but at least he could be grateful that his future parents-in-law both had the grace to keep their more serious disagreements private, unlike his own quarrelsome parents.

Albert took every chance to continue what he saw as his duty to educate the two young people for their future. He told Fritz that he ought to spend less time in military duties and more in familiarizing himself with contemporary government and politics. Vicky, he considered, still had much to learn regarding her role as an effective queen consort, and he devoted two hours each evening to coaching her. She wrote daily essays on history, literature and politics to be read and corrected by him, and to be taken to Prussia as a set of guidance notes to refer to in the years ahead. Aware that others could impart their knowledge of the sciences better than he could, he arranged for a governess to take her to South Kensington twice a week where she attended lectures by Faraday and Hofmann, and received private tuition from them.

At home Fritz was busy with preparations for his married life. That autumn he began to arrange the palace at Babelsberg, which had been chosen as one of their first residences. From England he went to Paris in December to pay a complimentary visit to Emperor Napoleon and allay his fears about the future of Anglo-French relations. Napoleon was regarded as a *parvenu* by most of his fellow-monarchs, and the one firm bond of royal friendship he had succeeded in making was with Queen Victoria. Now he feared that England might yield to Prussian influence, which would place her alliance with France in jeopardy, until the Foreign Secretary, Lord Clarendon, assured him that Queen Victoria's private attachment to the Prussian house had nothing to do with politics. Fritz did his best to reassure him, and the Empress Eugenie was captivated with her tall handsome guest, who was 'not without a resemblance to Hamlet.'[23] She was kinder than Mary Bulteel, Queen Victoria's Maid-in-Honour, whose first impression of Fritz had been 'that of a good-humoured lieutenant, with large hands and feet, but not in the least clever.'[24] Napoleon tried to make the visit pass as well as possible, but found that his guest's thoughts 'were always either at Osborne or Windsor'.[25]

On 16 May 1857 the engagement was officially announced. Three days later Queen Victoria opened Parliament, choosing the occasion for notifying the Commons and requesting financial provision for the marriage. The ministry's apprehension that the match would find little sympathy was unfounded; by a majority of 328 votes to 14, a dowry of £40,000 and annuity of £4,000 were granted.

A month later Fritz and Moltke returned to Britain. He and Vicky made their first public appearance together at the History of the Art Treasures Exhibition at Manchester on 30 June in a party which also included the Queen, the Prince Consort,* the Prince of Wales and Princess Alice. On the following day the Queen paid a second and strictly private visit, while the princes attended a reception at the town hall. An address was read to Fritz congratulating him on his engagement, to which he replied gracefully of his hopes 'that God's blessing may rest upon this union, in which to secure the happiness of the Princess Royal will be the dearest duty of my life.'[26]

---

* Prince Albert was created Prince Consort by Letters Patent in June 1857.

Later they went to Madame Tussaud's premises in London to inspect their newly-made wax likenesses; Fritz's was dressed in the Fusilier uniform of the Prussian Guards, while Vicky's wore a light blue silk dress decorated with lace and pearls. They posed for a full-length portrait side by side at a photographic studio in Regent Street, and accompanied the Queen to Ascot races. Music lovers were pleased when the family attended a performance of a Handel oratorio at the Crystal Palace and, led by Albert and Vicky, continually beat time with their scores. Theatre managers in the city did big business when every play which received royal patronage immediately afterwards drew vast audiences. The day before he left England, Fritz was presented with the Freedom of the City of London. Before resuming his military command at Breslau, he visited Berlin and noticed that souvenir shop windows were sporting cheap, poorly-executed busts of Vicky and himself.

The closing months of the engagement were not without their difficulties. First there was an argument over the composition of their future household, which was to consist solely of middle-aged Germans chosen by Queen Elizabeth and Princess Augusta. For Vicky it was a daunting prospect, and the Prince Consort had to ask them to include a few British girls of her age. Queen Victoria told the Prussian court that some of the German ladies might like to accept invitations to Windsor so that they and their future mistress could meet each other beforehand, a suggestion which was received coldly. Their secretary-to-be, Mary Seymour, was a daughter of Prince Albert's equerry, and Count Ernest von Stockmar, the Baron's son, had been chosen as their treasurer, despite Fritz's half-hearted protests that his presence at Berlin as a representative of the Coburg interest would be resented. Though he was to prove an invaluable adviser in performing a similar role for them as his father had for Vicky's parents, it might have been as well for the sake of their popularity in Prussia if the Prince Consort had taken some account of his future son-in-law's views. Albert insisted that the younger Stockmar was an ideal choice as one of the few people who knew both the English and Prussian courts well, as well as the Coburg family. Ill-disposed persons who called him an

English secret agent, he claimed, were troublemakers who must be ignored.

In his letters to England Fritz had reassuringly painted a rather roseate picture of Berlin's attitude to the marriage, which in fact was almost overwhelmingly hostile. Albert allowed himself to be taken in, appearing to believe that any criticism was largely manufactured by a fiercely xenophobic Berlin press, and naively wrote to Fritz that 'the people to whom you belong, and to whom Vicky is to dedicate herself, do not fear and hate English influence but will rather be pleased that your future wife is an English princess.'[27]

Later that year the Queen learnt that the Prussian court expected their future King's wedding to take place 'at home' in Berlin. It was not an unreasonable supposition, but she made plain to Lord Clarendon that this was impossible: 'Whatever may be the usual practice of Prussian princes, it is not every day that one marries the eldest daughter of the Queen of England. The question therefore must be considered as settled and closed.'[28]

By autumn King Friedrich Wilhelm IV had suffered a couple of strokes and was increasingly confused. His physicians declared him no longer capable of discharging the duties of a sovereign and Wilhelm was declared Regent for three months. It proved a mixed blessing for Fritz, as he was to discover when Augusta told them that she felt her opinions, or at least some measure of advice on matters of policy for her less intelligent husband, might be called for. Fritz found with dismay that her determination to be heard was making the atmosphere very difficult, with an exasperated Regent ordering her not to meddle and she becoming increasingly frustrated at being regarded as of no account. To be the only son and heir of such a mutually antagonistic couple was a thankless task. 'Sometimes when opinions differ it is wiser to pretend to agree so as not to irritate her still further,' he wrote to Vicky, as 'she is too autocratic a character to put up for any length of time with not having a say in everything now . . .'.[29]

Fritz arrived at Dover on 23 January 1858, two days before the wedding, and went straight to Buckingham Palace, where the court had moved from Windsor a week earlier to receive all the guests.

That evening he joined the family at a state performance of Shakespeare's *Macbeth* at Her Majesty's Theatre. After the final curtain the National Anthem was the signal for a massive burst of applause, followed by repeated calls for 'the Princess'. When the Queen took Vicky and Fritz by the hand to the front of their box, the cheering increased to a deafening roar.

Throughout the previous year Vicky's fond letters had dwelt increasingly on how much she would miss her father once they were married. The Prince Consort had found her such an apt pupil and valuable confidante that he would himself miss her deeply. Queen Victoria was inclined to be jealous of her daughter's intellect and the way in which she commanded her father's attention, and there had been the odd stormy scene in private between husband and wife; on the other hand, she was reproaching herself for having encouraged the girl to marry so early. Fritz knew his betrothed well enough to understand that, much as she loved him, for all her intellectual qualities she was still a very young seventeen, and would find it a terrible wrench to leave her closely-knit family. Walburga von Hohenthal, the orphaned daughter of a German diplomat, was chosen as one of her ladies-in-waiting and came to England to meet her about a month before the wedding. She thought her future mistress, who was only a year younger than her, still looked extraordinarily young; 'All the childish roundness still clung to her and made her look shorter than she really was.'[30]

As Fritz knew only too well, family and court life in Prussia could not be compared with the happiness found in England. He was aware of the bad impression made on their hosts by the other German princes with their uncouth manners and crude conversation. Even Prince Wilhelm had been tactless enough before Christmas by saying that as Regent he was too busy to attend the wedding, and only a desperate letter from Albert had persuaded him to change his mind.

St James's Palace, where the Queen had been married, was chosen again for her daughter's ceremony on Monday 25 January. Fritz was promoted that morning to Major-General of the Prussian First

Infantry Regiment of Guards, and arrived at the chapel in his new uniform. He was accompanied by his father on his right and his uncle Prince Albrecht on his left. Approaching the altar, he stopped near the Queen's seat and bowed to her and his mother, then knelt to pray at the altar steps. At that point Vicky, in a dress of white silk trimmed with Honiton lace, trembling and very pale, entered on her father's arm, both being escorted by King Leopold. She curtsied to her mother and Wilhelm, then Fritz came forward, dropped on one knee before her, and affectionately pressed her hand to his heart. Both spoke their responses firmly, which reassured the nervous Queen rather more than the Archbishop of Canterbury, who was so 'agitated', that he managed to omit several passages of the service, as he had done at the bride's confirmation. The ceremony was concluded with the *Hallelujah Chorus*, after which bride and bridegroom led the procession out of the chapel to the strains of Mendelssohn's *Wedding March*, the first time it was so used.

Returning to Buckingham Palace Vicky and Fritz appeared on the balcony, both with and without their parents, and after a wedding breakfast the young couple left by train for their two-day honeymoon at Windsor. Inside the castle, at last they found themselves alone together for more than a brief moment. After all the excitement of the previous few hours, surrounded by enthusiastic admirers and a phalanx of relations, it was unbelievably quiet, but they were glad to have a brief respite from being the centre of attention. Vicky would recall years later that they were 'two young, innocent things – almost too shy to talk to one another.'[31] Their parents were attending a state banquet at the palace, followed by a concert where the Queen and the Prince Consort were unable to appreciate the music properly as everyone within earshot was still talking about the wedding. Not until the small hours of the following morning did the exhausted mothers and fathers retire.

Next day the diarist Charles Greville noted that the ceremony 'went off yesterday with amazing *éclat*, and it is rather ludicrous to contrast the vehement articles with which the Press teemed (*The Times* in particular) against the alliance two years ago with the popularity of it and the enthusiasm displayed now.'[32]

On 27 January, having seen most of the guests depart, the rest of the family joined them at Windsor, and on the next day Fritz was invested with the Order of the Garter. On 29 January they all returned to London, and in the evening the Queen, the Prince Consort and the newly-weds again attended the theatre, the audience demonstrating their approval of the match once more by cheering the couple as they stood at the front of the royal box during the Anthem. On the following day a small drawing-room ceremony was held, and in the evening there was a private party for the bridesmaids and their families. Meanwhile Fritz was taken out to see the sights of London by night.

By now the glitter of the festivities was wearing thin. Fritz knew that behind the gaily smiling face Vicky presented in public, deep down inside she was filled with increasing anguish as the time approached to leave home. It would have taken a thoroughly insensitive bridegroom not to know that she would not find Berlin the most accommodating of environments after having been brought up in the happy yet over-protected family circle at Windsor, Osborne and Balmoral. She had had such a sheltered upbringing, and only 'dined out' once before her marriage – with her cousins. The capital of Prussia was hardly a place for an English adolescent girl who was known over Europe to be schooled in advanced political theory directly opposed to the views of her in-laws. He spent much of 1 February with his father-in-law, while Vicky made the most of this last precious day at home with her mother.

But for the newly-married girl the dreaded departure could not be postponed, and so the next morning there were tearful farewells on the stairs. The weeping Queen stayed at home, so it was left to the Prince Consort and the two elder boys to see Fritz and Vicky on their way. He wrapped a blanket tenderly around her shoulders to protect her from the wind and snow as they waved goodbye from their open carriage – a supreme sacrifice of comfort on such a bitter day – to crowds of well-wishers lining the city street. 'Be kind to her, or we'll have her back,' shouted a group of cockney draymen. At Gravesend they boarded the royal yacht, the *Victoria and Albert*; Fritz led Vicky to the cabin, where she clung to her father in a last embrace prior to the farewell. At the palace she had sobbed to the Queen, confessing that 'I think it will kill me to take leave of Papa'; and Bertie told the family that she was 'in a terrible state' when she had to say goodbye.[33]

As Albert sadly stepped ashore, he waited in vain for a few moments to see if they would reappear on deck. The only one in the small family group not to break down at the parting, he was too overcome to speak. The next day he wrote to his daughter, assuring her that his heart had been very full; 'I am not of a demonstrative nature, and therefore you can hardly know how dear you have always been to me.'[34]

After a stormy North Sea crossing, with Vicky's desperate home-sickness on her first night away from her old home made worse by storms and howling wind, they anchored at Antwerp to begin a series of celebrations and receptions planned for them on their way to Berlin. Fritz was relieved to see her put on a smiling face as she waved to the multitudes at Antwerp when he led her off the yacht. At Brussels they danced together at a ball given in their honour, and visited the cathedrals at Cologne and Magdeburg. This time Fritz could play the part of the well-informed guide, with their roles at Crystal Palace in May 1851 reversed.

One incident did nothing to enhance their German welcome. They stopped at Hanover to call on King Georg, son of Ernest Augustus, the last surviving son of George III, who had been heir to the British throne until Vicky was born. A gold dinner-service which had belonged to his father had been the subject of disputed possession until a British commission decided in favour of Hanover, much to Queen Victoria's anger. Vicky was a little piqued when this same service was used at table for the dinner given in their honour. Yet there were lighter moments, as when they stopped at Wittenberg where Field-Marshal von Wrangel, a veteran of the Napoleonic wars, welcomed them to Germany on behalf of the army. As he stepped into the carriage with them the train started with a jolt, and he found himself suddenly sitting in a large apple tart just presented to them. All three were helpless with laughter as Vicky called for their attendants to clear up the mess.

After breaking their journey at Potsdam to stay with Wilhelm and Augusta, they entered Berlin on 8 February, another day of bitter cold, in the state coach. The rest of the royal family had assembled to greet them at the Bellevue Palace, and for Vicky it was her first sight of King Friedrich Wilhelm IV and Queen Elizabeth. The latter was so taken aback at seeing this young girl in her low-cut dress without any wrap or coat running up the steps to greet them, apparently oblivious of the cold, that she temporarily forgot her hatred of England, and asked if she was not frozen. Back came the graceful answer with a ready smile: 'Completely, except my heart, which is warm.'[35]

As the Neue Palais was not ready, they were given apartments in the Berlin Schloss, the Prussian monarchy's traditional home, a maze of endless dark corridors connecting the vast rooms, where the winter wind whistled mercilessly down the chimneys. Though the state apartments had not been lived in since the death of Friedrich Wilhelm III, they were the setting for most of the court's social gatherings, receptions and dinners.

To Fritz, one palace or castle was no better and no worse than another. He had grown up in relatively spartan surroundings, without the modern conveniences of the palaces in England which Vicky had taken for granted. At first he found it a little hard to understand her bitter complaints about their lack of comfort. She had no cupboards in which to hang her clothes, no bath, and no lavatories; their carpets were dusty and threadbare; most of the family portraits were darkened beyond recognition by smoke from the old stoves, which provided the only source of heating. There was no proper lighting, and she was expected to read by a flickering candle, which struggled to stay alight in the teeth of Arctic winds penetrating the north-facing windows. She had only been in Berlin for a few days before her eyes were bright red, her nose was streaming with a cold, and she was getting chilblains in her fingers.

Out of Hohenzollern reverence for the dead, the building had been kept more or less as a shrine to the late King. The room in which he had breathed his last had been left undisturbed, except for the removal of his body, and this death chamber was situated between Fritz and Vicky's bedroom on one side and their sitting room on the other. The kitchen and servants' quarters were at the other end of the Schloss, so that the domestic staff had understandable cause for complaint at the distances they were expected to walk. Completely devoted to his wife, Fritz was sympathetic to her requests for making the place more comfortable, and he steeled himself to brave derision and ask for modest improvements to be put in hand. At his request a bath with running hot and cold water was soon installed, but not without a good deal of grumbling and derision from family and household alike.

Within a few days of arriving at the Schloss, he naively sent a telegram to his parents-in-law: 'The whole Royal Family is enchanted with my wife. F.W.' As the Prince Consort dryly remarked, the Berlin telegraph office must have been amazed.[36] They were certainly fascinated by her, for she had so little in common with them. She much shorter than they were; none of the princesses was less than five foot ten in height, while at her marriage she was a mere five foot two, and her small features made her look even younger than her age. Fritz's cousin Grand Duchess Olga, sister of Tsar Alexander II and Crown Princess of Württemberg, who resented anything and anyone English because of the Crimean war, was particularly ungracious to Vicky and asked her if she was sixteen before turning her back on her.

Like Augusta before her, she was surprised by their lack of interests, and could not even share her mother-in-law's appetite for tittle-tattle and endless parties. While she made friends with Marianne, wife of another of Fritz's cousins, Prince Friedrich Karl, her indiscreet conversations got her into trouble. After telling Marianne too freely about her walks in the Berlin slums and making indignant remarks about the poverty and wretched conditions she saw there, her words soon got back to the rest of her in-laws, who told her she had no right to complain about 'their' country like that. Vicky found herself confiding in Marianne because she felt so sorry for her. The latter was typical of the submissive Prussian princesses who knew their place. Her husband wanted sons who would grow up to be brave soldiers like him, and when she presented him with a third daughter he boxed her ears, leaving her with permanently impaired hearing. Vicky was horrified that the Hohenzollern women should accept such physical abuse as natural. Prince Friedrich Karl, she soon realized, was typical of the Prussian man who despised women and would always do so 'until he finds one that is his match and tells him the truth.' How she wished she could be the one to do so; he considered ladies 'as *un chiffon* to be well-dressed, and look pretty. To have stupid compliments and flattery paid them and to have children is all they are made for.'[37] How grateful she was that she had had the good fortune to marry the one shining exception to this rule.

Among her ladies-in-waiting Vicky had two more friends of her own age. Wally Hohenthal and Marie Lynar helped to enliven the times when Fritz was out all day after breakfast on military duties, and they could while away the hours playing the piano, painting, reading aloud to each other, and embroidering kneelers for the English church in Berlin. When not under the censorious gaze of the master and mistress of the household, they indulged in nursery games Vicky had brought to Prussia with her like draughts and ludo, or even hide-and-seek in the palace corridors. The more worldly-wise Wally could not resist the opportunity to tease her mistress, or Marie, with stories of *Die Weisse Frau*, the ghost of a long-dead family member which haunted the Schloss as she stalked the corridors, moaning to herself. One evening she was reading to Vicky in the drawing room when a door slowly opened in the wind. There were nearly girlish screams of terror at the prospect that they might have been interrupted by a real spirit presence. Though both girls were Prussians, they understood Vicky far better than her in-laws. They might resent her unguarded criticism of their country and her insistence that everything was done much better 'at home' in England, but unlike the princesses they knew better than to take offence.

Had it not been for their companionship, and the love of Fritz, these first few months of life in Prussia would have been almost impossible for Vicky. Though it is difficult to believe that she had had no warning, certainly from her husband if not from her father as well, she was thoroughly taken aback by the princes of whose family she had just become a part. They were a pompous, reactionary crowd – and unbelievably coarse as well. Fritz's uncles so delighted in 'improper jokes' at family dinner that even the hardened Prussian princesses sometimes found it hard not to blush. By comparison Prince Wilhelm seemed a kindly, dignified old soul, but Vicky was ashamed at his proud admission that his only interests in life were military – an astounding remark from a man so close to the throne. She found it hard to get used to Sunday dinners between 2 and 5 p.m. on the ground floor of the Schloss, attended by the whole family in full evening dress and decorations. Everyone was shocked when she once sneezed while standing behind the King's chair and Queen Elizabeth reprimanded her, only to be told that such attitudes were not to be found 'at home' in England.

Life in Prussia was a shattering shock to the system. In England she had been the second lady in the land after her mother and sovereign, and as the eldest of nine children a natural leader in the nursery. A gifted, quick-witted learner with intellectual powers that impressed even her demanding father, she had often been told that she was far cleverer than her backward, stupid, stammering brother Bertie, heir to their mother's throne. Now, a conscientious, eager yet immature girl of seventeen, her position had changed overnight. She had to take her place as the youngest of several princesses, who were almost without exception a dull, vacuous crowd, content to accept their lot as good for childbearing, prepared to fill their time with gossip and dinner parties. Her mother-in-law, who like her had also been given an excellent education and had a wealth of intellectual interests, had quickly learned to accept that the best way to a trouble-free life was to conform to type, argue with her husband when she must, but make the best of her situation as she could. Occasionally Augusta unbent sufficiently to draw Vicky aside and tell her not to think ill of her, 'if I saw her lose command over herself' after family rows, but such intimacies were rare.[38]

If Vicky had been welcomed into the Prussian household with consideration or respect, with her father-in-law the first to ease her path, then the subsequent story of her married life would surely have been very different. In a strange environment and desperately homesick, she was intelligent enough to tread carefully at first. Yet it would have been remarkable if she had not taken refuge in everything which reminded her of home. Fritz warned her as gently as he could to be more circumspect in the presence of her in-laws, but he was powerless to smooth her path against the generally conflicting advice from her parents' frequent, voluminous letters. 'Your place is that of your husband's wife, and of your mother's daughter,' the Prince Consort reminded her rather ambiguously three weeks after her wedding. 'You will desire nothing else, but you will also forego nothing of that which you owe to your husband and to your mother'.[39] He never ceased to imply that she had a mission in life to hold steadfast to the political opinions which he had inculcated in her. Queen Victoria was equally forthright in reminding Vicky of her duty 'as my daughter and Princess Royal',[40] by following English practices in her own personal life, regardless of whether they would cause any resentment. How she was supposed to reconcile these commands from her mother with her new status as a Prussian princess by marriage was never explained.

Thus were sown the seeds of the problem that would plague Vicky for the rest of her life. She was blamed for being tactless, and persistently going her own way in the face of hostility from her in-laws. Constantly hectored from a distance by parents determined not to let go, it was almost impossible for her to do otherwise. As a girl of seventeen who had led a very sheltered life by anyone's standards, she had no opportunity to stand back and look at matters from a distance. An older, more self-confident princess in her position could have perhaps decided that her parents would do better to let her recognize that her loyalties had shifted with marriage and should be kept in their place, but for Vicky this was easier said than done. Her father never ceased to try and guide her political attitudes and opinions, while the Queen seemed more intent on controlling her daughter's personal life as a married woman as much as possible. She demanded frequent, preferably daily, return letters about every detail of her routine and new life, and her daughter's views on her Prussian relatives. Far from helping her to stand on her own two feet, such requests, or rather orders, weakened her confidence, confused her loyalties, and undermined, even came close to destroying her judgment.

Ever eager to learn, she had been positive that all she needed to do in her new home was to apply the lessons her father had taught her, and all would be well. She had not yet absorbed his ability to see matters as part of a broader picture, and distinguish the unimportant from the essential, the matters of the heart from those of the head. If she had acquired such insight, the damage to her future need not have been so great.

Utterly devoted to his wife, Fritz was determined to make a success of his marriage where his parents had conspicuously failed. Augusta had long since ceased to stay in Berlin after the social season any longer than court etiquette demanded, preferring to live alternately at Weimar, Baden, or her country palace in Koblenz. While he sympathized with his mother, he took the lesson to heart. He did not want such a life for himself and Vicky, and though he was nothing like his male relations who merely regarded their wives as brood mares, he could have been excused for wondering whether he had in effect married not just a wife but his wife's parents as well.

Though the young couple had had little opportunity to get to know each other well, he was genuinely in love with her. It was a relief to spend what time he could with a loving wife instead of with his quarrelsome parents and uncles. When they did not have to endure the company of their relations, he enjoyed reading to her in German from his favourite histories, and listening to her reading, usually in English, from newspapers sent to her regularly from London, or from her treasured set of Shakespeare bought with her pocket money as a girl. Yet such precious evenings were rare. They had only been in Berlin for a few days when his father thoughtlessly ordered him to take part in yet another course of military training, so often the only part of the day they spent alone together was breakfast.

If he had hoped that his married status would have made any difference to his relationship with his parents, he was to be disappointed. The Prince Consort was right to complain that his son-in-law was a victim of Prussian 'army-mania', but he was living in a dreamworld if he seriously expected his letters to both Fritz and

Vicky to request that he be given more training as heir-presumptive – attending council meetings, studying state papers, and the like – to have the intended effect. There was no point in approaching the King, now under constant medical attention, so Vicky plucked up courage and asked Prince Wilhelm to consider giving his son a role commensurate with his status. As she had feared, he angrily told her to mind her own business. Very set in his ways, the Prince refused to accept that statecraft, even for a future sovereign, was more important than the army rituals of drilling and marching day in and day out. It was of apparently no consequence that he was over sixty and his son was probably not so far away from the throne. This may have been the main reason for his obstinacy, for in his moods of despondency Wilhelm feared that there could be a hereditary element to his brother's illness. Little more than a year younger himself, he felt that his days might be numbered as well.

'Perpetual learning saps energy,' the Prince Consort had written to Augusta, 'and Fritz has arrived at an age when he ought to be at work, I mean, on something really useful. He feels this himself, for he spoke to me at Windsor about his desire to be drawn by his father more into active business. He was shy of suggesting it to him for fear of appearing ambitious or pushing.'[41] Years of marriage to the obstinate Wilhelm had taught Augusta that to try and intervene herself would be futile. She continued to scold and bully her son, venting on him all the irritation her husband caused her. At first she was civil and occasionally kind to Vicky, but jealousy of her soon overcame all other considerations, and it was not long before she treated her unpleasantly as well. Had she cared deeply for Vicky she would have behaved with more understanding, but she probably assumed that Vicky was young and malleable enough to accept her fate and, after initial resistance to the mores of royal life at Berlin, would resign herself to conforming with the status quo at court. If so, she greatly underestimated the resilience and determination of her son's wife. They stayed with her for a few days in April in Weimar, and though they had been looking forward to the visit, Augusta was rude to family guests and servants alike, the atmosphere was frigid and uncomfortable, Fritz caught a heavy cold, and they were given separate rooms on different floors. They were only too glad to return to Berlin afterwards.

In May they moved to Babelsberg, their summer palace at Potsdam, sixteen miles south-west of Berlin. The interior was almost as uninviting as the Berlin Schloss, with heavy tasteless furniture and ungainly hothouse plants, and they were not allowed to make any major alterations, apart from hanging their own photographs and a selection of Vicky's paintings. However it had the advantage of being in a more picturesque woodland setting, overlooking the river Havel and open countryside, and it was closer to Fritz's military headquarters where he had to report daily. A couple of days after their arrival Vicky slipped while coming downstairs, as she moved to get out of the way of a lamplighter who was going up. Not wishing to make a fuss, she attended the opera as planned that night, but next day found that she had sprained her ankle, which was painful and swollen. Though it was soon better, Dr Wegner was anxious, as he suspected she was carrying her first child.

The Prince Consort had just told her that he was about to visit Coburg, and hoped she could meet him there. As the doctor forbade her to travel, he came to visit them at Babelsberg at the beginning of June. On the next day the King, Queen, Wilhelm and Augusta drove over from Charlottenburg to see him. Though he was distressed at the deteriorating appearance of King Friedrich Wilhelm IV, he was pleased by the evident mutual love and affection of his daughter and son-in-law, telling Baron Stockmar that 'the harmony between the young people is perfect.'[42]

By this time Queen Victoria knew that her daughter was *enceinte*. This 'horrid news', she wrote tactlessly, 'upset us dreadfully. The more so as I feel certain almost it will all end in nothing.'[43] A more tactless, less graceful remark to an anxious eldest child expecting her first baby would be hard to imagine. Some weeks later she warned Fritz that what filled him with joy 'brings me sorrow and anxiety, for it is bound up with so much suffering and danger for the poor and very young mother!'[44]

In August the Queen and Albert came to Babelsberg, where they made an effort to recreate the happy family evenings at Windsor in which Fritz had revelled as a guest. Remembering those not-so-distant days, he leant over the piano turning the pages of the music while Vicky and her father played and sang duets. He introduced them to various Prussian notables such as the scientist Alexander von Humboldt and 'old Wrangel', who could still talk of nothing but how glad he was that Fritz had chosen Vicky, who was a 'blessing to the country'. The only character to whom the Queen and Albert found it difficult to be civil was the reactionary Prime Minister Otto von Manteuffel, whom they privately blamed for Fritz's enforced political ignorance; they found him 'most unpleasant, cross, and disagreeable'.[45]

However the minister's office was coming to an end. Even the omnipotence of a Hohenzollern King had its limits, for the monarch was now increasingly unintelligible, jumbling his words, losing interest in everything, and behaving like a man barely awake. In October Wilhelm was granted the full powers of Regent, with a royal decree conferring the position upon him, and Fritz attended a ceremony in the Berlin Schloss at the end of the month in which his father took the oath 'to exercise the royal authority to the best of his ability as Regent with sole responsibility towards God,' and observe the constitution of 1850.[46]

Hopes of progress seemed justified when Wilhelm asked Manteuffel to resign, creating him Count and a life member of the *Herrenhaus*. In his place Prince Karl Anton Hohenzollern-Sigmaringen, a member of the Catholic branch of the family and a pronounced liberal, was asked to form a government. The next election produced a large liberal majority in the *Landtag*, and on the new minister's advice Fritz was allowed to attend meetings of the house. In addition Privy Councillor Brunnemann was appointed his political secretary in all but name, with responsibility for keeping him informed on state affairs.

Prince Karl Anton had been a guest at Fritz and Vicky's wedding, and was a favourite of Queen Victoria and the Prince Consort. Vicky openly expressed her delight at this change, which she thought a most important step '& one which will satisfy all the nation, please all patriotic men, raise the Prince in the eyes of all, make his work easier for him, in course of time I hope restore the country to its place and position in Europe'.[47] Unfortunately she made plain her delight not only in private letters to her parents, but also verbally to one of the gentlemen at court. Repeated and exaggerated, her words got back to members of the conservative party, who had viewed the dismissal of their champion Manteuffel with distaste. Such indiscretions did nothing for her popularity, and neither did it help her when the Prince Consort unwisely sent the Regent letter after letter of unsolicited advice on liberalizing the Prussian government, most of which he threw away unread.

Vicky still had problems with her mother, who persistently reminded her that she must never forget what she owed her country, in other words, England; 'never forget those duties which you owe to it as well as to your new one!' There was nothing, she maintained, in 'these two-fold affections and duties which need ever clash; the interests are so much, and will in time get more united.' They reached a crescendo when the Queen expressed indignation at the 'extraordinary' Prussian custom that a lady who was *enceinte* could not stand as godmother at a christening; 'above all promise me never to do so improper and indecorous a thing as to be lying in a dressing gown on a sofa at a christening! as my daughter and an English Princess I expect you will not do it. . . . Let German ladies do what they like but the English Princess must not.'[48]

Vicky had been placed in an impossible position. She told her mother quite rightly that while letters from home were a delight as well as a comfort to her, this 'extended correspondence' was taking up a good deal of her time.[49] Her first duties, she had to point out, were in Prussia, and in fulfilling them to the utmost she was merely doing what her own country would wish and expect. 'It would seem strange if a German princess married in England and insisted on having a christening there with the same customs observed as in her home. I fear I should make myself justly disliked if I showed a contempt for a custom which is after all an innocent one'.[50]

Ernest Stockmar warned his father about Vicky's problems and the Baron wrote to Lord Clarendon, who was visiting Berlin at the time, asking for his help. The Queen, he said, 'wishes to exercise the same authority and control over her that she did before her marriage and she writes her constant letters full of anger and reproaches . . . and of her forgetting what is due to her family and country, till the poor child (as Stockmar called her) is made seriously ill, and put in a state dangerous to her in her actual condition.'[51] The old Baron was evidently a little conscience-stricken, being as responsible as anyone else for having repeatedly advocated the marriage of Vicky and Fritz in the first place, and was now alarmed at the young wife's plight. He asked Clarendon to discuss things with the Prince Consort, who admitted that he was perturbed at the Queen's 'aggressive system'. He had tried, without much success, to moderate the demands his wife was making on their daughter with her insistence on never-ending daily letters home. Unfortunately, he admitted, it was necessary to acquiesce to Queen Victoria to a degree, lest she should become too 'excited to an opposition to her will', and the madness of George III might be unleashed in her. However, that he said something to her on the subject can hardly be doubted, for her letters became less hectoring in future.

There was another unfortunate legacy which Queen Victoria had left her eldest daughter. Vicky's ignorance of the facts of life and her mother's insistence on the proprieties left her totally unprepared for motherhood. That June she had written of her pride at the very thought of 'giving life to an immortal soul',[52] but in the process her pride, physical strength and fortitude would be tested to the utmost.

THREE

'You belong to your country'

Fritz and Vicky moved into Unter den Linden, Berlin, their official winter residence, on the eve of her eighteenth birthday in November 1858. Though she was unwell throughout autumn and winter, her physician Dr Wegner saw no grounds for concern. Regretting her inability to attend the birth herself, Queen Victoria sent Dr James Clark to Berlin. He had attended her last confinements, and when he examined Vicky, he likewise assured them that she would be her normal self again once the baby was born. Only the experienced midwife, Mrs Innocent, had any idea of what was in store. Arriving in Berlin soon after Christmas, she took one look at the expectant mother and feared they were 'in for trouble.'[1]

On the advice of Baron Stockmar and King Friedrich Wilhelm's personal physician, Professor Johann Schönlein, Prince Wilhelm engaged the services of Dr Eduard Martin, a professor of gynaecology and obstetrics at the University of Berlin, as the man best qualified to assist. There was some professional jealousy between both men and Wegner, more courtier than physician, was reluctant to jeopardize the sensibilities of his royal patient by conducting the necessary examination, even at the risk of allowing nature to take its course by letting her and her child die. Mortality in childbirth was frequent and his professional reputation in Berlin would probably not have suffered had this been the outcome.

For several days Vicky had suffered from what Fritz discreetly called 'pains of an unusual nature' which had given them more than one false alarm. Her labour began shortly before midnight on 26 January, and he called Mrs Innocent. Soon Drs Wegner, Schönlein and Clark, the German midwife Fräulein Stahl, Countess

Blücher, and Countess Perponcher, a lady of the bedchamber, were all on hand. Countess Blücher, an Englishwoman married to a German, was a confidante of Queen Victoria and Princess Augusta, and one of the few women in Berlin whom Vicky trusted implicitly. From her the mother-to-be had an urgently-needed crash course in the 'intimacies' of childbirth that Queen Victoria, with her disgust for anatomical details, had never given her daughter. Vicky put on some warm loose clothes and paced to and fro, supported by Countesses Perponcher and Blücher, and Fritz himself. That the father-to-be remained with his wife for so long before and during the birth was extremely unusual for the time. As the labour pains increased in severity, Wegner examined the patient and noticed that there was something not quite right about the position of the child. He sent a messenger to summon Dr Martin at once, and he reached Dr Martin's residence as he was getting into his carriage, about to give a lecture at the university. At around the same time he received a note written by Fritz the previous evening, asking him to come and attend without delay as his wife was about to give birth. Instead of being handed to Dr Martin, as was presumably the intention, this note was posted in the mail.

To his horror Dr Martin found Dr Wegner and his German colleague or colleagues in a corner of the room while the distraught Fritz held his semi-conscious wife in his arms, having put a handkerchief into her mouth several times to prevent her from grinding her teeth and biting herself. He administered chloroform and a baby boy was born at 2.45 p.m. Once he had delivered the baby, Martin devoted his attention to saving the mother, who was very weak. Fraülein Stahl was the first to notice that the infant had not yet uttered a sound, and she feared it was dead. She and Martin tried every method they knew, culminating in increasingly vigorous slapping, until at last a cry came from his lips. Fritz had fallen, exhausted and close to fainting, on the bed next to that of his wife. On hearing Martin's dejected tone of voice as he announced the child was a prince, he too thought his firstborn was dead, until to his relief he heard the baby crying in the next room.*

Though the child was alive, he was clearly not physically normal, and his left arm hung limply from its socket. The doctors referred to this injury in their reports on the birth, without considering the possibility of mental trouble. Recent medical analysis of their accounts has suggested that his hyperactivity in later life, and maybe a degree of brain damage, were caused by a 'reduced blood flow to the brain during delivery'.[2]

'In truth I could not go through such another',[3] Dr Clark admitted to Queen Victoria. The young mother wrote to Queen Victoria praising Dr Wegner's tact and discretion, though she did not know what she would have done without Clark. Dr Martin, to whom she had initially taken a violent dislike, was 'an excellent man' in whose skill she felt 'the greatest confidence',[4] but she could never absolve him completely from blame for the 'bungling way' in which she was treated.[5]

The christening was postponed to give Vicky enough time to recover, and the infant was given the names Friedrich Wilhelm Victor Albert at a ceremony on 5 March. Though still weak for several weeks after her confinement, she was thrilled to be a mother, with none of Queen Victoria's aversion to 'ugly' small babies and the 'animal-like' characteristics of pregnancy. 'I am so thankful, so happy, he is a boy,' she wrote. 'I longed for one more than I can describe, my whole heart was set upon a boy and therefore I did not expect one.'[6] However it was hardly surprising that her natural pride as a first-time mother was wounded, and she must have reproached herself at having presented her husband with a son and heir who was not physically perfect.

---

* Accounts of events leading up to the confinement and birth in Daphne Bennett, *Vicky* (p.84ff), Hannah Pakula, *An Uncommon Woman* (p. 124ff), and John Röhl, *Young Wilhelm* (p. 4ff), all differ slightly but in crucial details. The above is based primarily on the latter, which as the most recently published and most detailed summary, based on the widest range of unpublished sources, can be regarded as the most accurate.

Twelve months of life in Prussia had shaken her self-confidence, and to make matters worse her baby and the future King – assuming he survived – was physically handicapped. On hearing of the birth an excited Prince Wilhelm told his family that they had 'another fine young recruit'; when he knew more, he told Fritz coldly that he was not sure if congratulations on the birth of 'a defective prince' were in order. It was an unpromising start to motherhood for Vicky, but she adored her child and was bitterly upset when Augusta would not allow her to breast-feed him herself. Not content with insisting that Vicky should hand him over to a wet-nurse, in later life she told her grandson that his mother could not bear to nurse him because she found him repugnant with his misshapen arm.

In the spring they moved into the Neue Palais at Potsdam, where Vicky could work on transforming musty, long-uninhabited rooms into a comfortable home, and restoring the overgrown garden. This change of residence coincided with matters taking a turn for the worse in central Europe, when Emperor Napoleon sought to use Italian unification to further his territorial ambitions. He agreed to help Piedmont in its war of independence against Austria in exchange for the Piedmontese states of Savoy and Nice. Austria, confident of military superiority, issued an ultimatum to the Sardinian government – disarmament or war – and invaded Piedmont at the end of April 1859, whereupon Napoleon sent the French army to join the Italians. Most of Europe was neutral; Napoleon's intrusion was hard to justify, but Franz Josef was undeniably the aggressor. In Germany, however, where any French action was automatically suspect, opinion was naturally pro-Austrian; and victory for Italy and France, the German military knew, might lead to further French aggression on the Rhine.

As a gesture of solidarity with the Austrian Emperor the Regent ordered partial mobilisation. Fritz, a trained soldier bored by enforced inactivity, had been waiting for the moment. He believed that Prussia's reputation as a faithful ally was on the line, to say nothing of his own honour as a prince and officer. Vicky could not understand such an argument; to her it was 'fine' for the men to talk of defending their country, 'of a soldier's life being the only one that becomes a man, that death on the field of battle is the thing they wish for; they don't think of their poor unhappy wives whom they have taken from their homes and whom they leave at home alone.'[7]

While Fritz was preparing for the campaign in May, Vicky paid her first visit to England as a married woman, reluctantly leaving Willy with his nurse as Dr Wegner refused to let her take him. She was gratified to find a new bond with her mother; both women had had new babies comparatively recently, Queen Victoria's youngest child Beatrice being only two years old. Now Vicky felt they were more like sisters than mother and daughter, noting with mild astonishment that they seemed more in harmony than ever before; 'Mama shows a kindness & love for me that I have not hitherto known'.[8] Perhaps she was subconsciously acknowledging that during childhood she had never felt herself to be her mother's favourite. She desperately missed Fritz, writing to him that in her old room 'I experienced the happiest moment of my life when you took me into your arms as your wife and pressed me to your heart; when I even think of that moment my heart beats madly and I have a terrible longing for you, and I think I would hug you to death if I had you here now.'[9]

Meanwhile Fritz was given command of the First Infantry Division of Guards. They were still on their way to the war zone in Italy when news reached them of Austria's defeat at Solferino on 24 June, and the subsequent peace treaty at Villafranca a couple of weeks later. Without having even seen a shot fired, he angrily returned home. A commission was appointed to oversee urgent army reform and he attended each meeting of the new military council, pledging himself to making the Prussian forces invincible. If Austria, confident of victory, could be defeated so heavily, then so could the Prussians if they suddenly found themselves at war. For several days, from dawn to dusk, he drilled and marched his troops with a severity they had never before known of him.

Her husband's sudden obsession with the army was the least of Vicky's anxieties during what was becoming a difficult summer. In July she expressed a wish to consult a surgeon about Wilhelm's arm which had failed to respond to gentle exercises, cold baths, and 'invigorating embrocations' that the doctors assured her would help. When his arms were measured at the age of six months the left was about a centimetre shorter than the right, and she was warned that this disparity would increase with time. Dr Langenbeck diagnosed a course of 'animal baths', with his arm being inserted twice weekly for half an hour in a freshly-slaughtered hare, a gruesome-sounding medieval remedy which was supposed to transfer the warmth and vigour of the animal to the arm. A less drastic solution was to tie his right arm to his side and leg for an hour each day to encourage him to use the left, but all he did was lie on his back on the floor and kick his legs in the air. He could not crawl, and not until he was fifteen months old did he take his first unsteady steps unaided.

Worries about her deformed child were one thing; concern for her father was another. While visiting England in May she had been alarmed to see the Prince Consort looking so tired and aged. It was the last straw when Fritz returned home from his campaign that never was, angered by what he called Germany's humiliation, blaming the Austrians for reaching an agreement without consulting their Prussian allies, and thinking of nothing but the army. She impulsively dashed off a desperate letter to her father asking what to do. He replied that she must remind Fritz that Prussia was less important than Germany; it was childish of him to behave as if the state was on the verge of war, and such action could bring the whole of Europe into armed conflict.[10] However in his present frame of mind, war would have been welcome to Fritz, to obliterate the humiliating aftermath of the abortive Austrian campaign.

That autumn he went down with influenza, only to be roused from his bed before he was better. The Regent had just published plans for army reform, demanding among other things an increase in conscription from two to three years, with extra taxation to finance it, and abolition of the *Landwehr*, a territorial army drawn mostly from the middle classes. Fritz was furious at not being consulted, and without waiting till he was well again he confronted his father. The latter, knowing his reforms would not meet with the Liberals' approval and that he would have a struggle to see them through, took all his anxiety out on his son. He called Fritz a meddlesome amateur, while Fritz accused his father of keeping him out on a limb. Suffering badly from insomnia, he would get up at night and sit in a chair with a book until he dropped off; in the morning he woke up stiff, still tired and depressed.

Vicky had to persuade him to come to England with her for a change of air. Leaving Willy again with his nurse, November saw them back at Windsor, celebrating the Prince of Wales's eighteenth birthday and spending family evenings in the rooms where they had enjoyed their honeymoon. Fritz was soon at his most relaxed, and ill-inclined to argue with his weary-looking father-in-law. At the same time, the royal household were getting to know and like him even better. Prince Arthur's governor, Major-General Elphinstone, had met him the previous year and found him a typical arrogant Prussian prince, but on this occasion they had a friendly conversation and afterwards the governor noted that 'there was none of the hauteur I had previously ascribed to him.'[11] Fritz was never haughty, but shyness on previous visits to his wife's family had made him appear aloof to those who did not know him well.

From the welcoming atmosphere of Windsor they returned to Berlin for a Christmas made intolerable by Wilhelm and Augusta's endless squabbles. The reform proposals were now common knowledge, and everyone saw the Regent's programme, supported by all but the most moderate conservatives, as the military caste's attempt to eliminate any 'middle-class element' from the officers in order to achieve complete control of the army. In pursuit of their aims they would not stop at overthrowing the Liberal ministry or even the constitution if necessary, and Wilhelm threatened to resign his position as Regent if thwarted.

After what he had seen in the forces during the previous summer's mobilization, Fritz was sympathetic to his father's reforming zeal. The number of recruits had not risen since 1815, despite a considerable increase in the Prussian population since then, and for Prussia to pursue what might be regarded as a 'progressive' policy, it had to have a strong army. Nevertheless he did not support abolition of the *Landwehr*, he had been deeply hurt by his father's failure to consult him on the proposals before publication, and he was dismayed at the unconstitutional obstinacy that was leading to a private war between the army officers and the liberals. Yet it did not stop him from being dragged into the controversy in the most unpleasant way possible. One morning he was summoned in secret to an anteroom in the council chamber, where some of the bolder conservatives and liberals were waiting for him. Tired of the Regent's intractability, they intended to overthrow him and put his son in his place at the head of an army dictatorship. They had sorely misjudged Fritz's character, for he had never been so shocked in his life. Without stopping to think of the consequences, he went at once to his father and told him everything. The Regent accused his son of treason, of instigating the conspiracy, and on being faced with failure, losing his nerve and confessing in order to save his skin.

Fritz and Vicky felt that much of the ill-feeling between father and son was caused by jealousy. Their marriage was that rare, maybe even unique thing – a happy Hohenzollern marriage. It was simply not the done thing for husband and wife to go driving, walking, and going out in the evening together. None of the other princes or princesses even accompanied each other to church or the railway station. Fritz had always suffered from the cold, though he could not stand hot rooms as he kept losing his voice in them, and had the sense to wear a cloak or drive in a closed carriage during the bitter Berlin weather, much to the scorn of his relations. This, they said behind his back, could be ascribed to the influence of his English wife. It was hardly surprising if Prince Wilhelm looked at his daughter-in-law, saw the ghost of Elise Radziwill, and allowed himself to think of what might have been if he had not bowed to family tradition. In one sense, fate had dealt his son a better hand.

On 24 July 1860, after an easier pregnancy, Vicky gave birth to a daughter, who was christened Victoria Elizabeth Augusta Charlotte the following month. In the family she was known as Charlotte, in honour of the Regent's favourite sister the Dowager Tsarina of Russia, who died four months later, and after her father's favourite cousin and boyhood companion.

Charlotte was normal in every way, unlike her brother. Though he was a lively, cheerful infant, his stunted left arm still had little life in it, and he could hold a stick only with difficulty when it was pressed into his tiny fist. His right arm was regularly tied down to encourage him to use the other, and he was given a small drum to beat with his powerless left hand, to make him become conscious of the undeveloped muscles in his arm. In her letters to England Vicky had mentioned his trouble and her hopes that it would mend with time and treatment, and so far she and Fritz had managed to avoid a meeting between the boy and his maternal grandparents. But by autumn 1860 they were increasingly impatient to see him, and Vicky realized she could not keep them apart any longer. The Prince Consort was making plans for a visit to Coburg with the Queen and Princess Alice, and hoped they could all meet there in the second half of September.

The rendezvous got off to a bad start when the elderly Dowager Duchess of Coburg, Albert's stepmother, died as they were on their way to meet her. On 25 September Fritz and Vicky met Duke Ernest at Coburg station to await the royal party, and at last the Queen saw her grandson. She noted in her journal that he had his father's eyes and his mother's mouth, and for their sake she did her best not to look at his arm. It was the only saving grace of this German excursion for the Queen and the Prince Consort, as a few days later Baron Stockmar and Duke Ernest warned Vicky and Fritz that the Prince Consort was in a fragile state. He had just been involved in a minor coach accident and was physically unharmed but suffering from shock, convinced he would never see his birthplace again.

In November the Dowager Tsarina of Russia, sister of the King and Regent, passed away, and it was expected that the King would soon be released from his twilight existence. On last seeing him in June Fritz and Vicky had been horrified by the 'human ruin' lying in a bath chair with his left hand, arm, and both legs tied up, unable to speak or direct his eyes to look at anyone, showing no signs of consciousness except for looking up feebly to his right. By Christmas he was dying.

Soon after midnight on New Year's day 1861, they were summoned by telegram to Sans Souci to join the rest of the family at his bedside. After a few hours of waiting, Vicky was overcome with exhaustion and nodded off on a sofa while Fritz and the others, clad in black, paced up and down. They stayed till late afternoon, when Vicky was feeling so sick and faint that Fritz sent her back to the Neue Palais to bed. He remained at the vigil with the rest and was still there when the King breathed his last soon after 1 a.m. on 2 January 1861. His nephew and niece were now Crown Prince and Princess Friedrich Wilhelm.

When Vicky returned to the death chamber to bid him farewell, she could hardly bring herself to leave the scene. 'There was so much of comfort in looking there at that quiet peaceful form at rest at last after all he had suffered – gone home at last from this world of suffering – so peaceful and quiet he looked – like a sleeping child'.[12] Overcome with sympathy for the widowed Dowager Queen Elizabeth, complaining sadly that she was 'no longer of any use in this world', Vicky sat with her for a while. Having been one of the most hostile towards Vicky on her arrival at Berlin, she was immediately disarmed by her tenderness and obvious concern. From then on she made it clear that the Crown Princess had been the only person to take any notice of her, and it was a kindness she never forgot. Much to Augusta's fury, when Queen Elizabeth died twelve years later she broke with Prussian tradition, and instead of bequeathing her jewels to the crown she left them to Vicky.

King Friedrich Wilhelm IV had added a codicil to his last will and testament, urging his successors to the throne to refuse to take an oath to uphold the constitution. The Prince Consort was shocked that the King should have 'tried to provoke a breach of faith even after his death'[13] and even more by the court camarilla's efforts to put pressure on his successor to comply with this out of respect for his brother. To his relief King Wilhelm rejected their advice, saying he felt it his duty to conform to the Prussian constitution albeit reluctantly, on the grounds that it would be dangerous to oppose it.

A few days after his accession Queen Augusta advised Baron Schleinitz, the pro-French Minister for Foreign Affairs, to persuade the King to send Emperor Napoleon a fraternal letter of good wishes before he received the formal announcement of his accession, in order to establish closer Franco-Prussian relations. She enclosed a draft of the message, composed by herself, which she thought should be sent. Schleinitz replied to both King and Queen in favour of the scheme but the messenger muddled the letters, handing the King that intended for his wife and vice versa. Wilhelm was furious that she should 'meddle' in what he considered was no concern of hers, and she threatened to retire permanently to her summer residence at Koblenz. Only the tactful intervention of Fritz, persuading them to put their differences aside for the sake of the crown, prevented a worse breach.

The Prince Consort saw King Wilhelm's accession as the time for another attempt to write and influence him with his ideas. A free, united, outspoken Germany alone could win respect abroad, he told Vicky, while 'a reactionary tendency in Berlin would play havoc with everything.'[14] He had been further encouraged by the sudden death of the feared Gerlach, one of the old ultra-conservative guard, who had caught a chill at the King's funeral in January. Impatient with this thinly-veiled interference, the King threw Albert's letters into the fire without a second thought, scolding Fritz and Vicky bitterly as he did so.

To Fritz the Prince Consort suggested that his father ought to be crowned in Berlin to mark the beginning of the 'new era', instead of at the old capital Königsberg, the setting for all coronations since the Elector of Brandenburg had been crowned King Friedrich I of Prussia in 1701. Fritz told the King, who promptly snapped that everyone was plotting his downfall. The new King of Prussia, now answerable to nobody, was no more likely to take advice from his son and young daughter-in-law than from the liberal Coburg prince so despised and feared by his reactionary ministers. Any hopes they might have had of influencing him were undermined by his belief that the ministry wanted him to abdicate on account of his age and inflexibility over the army reforms, and that Fritz could not wait for him to step down and wear the crown instead. Nothing was further from Crown Prince Friedrich Wilhelm's wishes, but the King simply did not want to know.

Albert was particularly disappointed that King Wilhelm, first and foremost a military man, made it evident he was more interested in his army, which to him was the source of Prussia's strength, than in nationalist aspirations. His unwillingness to take a leading role on behalf of Prussia in German affairs irked Fritz and the liberals. Albert maintained that Prussia must first become 'the *moral* leader of Germany before it can raise itself as a power in Europe and this will not happen by adoption of hasty policies or by making outrageous claims; but by adoption of a bold, confident, truly German and completely liberal policy that corresponds to the needs of our time and the needs of the German nation, which will in turn make it impossible for any of the other German states to adopt any alternative course.'[15]

Fritz had several new duties as Crown Prince, in addition to his military work which occupied the mornings; there were council meetings to attend, deputations and audiences to see, and his father's papers to arrange. Resignedly, Vicky wrote to her mother that sometimes she saw little of her husband from one day to another, and often she did not know whether he was in the palace or not; they might as well not be married. As Crown Princess, she also had her share of audiences, to say nothing of extra demands made on her by Queen Augusta. Her mother-in-law's tyranny was a heavy cross to bear. She professed to be a close intimate of Queen Victoria, and both corresponded regularly; as the well-known liberal of the family, Augusta should have been Vicky's ally at court. Instead she took full advantage of her new position as first lady of the land, demanding that her word in all social matters must be regarded as law. Vicky was piqued at being treated as a kind of reserve lady-in-waiting, at her beck and call at all hours. It would have been easier to accept if Augusta had treated her with more warmth, but the elder woman's jealousy of the young, attractive Crown Princess with a lively personality to match meant little chance. Augusta resented the fact that Vicky was always ready to steal her thunder, or so she thought, and that the elderly King Wilhelm might not reign for long, leaving her as Queen Dowager without any influence. This was a problem with which Fritz could not help. To put up with his mother as meekly as possible was the lesser of two evils, as he told Vicky; 'If it keeps Mama quiet, it is in everybody's interest'.[16]

Vicky paid a short visit to England in March after the death of her maternal grandmother the Duchess of Kent, to find her mother temporarily bowed down by grief and her father almost worn out by the extra work this bereavement had added to his never-ending chores. She and Fritz went again in the summer by which time the atmosphere had improved, particularly as they were sure they had found the wife for Bertie, the charming young Princess Alexandra of Denmark. There was one major political drawback, namely the fact that her father Christian was heir to the throne of Denmark, which like Prussia also had a claim to the duchies of Schleswig and Holstein. Fritz declared gloomily that a marriage between his brother-in-law and a Danish princess would be contrary to Prussian interests, but there were no other suitable prospective brides in sight. While they were in England Fritz was suddenly summoned home after a student had attempted to assassinate the King, but the bullet had only wounded him lightly in the neck.

In September the Prince of Wales came to stay so he could attend the autumn manoeuvres at Koblenz with Fritz, and join them on a visit to Speyer Cathedral. It was arranged that he would meet Princess Alexandra while they spoke to her parents, Crown Prince and Princess Christian of Denmark. Bertie and Alix appeared taken with one another and it was a relief to Vicky to feel that she was helping to solve one family problem. It was some consolation for the increasing anxiety over the effect that army life was having on her husband. When appointed regimental Commander by his father during the manoeuvres of 1860 he could hardly contain his delight, telling Vicky excitedly of its status as the oldest regiment in the entire Prussian army and of its previous campaigns. Though she was pleased for him, she worried about his late nights and long absences from home, and the consequences for his health, reminding him that he was supposed to save his strength for the future when he would occupy a greater position. A tired, weak spirit and agitated nerves, she warned, 'can only weaken the mind – impairing judgement & blurring clear thought.' He only had to look at his father and mother for examples, she went on; 'you belong to your country & cannot, indeed must not, squander your strength this way!'[17] Such

61

words might almost have been her father's. Ironically his parents were destined to live to a great age, while at the time she wrote this letter, her chronically overworked father had less than four months ahead of him.

Fritz's thirtieth birthday, 18 October 1861, was chosen as the date for King Wilhelm's Coronation at Königsberg. Vicky, dressed in ermine and white satin with a gold-embroidered train, was utterly dazzled by the vivid colours of the scene; 'the chapel is in itself lovely, with a great deal of gold about it, and all hung with red velvet and gold – the carpet, altar, thrones and canopies the same.'[18] Fritz looked resplendent in his Silesian Grenadier uniform and mantle of the Black Eagle, which reached from his shoulders to the ground. The following day at a ceremony at Königsberg he accepted the Rectorship of the Royal Albertus University, an office previously held by the late King. Vicky was appointed Colonel-in-Chief of the 2nd Regiment of Hussars, which made her laugh at first; she thought it was a joke, as 'it seemed so strange for ladies'.

In the two-day whirlwind of festivity, Fritz did not immediately appreciate the unconstitutional implications of his father's coronation speech – 'mindful of the fact that the crown comes from God alone.'[19] It was a defiant assertion of the Divine Right, and a snub for liberals everywhere. While Fritz thought his father's views foolhardy, he had learnt from past experience that arguing with him on the subject, no matter how good his intentions, was a waste of time; it only reinforced the old man's stubborn convictions.

The fatigues of the coronation ceremonies left Vicky with a heavy cold, accompanied by high fever and an abscess in her ear. Among the symptoms of her illness which Fritz noted in his diary were acute pain in the left eye socket and nerves in her head, and 'horrible stabbing pains' in her ears which lasted for days 'despite leeches & warm compresses & medicine'.[20] At one stage Dr Wegner wrote to warn Queen Victoria that her daughter's life might be in danger. She was confined to bed for over three weeks, and Queen Augusta was angry when told that her daughter-in-law was not fit enough to accompany her at her social engagements. Even a planned twenty-first birthday party for Vicky was out of the question. Yet despite her poor health she was not blind to the strain leaving its mark on her husband. When he left Berlin in November for military service in Breslau he was obviously far from well, his complexion yellow and fatigued. Queen Augusta, her 'immensely strong constitution' and her hunger for society life were largely to blame, her nerves in a 'perpetual state of excitement'. Fritz suffered his mother's domineering manner in silence, feeling it his duty to let her have her way, as it kept her happy, and this was in everybody's interest.

On her birthday Vicky received a letter from her father bestowing his blessings on her, in typically Albertian phrases: 'May your life, which has begun beautifully, expand still further for the good of others, and the contentment of your own mind!' It ended with a warning; 'Without the basis of health it is impossible to rear anything stable. . . . Therefore see that you spare yourself now, so that at some future time you may be able to do more.'[21] It was one of the last letters, perhaps the last, he ever wrote to his favourite child. Perhaps he realized that time was not on his side; in view of subsequent events, his words had a hollow ring.

Three weeks later, on 13 December, Fritz received a telegram from the Prince Consort's private secretary, Sir Charles Phipps, asking him to prepare Vicky for her father's imminent death. Overwhelmed by work and anxiety, his constitution undermined by perpetual ailments, Albert had contracted pneumonia and was now in bed at Windsor Castle with typhoid fever. Trying to control her forebodings of imminent tragedy for the sake of appearances, Queen Victoria wrote optimistically to Vicky that he was ill but would soon be better. On 15 December the news reached Berlin that he had died on the previous evening. 'Why has the earth not swallowed me up?' was Vicky's reaction in her next letter to her mother. 'To be separated from you at this moment is a torture which I can not describe.'[22]

The Prince Consort's death deprived his eldest daughter of her foremost mentor, the most stable element in her life, the person who understood her better than anyone else, the only one whom she deemed capable of guiding her in her role as an English princess in a hostile foreign land. Only twenty-one at the time of his death, she was still learning to judge people and situations properly, still impulsive and inclined to jump to conclusions. Deprived of his leadership too early, it took her a long time to come to terms with her loss, and she was left with the unrealistic burden of trying to live up to her image of him. In some ways he had been her saviour, for even King Wilhelm and Queen Augusta had to take note of his words when he came to her defence, even if they betrayed considerable impatience with his 'interference'. She was aware that they regarded his death as more of a deliverance than anything else, and that there was no more than empty formality in most of her in-laws' expressions of sympathy and regret.

As the eldest child she felt herself under an obligation to try and give emotional support to her grief-stricken mother, who feared (as did her second daughter Alice, and some of the senior ministers) that the shock of bereavement might deprive her of her reason. Though devastated by her own grief, Vicky realized what her mother had lost, and tried to convince her that Papa had been too good for this earth; he was better off at eternal rest, and his death was God's will. No less importantly, she did her best to make her mother realize that Bertie's liaison with an actress, which the Queen had convinced herself broke his father's heart, was a foolish escapade but certainly not a capital offence. The Queen rebuked her daughter for preaching, assuring her that she might continue to lead 'an *utterly extinguished* life, but it will be *death in life*.'[23] She continued to write to her nearly every day, still expecting regular replies as before. Albert's letters had shown some political understanding of the Prussian character, albeit somewhat removed, but the Queen's emotional outpourings had none of her husband's restraint.

A more detached observer would have realized that the Prince Consort had done Fritz and Vicky, particularly the latter, an inadvertent disservice by his support. Though well-intentioned and high-principled, it virtually amounted to subtle interference in Prussian affairs. As a Coburger by birth and an Englishman in practice, if not in personality, by marriage, it was arguably not for him to try and take Prussia towards the goal of the liberal united Germany which he, Baron Stockmar and King Leopold all longed to see; and,

as Fritz had pointedly said to Vicky in a heated moment, it was not
his business to try and rule the land through King Wilhelm. It was
equally injudicious of him to make himself the pillar of support on
which they leaned and to whom they looked for advice. He should
have seen that the day would soon come when he was no longer
there to help them, especially as he was a sick man for the last few
months of his life; and, to use his own expression, did not 'cling to
life'. His plan had been for their secretary, Ernest von Stockmar, to
assume this counselling role gradually himself, but this revealed as
much as anything else his lack of understanding of both situation
and character. The Stockmars, father and son, were viewed with just
as much suspicion in Berlin as the Prince Consort himself, and by his
mere presence, their secretary in turn made Fritz and Vicky distrusted by the court camarilla. Moreover the younger Stockmar
lacked his father's drive and visionary outlook. The Prince misjudged
his character in the same way as he had that of King Wilhelm, both
as prince and sovereign, tending to see what he wanted to see till it
was too late.

Lastly, though few statesmen of the day had a more astute grasp
of constitutional politics than Prince Albert did, his textbook
knowledge of Prussian court life was based on hearsay and not
experience. Not having lived in Berlin, he was incapable of
understanding the conditions Vicky found at court after her
marriage, from the stiff etiquette and narrow-minded elderly
princes, to the deep-rooted distrust of any connection with
parliamentary government. That she had inherited much of his
analytical mind and way of thinking was her great misfortune,
according to Mary Bulteel, she 'divided everything into three heads,
turning them about so much that she often came to a wrong
conclusion.'[24] Men like the liberal-minded Max Duncker, appointed
political adviser to Fritz earlier in 1861, lacked Albert's intellectual
foresight but were better placed to advise, as they knew Prussia from
first-hand experience.

Vicky still had much to learn about dealing with people. Wally
Hohenthal was dismayed at her readiness to take 'violent fancies' to
others. 'She used at first to think them quite perfect and then came

the bitter disillusion. She also took first-sight dislikes to persons, based often only on a trick of manner, or an idle word dropped about them in her presence, and thus she often lost useful friends and supporters. She was no judge of character, and never became one, because her own point of view was the only one she could see.' Her husband, Wally noted, was 'undeveloped for his age', and it was evident whose was the stronger character.[25] Fritz's adjutant, General Lothar von Schweinitz, who had accompanied him to England in 1858 and attended the wedding, recalled that after the bride said goodbye to her English family, she took her husband energetically by the arm and led him to the railway carriage, adding that she 'led him all through life in the same way'.[26]

Dr Wegner forbade Vicky to visit England at once and comfort her mother, as she was in the early stages of her third pregnancy, and still convalescent at the time of her father's death. Fritz went instead, and the Queen unburdened her grief to him as she described her husband's last hours in detail. Brokenly she told how his illness had started and progressed; how he had been reconciled with the wayward Bertie after his liaison with a young woman while at Curragh earlier in the year; how she had held his hand to the end, only realising that he had passed away by the spiritual look on his face. Then, taking his hand and leading him into the bedroom she showed him the corpse dressed in a blue overcoat, his hands holding a photograph of the Queen. He stayed for the funeral at St George's Chapel, Windsor, on 23 December, at which he and the Prince of Wales were chief mourners.

Vicky felt particularly isolated while he was away, but in February 1862 she was given her chance to go to Windsor. If she found it an impossible task trying to comfort the inconsolable Queen, both women benefited from the emotional reunion. As a young wife who remained as passionately in love with her husband as she was the day they were married, she understood her widowed mother's plight better than anyone else as she described the sense of loss to Fritz; Papa's empty room, empty bed, how she slept with Papa's coat over her, the red dressing gown beside her and some of his clothes in the bed. She herself desperately missed her father's ready good morning and good night, and it almost seemed to her 'as if the sun had stopped shining'.[27]

Others in Prussia thought the sun had stopped shining on their Crown Prince and Princess as well. Shortly after Christmas rumours began to circulate that he had fallen for the attentions of an attractive lady at court, and that his jealous wife was leaving for England where she would begin divorce proceedings against him. To their fury Baron Stockmar and other members of their household received letters asking if there was any truth in these stories, which Fritz blamed on the machinations of the arch-conservative *Kreuzzeitung* party. Such slanders were without foundation, nonetheless credible as nobody had any illusions about the unhappy marriage of the King and Queen, or of his brother Friedrich Karl and his much-bullied wife Marianne. Nevertheless these malicious whispers marked the beginning of a persistent campaign against the 'non-Prussian' Crown Princess, accused of being an agent of another power, dominating a mild-mannered weak husband. It was something they had to learn to accept, or live with at any rate.

Prussian elections in December 1861 had produced a greatly increased liberal majority, hostile to military reforms. After discovering that extra funds had been fraudulently diverted towards the army, the ministry insisted that all such expenditure should be strictly accounted for in future. Despite Fritz's warning that to dismiss the ministry would exacerbate any conflict between crown and parliament, and that its presence was vital for the maintenance of the fragile balance between the most reactionary conservatives and radical liberals, the King dissolved the *Landtag* in March, replacing the liberal ministers with conservatives, led by Prince Adolf von Hohenlohe-Ingelfingen. Though the new Minister-President was a moderate by conservative standards, his appointment was still welcomed by the *Kreuzzeitung*.

Vicky warned Fritz in a letter that if the King looked to the conservatives to solve the crisis, 'then all bright hopes are finished during his reign, for if he once gets into the hands of those people, he will never get away while he is alive.' The best he could do, she recommended, was for him to keep away from parliamentary sittings in the event of an anti-liberal government. 'You owe it to your future, to the country and to your children to keep aloof from everything which might lead the people to have an erroneous idea of your political convictions, or that might shake the confidence which you have won by your liberal attitude and your collaboration with Ministers holding those opinions.'[28]

In a meeting with the King that same month Fritz made clear his complete agreement with 'essential liberal policy for internal and foreign affairs' – basically, no ill-considered reform of the army and taxation at home, and closer links with the rest of Europe. The King reproached him for being hand-in-glove with the Liberals, warning him that as Crown Prince he was placing himself in jeopardy with his liberal views, especially as the press was rather tactlessly describing his attitude as being in opposition to his father. Fritz was angry and bewildered; surely there was a wide difference, he wrote to Vicky, between the freely-expressed opinions of an unbiased person, such as himself, and an opponent deliberately setting himself up against the King.[29] The liberals wanted him to break with the King, while the military establishment were rumoured to be planning a coup in favour of the King's brother Prince Friedrich Karl.

It was in these months that Vicky's influence on him began to make an impact. Mild, good-natured but indecisive, Fritz was upset by family quarrels and often caught between both sides of an argument, and Vicky reinforced his belief in his own opinions, giving him a measure of badly-needed self-confidence. With a bullying father and an indifferent mother, neither of whom had cared about him nearly as much as Queen Victoria and Prince Albert had about each of their brood of nine, he badly needed somebody in the family to give him support, encouragement and faith in the future. The Prince Consort had done so to the best of his ability, and Vicky vowed to do likewise. A Crown Princess of Prussia carrying out such a sacred trust from her late father, her Hohenzollern in-laws feared, would be a formidable character. Some of them saw it would be in their best interests to try and minimize her influence on their Crown Prince, or failing that, use attack – in other words, attacking her reputation – as the best form of defence.

Husband and wife had always differed in their outlook to a degree, and always would. Vicky had inherited her father's conviction that Prussia needed to adopt a more liberal constitution before aspiring to German leadership, and shared the policy of more left-wing members of the *Landtag* who wanted Prussia to adopt parliamentary democracy along British lines. This was too radical for Fritz, a supporter of German unification first and liberalization second. For Prussia to emerge as leader of the German states, it needed to subjugate the opposition of other German rulers to unification under it, if necessary by force. Moreover he took issue with the liberals who aimed to increase parliamentary power at the crown's expense. As far as he was concerned free expression, free trade and popular education could be attained without altering the constitution or subordinating the monarchy's powers to parliament. The assembly's role was to defend existing laws and institute progressive reforms as long as they could be achieved through mutual cooperation between crown and parliament.

Fritz was more cautious than his wife, more introspective, reluctant to embrace conflict and controversy; she was impulsive, impatient, and as she readily admitted, loved a good fight. A few more years of guidance and restraint from her father might have taught her the wisdom of proceeding more slowly and surely, of seeing situations with a more elastic judgment. She was irritated by her husband's apparent unwillingness to use his position to initiate or promote liberal changes in Prussian policy, not fully appreciating that his position as heir to the throne prevented him from doing so. All he could do was attend meetings of the crown council and council of ministers as an observer, and act as his father's representative abroad. Such minimal power and influence as he thus had were also exaggerated by his liberal supporters, who like Vicky often expected him to be able to provide more than he could deliver. Years of experience eventually persuaded her to see matters more his way, and she revised her outlook as inspired by her father, who had gone to his grave insistent that Prussia should be the self-appointed champion of morality and legality, peacefully attracting other German states to the concept of unification under Prussian leadership. In due course she accepted the policy of other German liberals who advocated decisive action on behalf of the nationalist cause whenever Prussia faced a foreign policy crisis, thus revising their ideas on moral conquests to suit the situation. Force was only permissible if used to advance the liberal-national goals of unification, self-determination of the German people under foreign rule, and the preservation of constitutionalism.

It was unfortunate that she had been temporarily thrown off balance by her father's premature death. In the months immediately afterwards, she clung so tenaciously to his example that for a time it was impossible for her to see that Prussia's future developments would have eventually resulted in him revising his opinions.

With so much unpleasantness at home, Fritz was glad to go regularly to England, although he doubted the wisdom of Queen Victoria in allowing a foreign prince to deputise for her so frequently, and he regretted having to leave Vicky behind. He opened the second international exhibition in May, in his capacity as President of the Exhibition Commission appointed to prepare Prussia's role in the display, and a few days later he was a special guest of the Royal Academy of Arts at their annual dinner. The other guests were impressed by his speech with his clear grasp of the English language, in which he dwelt on his genuine love of his wife's country. Queen Victoria claimed that her grief made it impossible for her or her children to participate in such festivities, but as Fritz had feared, the English public was not over-impressed with the spectacle of a German prince performing such public functions in England.

Meanwhile there were growing rumours that Bismarck might be appointed as the 'strong man' to come and solve the crisis his own way. As federal representative at Frankfurt and Prussian representative at St Petersburg, his name was already a byword for abhorrence of Britain and liberal government, and the Prince Consort had vetoed his nomination for Prussian ambassador in London the previous year, on the grounds that a man who had taken such a pro-Russian stance during the Crimean war was no friend of England. Vicky was aware of his reputation as an unprincipled character and dreaded the consequences if he was appointed, while Fritz knew him to be his mother's 'deadly enemy', and hoped at least for her sake that he would not be summoned. Bismarck had written and circulated a report of his meeting in London with Lord Palmerston and the Foreign Secretary Lord John Russell, in his capacity as Foreign Minister, calling the English constitution contrary to his principles, as it stipulated that the crown's advisers should come from the parliamentary majority's ranks, thus allowing for 'great and permanent encroachments' on the royal prerogative. This despatch, Fritz wrote, was a grim foretaste of what might be in store for them 'if that man were sooner or later to control the destinies of Prussia!'[30]

As she was in the eighth month of her third pregnancy Vicky was unable to attend Alice's wedding, held privately in the dining room at Osborne on 1 July with Fritz as best man. On 14 August her third child, Henry Wilhelm Albert, was born. Queen Augusta thought that he would be known as Albert, as a name which 'really ought to be handed down as a legacy from the never-to-be-forgotten grandfather – and I believe that Queen Victoria expected it too.'[31] However he was called Henry in the family.

By this time the political crisis was reaching deadlock. Further elections in May had resulted in a heavy defeat for the conservatives, with corresponding gains for the liberals and progressives. Any compromise between the King's ministers who defended his prerogative and his reform programme, and the elected parliament, 85 per cent of which were members of the opposition, appeared out of the question. The King vowed to prevent any parliamentary attempt to undermine his prerogative, while the *Landtag* was determined to reject the military budget and impose parliamentary government on the crown. Some liberals, prepared to hold out an olive branch, offered to abandon their opposition if the government agreed to accept their demand to reduce the term of military service from three to two years. The King would not yield, telling them he would rule without a military budget, but his ministers rejected this on the grounds that he would be placing the crown in violation of the constitution. Roon advised him to summon Bismarck and give him a cabinet post, or entrust him with the reins of government in order to strengthen the case of the crown, but he declared that he would rather abdicate.

On 17 September the *Landtag* was called upon to vote the measures en bloc, and defeated them by 308 votes to 11. Anarchy was everywhere, the King raged, and he would sooner abdicate than yield. General Roon, Minister for War, advised that either they could stage a *coup d'état*, and authorise illegal collection of taxes in defiance of the constitution, or else he would call Bismarck to take over the government. Next day he sent the latter a telegram urging him to return at once.

Fritz and Vicky had gone to see Queen Victoria at Gotha, but the King recalled Fritz to Berlin because of the impending crisis. On 18 September, with tears in his eyes, he showed his son the deed of abdication and the draft of the speech in which he would announce that he was relinquishing the throne. It was a carefully-considered decision; God and his conscience, he said sadly, would not allow him to do anything else. If the ministry refused to accept his reforms, he would make way for his son.

Fritz, astonished, was overcome with sympathy for the 'poor broken old man'. This was no threat to abdicate in the heat of the moment, and he did not appreciate that his father was only doing so because he knew that Fritz himself would spare no effort to implore him from taking such a drastic step. Moreover he was worried about the precedent that would be set if a Prussian sovereign could be forced or cajoled into abdication like this as a result of parliamentary decisions, and the threat it would pose to dynasty, crown and country. Much as he respected the institution of parliamentary government and the constitution, he revered the crown still more.

Though he was nominally opposed to the two-year term of military service, he tried to impress on his father that conceding on the two-year term would not be comparable with the consequences of relinquishing the throne. He tried to convince the cabinet to support the King so that abdication could be avoided, but the ministers remained resolutely divided on the two-year service term. He spent the next forty-eight hours trying to mediate between the King and his ministers, brokering a compromise; conceding part of the way on military training would be far preferable to abdication.

That evening he wrote to Vicky, who had remained in Gotha with Queen Victoria and Lord Clarendon, and explained everything; she was equally taken aback, but she guessed that the King was playing for high stakes and understood his son only too well to know what Fritz's answer would be. Why, she suggested, should they not take the chance? They must not think of themselves, but of the fatherland and of their children who would otherwise one day have to make good where they had failed. If the King felt he could not take the necessary steps to restore order and confidence in Prussia without going against his conscience, she said, it would be only 'wise and honest' to leave it to others who could take over such duties without burdening their conscience. She could see no way out, and considered he should make the sacrifice for the sake of their country; if he did not accept his father's decision, she believed that he would come to regret it one day.[32]

Unlike her husband, she was glad that things had come to a head. For once they could do more than remain silent in the face of such drastic circumstances. 'What is expected of you as a dutiful son and subject is so very difficult and severe, but this cannot be compared to what you would have to contend with if you stood idly by watching your father forfeit his popularity (a process that is already underway) and watching errors being committed that could threaten crown and country!'[33] To her it was a golden if unexpected opportunity to see her husband's accession lead to the establishment of government in Prussia after the British example.

Fritz was not ready to embrace such radical changes, one of his reasons for opposing his father's threat to abdicate. He knew that as King he would find himself caught between liberal and conservative forces, and would be confronted by entrenched reactionary opposition to his liberal views. It had already been made clear to him that the army would not let him ascend the throne if he allowed himself to become too closely identified with liberal aspirations, if only by means of a military conspiracy to remove him from the line of succession in favour of Prince Friedrich Karl, who would willingly be a tool of the Junkers and their clique. At the same time he would have been reluctant to cooperate with the radical liberal majority in parliament. His father's abdication would have signalled the liberals' victory in the constitutional conflict, and the first item on their agenda would have been demands for genuine parliamentary government. As he had no intention of sacrificing any powers of the crown to parliament, further conflict between both sides would have quickly followed. Moreover to find himself unexpectedly King of Prussia, by means which ran counter to his respect for the natural laws of succession, with a crowd of hostile reactionary ministers, a former King watching his every move, and a Queen Consort unpopular with the Court and her in-laws, would have been impossible.

On 22 September Bismarck met the King, to be told gravely that if they could not come to some understanding, the act of abdication would be published forthwith. Bismarck had only one answer: 'royal government or the supremacy of Parliament'.[34] Next day he was proclaimed Minister-President of Prussia. The fears of Vicky and Fritz were confirmed; for the immediate future, while King Wilhelm reigned, Bismarck would rule. It was an appointment destined to have unforeseen consequences, not only for the hapless Crown Prince and Princess of Prussia, but also for both the map and the history of Europe for over half a century.

FOUR

'Youth is hasty with words'

Vicky and Fritz were certain that if Bismarck was appointed, he would exacerbate the crisis by violating the constitution in order to secure the King's army reforms. People everywhere, they knew, would be suspicious of reaction, distrust would be aroused on all sides of the political spectrum, and the King would have many difficult moments as the result of appointing such a 'dishonest character'.[1] In the Minister-President's maiden speech to the parliamentary finance committee, he said that the German people looked to Prussia not for liberalism but for power. Prussia's frontiers, as fixed by the Congress of Vienna, were not suitable for healthy development; her goal was the development of its power, and the great questions of the time would not be solved by speeches and majority decisions – that was the great mistake from 1848 to 1849 – but by iron and blood.[2] His words were less a call to arms than an appeal to the *Landtag* finance committee to fund military reforms, as Prussian ability to assume leadership of the German confederation depended not just on military power but also on alliances and a strong foreign policy to weaken the alliances of Prussia's enemies. His political adversaries, as well as subsequent German historians, saw it as his determination to achieve unification by war, and his implicit threat to resort to such means was clearly seen.

There was another, more personal problem for Vicky and Fritz. Earlier that month the Prince of Wales had been betrothed to Princess Alexandra of Denmark. Her father Prince Christian was heir to the Danish throne, and on his accession the Schleswig-Holstein question would almost certainly create controversy. The duchies of Schleswig and Holstein, the latter with a large German population, had been ruled by Denmark since the London Protocol

75

of 1852. With the growth of German nationalist feeling, the citizens of both were increasingly restless and the death of the present King, Frederik VII, would bring demands for recognition or self-government to a head, particularly on the part of Holstein and German areas of Schleswig, objecting to the administration of their Danish overlords. By marrying her heir to one of the country's princesses, Britain was making her Danish sympathies evident. The knowledge that Fritz and Vicky had helped to bring the marriage about, probably thanks to the indiscreet Duke of Coburg, did nothing for their popularity in Prussia. The Duke, a fervent champion of German unification, called the match a 'thunder-clap' for Germany,[3] and warned his niece that she had harmed herself as a result.

Fritz and Vicky were anxious to distance themselves from Bismarck's government and policies. Though a fortuitously-timed holiday away from Berlin might have been seen by some as politic but cowardly withdrawal, they would not have been able to do anything to advance the cause of liberalism by staying in Berlin at this difficult time. Queen Victoria had invited Alix to stay at Windsor in order to get to know her better, and wanted Bertie out of England. He was borrowing the royal yacht *Osborne* for a Mediterranean cruise, and it was suggested that Fritz and Vicky should join the party, in order to demonstrate that the Crown Prince's absence from Germany would prove to the liberals that he neither condoned nor took part in plans by the new government to violate the constitution.[4] They did not give it a second thought, and though the King complained when they asked his permission to go, he was glad to see the back of them. The presence of his 'disobedient' son and daughter-in-law in Prussia during the constitutional crisis was not required.

Before their departure, on the advice of Vicky and Ernest von Stockmar, Fritz had written to Bismarck warning him that any attempt to violate the constitution would create an atmosphere of mistrust between crown and people, which would stifle the government in its domestic and foreign relations. Any solution to the conflict, he emphasized, must be achieved according to the constitution and the will of the people.

They left Coburg on 6 October, and sailed from Marseilles a fortnight later. During the next few weeks they explored the ruins of Carthage, visited the Bey of Tunis, lunched in the open air at Syracuse in a grove of orange and lemon trees, gazed at the bay of Naples while Vicky sketched, and walked up the dormant Mount Vesuvius. Fritz guided her round the art treasures and churches at Rome, and they went to see the Pope. Afterwards the pontiff told Lord Odo Russell, English representative at the Vatican, that in the whole of his long life he had never been more favourably impressed by anyone than by the Crown Princess of Prussia. Vicky may have been similarly impressed by the Pope, but she was very scathing about what she called the 'dumb foolery' of High Mass – priests dressing and undressing, bobbing up and down, and mumbling Latin so fast as to be unintelligible, a ceremony which almost made her laugh.

While they were away Bismarck had sought a compromise with parliament, as he hoped that the strife could be settled if minor concessions were made to the liberal opposition. Like Fritz, Bismarck was not opposed to the two-year service term, and he arranged a plan whereby conscripts could purchase their release from military service after two years, any funds thus raised to be used to attract volunteers; those who could not pay would serve a third year. This scheme was anathema to the King, who claimed that anything less than the three-year term would be fatal to the army. Bismarck then suggested a further concession to the opposition by offering cabinet posts to three senior liberal deputies, but they insisted on the two-year term as a condition of acceptance. Though Bismarck told the liberals in private that he would secure the King's consent to the two-year term, the liberals, well aware of their sovereign's stubbornness on the issue, refused to enter the government.

Having failed to effect a compromise between crown and parliamentary opposition, Bismarck had to find an alternative solution. On the King's orders he withdrew the budget for 1863, which had been submitted to parliament with that for the previous year, thus preventing the opposition from voting down funds for the 1862 army reorganization. In a speech before the budget committee, he declared that if parliament refused further funds for the new year he would rule without a budget, a measure justified by the fact that parliament had no exclusive power over military estimates. It was therefore imperative that an agreement with the crown should be reached. Rejection of the budget by either power constituted an emergency, which empowered the government to govern without a budget, as the crown retained all rights not expressly allocated to parliament by the constitution. When progressive party member Rudolf Virchow declared that it was unconstitutional for the government to rule without a budget, Bismarck answered that the constitution made no provision for what was to happen if it was rejected by parliament. As the constitution was deficient in this aspect, the government was obliged to prevent a standstill of all business, and must continue even if that implied expenditure without lawful parliamentary enactment. This failed to persuade the liberals, who accepted the financial estimates for 1863 but rejected the figures for military expenditure. Bismarck dissolved parliament on 13 October, proclaiming a state of emergency and announcing that the government would rule without a budget approved by parliament, submitting a bill of indemnity only when normal conditions were resumed.

After the dissolution he assured Fritz that, while his ministry would continue to do everything possible to resolve the conflict in a manner satisfactory to all, parliament's uncooperative attitude could result in measures incompatible with the letter of the constitution. As minister-president he was frustrated by the perpetuation of the conflict and felt that the situation was becoming untenable, but even so he said he was committed to removing all barriers to compromise between crown and parliament. While professing a desire to work amicably with the Crown Prince, insisting that he was no reactionary and had no allegiance to any political party, nor any objection to the liberals, he had to take care not to adopt a liberal policy lest parliament interpret this as submission of the government to the will of parliament.

The Prince and Princess of Wales were married on 10 March 1863 at St George's Chapel, Windsor, with Vicky and Fritz among those present, Fritz as the groom's best man. Highland-clad Willy took advantage of the occasion to give a foretaste of his future behaviour towards the family in England. Bored during the long service, he threw the dirk from his stocking on the chapel floor; when his uncles, twelve-year-old Arthur and nine-year-old Leopold, scolded him, he retaliated by biting them in the legs. Vicky and Fritz were pleased to hear that the King had kept a promise which he had verbally given them and attended a dinner given by the British Ambassador at the embassy in Berlin that same evening to celebrate the wedding. Bismarck had warned him that in view of Prussia's attitude towards Denmark it would not be prudent, but to no avail.

Fritz's suspicions that Bismarck believed in the maxim 'might is right' were confirmed by his intervention against the Polish rising in the spring of 1863. Poland was a state east of Prussia, partitioned between Russia, Prussia and Austria, whose government considered such an arrangement was justified as the Poles could not be expected to provide strong government themselves. Throughout Germany, among radicals in Austria, and most other European nations there was much sympathy for the Poles, victims of Russian oppression. Vicky and Fritz shared the Liberals' anger when Bismarck signed a treaty with Russia promising Prussian aid with putting down any trouble. It was tantamount to a declaration of unprovoked war, as the rebels had not taken up arms against the Prussian government, but only against the repression of Tsarist rule, and their action was confined to Russian Poland. Bismarck, however, told an aggrieved Fritz that, one day, they would be glad he had sought the Tsar's gratitude. Ignoring the liberals' demands for a declaration of strict neutrality, he mobilized Prussian regiments in the Eastern provinces to help crush the insurgents if necessary.

By the spring of 1863, observers said that liberals were becoming alienated from the dynasty by their Crown Prince's passive attitude towards the new regime, and some wanted him to be supplanted in the line of succession to the throne by his brother-in-law Frederick, Grand Duke of Baden. To save his reputation, he would be advised to break his silence. Further pressure to do so came in May when the King and Bismarck dissolved parliament after the opposition claimed a right to free speech without interruption from government ministers, and Bismarck proposed to issue an edict against the liberal press in a meeting of the ministerial council in May 1863. Fritz knew it was difficult to justify a decree against the press on constitutional grounds, and while he did not oppose it at the meeting, he made his feelings on the subject clear to his father.

On 31 May, before beginning a tour of military inspection in East Prussia, Fritz, fearful of what might happen next, wrote to his father begging him not to infringe the constitution, in return for keeping a promise not to oppose his views openly. Out of respect for his father, and a wish not to be identified with the opposition which wrongly considered him as one of its own, he had held his silence; but he felt justified in abandoning passive resistance on the grounds that it was his duty to speak if the King's prestige and the welfare of Prussia were under threat. Such a measure, he said, was against the integrity of the constitution and would seriously endanger the standing of the crown. Vicky assured him that one day his father would thank him for telling him the truth and having the courage to act in accordance with his own opinions; 'when feelings of duty and conscientiousness collide with your obligation to be obedient, you must satisfy the demands of your conscience *before* those of your father and King.'[5] The King replied that Fritz's 'opposition speeches' had spread abroad; now he had a chance to redeem himself by keeping his distance from the liberals and radicals, and allying himself with Conservative opinion.

A decree was to be published empowering the suppression of newspapers and periodicals 'for persisting in an attitude endangering the commonweal'; the offences listed included 'undermining respect and loyalty towards the King' and 'exposing to hatred or contempt state institutions'.[6] As the constitution guaranteed freedom of the press, Fritz replied on 3 June that he considered the cabinet proceedings illegal and contrary to state and dynastic interests. Receiving no reply to this, he wrote again the following day, apologizing for causing his father pain, but standing by his protest against such infringement of the constitution. He and Vicky were not alone in their views, which were shared by several of Bismarck's colleagues.

Undeterred, the King dissolved parliament and signed an edict silencing the opposition press. The liberals protested that this measure was unconstitutional as it was created while parliament was still in session and there was no 'unusual emergency', and on 4 June the Berlin city council voted to send a delegation to the King registering its disquiet at the government's arbitrary behaviour. All protests were immediately suppressed by the government. None of the ministers bothered to notify the Crown Prince or Princess of the edict, and like everyone else they only learnt of it from the newspapers. Fritz immediately wrote to his father expressing his dismay. Unlike the liberals he did not attack it as unconstitutional, but he said that it went against the 'true spirit of the constitution.' While admitting that the opposition press posed a threat to the government, he suggested that the menace could have been assuaged without going to such lengths, and recommended that the decree should be rescinded as it would incite the opposition to further protest.

Vicky thought this response was too mild. When Fritz arrived in Danzig on 4 June, she and Leopold von Winter, Mayor of Danzig, argued that he stood to lose as much as his father in popular support unless he spoke publicly against the decree, adding that his silence on the subject would be interpreted as approval. His decision to speak on the subject was reinforced by the dismal mood of the public at Danzig, as he realized that they interpreted his silence as approval of the press edict.

Vicky was adamant that he should not remain silent any longer. A parade by the Danzig garrison in his presence on 5 June was followed by a reception at the town hall. Winter, a former Berlin chief of police, had suggested that the Crown Prince ought to declare his views openly. Welcoming his royal guest on the platform he apologised for the lukewarm festivities in the town, owing to the gloom they all felt over the decree. Fritz then rose to his feet and said how he regretted the conflict between government and constitution. He knew nothing of the decrees; he was absent at the time, 'and took no part in the deliberations which led to these ordinances. But we all, and I myself most of all, since I know best the noble and paternal aims and lofty sentiments of His Majesty the King – we all have confidence that . . . the kingdom of Prussia is advancing steadily towards that greatness which Providence has destined for our nation.'[7]

His delivery of the address left him with mixed feelings. While he was glad to have a chance of proving his sincerity to the liberal cause, making it known that he was opposed to Bismarck and his unsavoury policies, and proving to the world that he had no part in his schemes, he feared that the speech could result in a complete break with his father. The King considered it verging on treason, writing him 'a furious letter, treating him quite like a little child; telling him instantly to retract in the newspapers the words he had used at Danzig, charging him with disobedience, etc., and telling him that if he said one other word of the kind he would instantly recall him and take his place in the Army and the Council from him.'[8] Fritz refused to retract his words, as he was well aware of the consequences of his behaviour, and asked his father to understand that he was standing by his convictions. As an officer in the army he was technically guilty of insubordination, and under military law liable to imprisonment. A precedent existed in the case of another Friedrich of Prussia in the previous century; as Crown Prince, Friedrich the Great had been imprisoned by his father for similar resistance.

The King's brother Karl suggested that he should be confined in a fortress, but Bismarck knew that to make a martyr of the Crown Prince would do much for liberal opinion in Prussia. He cautioned the King that imprisonment or any kind of persecution would make the Crown Prince a martyr to the liberals and strengthen their resistance against the government; 'deal gently with the young man Absalom' was his view. It would be more prudent to issue a sharp warning that any repetition of the Danzig speech would not be tolerated. He also persuaded the King to let Fritz continue the military inspection tour, since any deviation from his schedule could give the impression that he was planning further acts of insubordination. Finally he recommended that in future the Crown Prince should be kept busy with ministry meetings and affairs of state so there would be less chance for him to have any contact with his liberal advisers.

The King accepted this and wrote to Fritz, informing him that he was free to share the opinions of the opposition, but not to make them public. He was prepared to forgive the Danzig episode as long as his son promised not to broadcast anti-government views again. Fritz was prepared to accept his father's terms for reconciliation as he had no intention of criticizing the government again, much to Vicky's disappointment. 'A year of silence and self-denial has brought Fritz no other fruits than that of being considered weak and helpless,' she wrote to Queen Victoria. 'The Liberals think that he is not sincerely one of them, and those few who think it, fancy he has not the courage to avow it. He has now given them an opportunity of judging his way of thinking and consequently will now again be passive and silent until better days come.'[9]

In London *The Times* claimed that the Crown Prince had 'cleared away the mist of doubt which hung around him and dimmed his popularity, that he greatly improved his position before the country, and gave, for the future, an implied pledge precious to the people and most important to his dynasty'.[10] This was an exaggeration, as the German liberals criticized him for his remark that he knew nothing about the discussions that brought the press decree about. They knew he attended crown council meetings and that he must have known the edict was under consideration, so in their view his comments cast some doubt on his sincerity. Queen Victoria unequivocally endorsed their action, telling her daughter that she was 'the best and wisest adviser he could have, and the worthy child of your beloved father who will look down approvingly on you.'[11] Such encouragement was not best calculated to make Vicky act with caution in the future, but she was right to explain that the intention of the Danzig speech was 'to convey in a clear and *unzweideutig* (unambiguous) way to his hearers, that he had *nothing* to do with the unconstitutional acts of the Government – that he was not even aware of their being in contemplation!'[12] Liberals also criticized his endorsement of his father in the speech, which to them seemed uncalled for as the King endorsed Bismarck's decree.

Despite their reservations, some prominent liberals tried to persuade Fritz to deliver a more unequivocal statement of opposition to Bismarck's government. The Grand Duke of Baden and his foreign minister, Hans von Roggenbach, advised him to resign his military posts or refuse to perform any more official functions till the ministry ceased its unconstitutional business, and one liberal deputy, Karl Mathy, said he hoped the Danzig speech would be but the first in a series of statements against the Minister-President's policies. Queen Victoria also encouraged her son-in-law to show his disapproval by breaking off his military inspection tour forthwith, absenting himself from Prussia and coming to England. 'He cannot satisfy his father by half measures,' she wrote to Vicky, 'and he may compromise his and his children's position if he does not clearly show to the country that he not only does not belong to that party, but highly disapproves what has been done!'[13]

Knowing that any sudden end to his tour would constitute another act of insubordination, Fritz prudently declined the invitation. Any further anti-government statements, he realized, would push him into the arms of the progressive party. If the progressives wished to claim him as one of their own, he believed, he would not be able to restrain them any more than he could prevent Bismarck's efforts to bring him over to his point of view. Having made his views plain at Danzig, he refused to say or do any more as he did not want to set himself up as a leader of the opposition. Before the speech, he had foreseen that any protest on his part would be bound to create confusion. His much-criticized homage to his father was meant to convince everyone that the King had not turned against them, and to hold out hope that in time he would reverse his support for Bismarck's damaging unconstitutional methods. It was intended as a gesture of faith in the King, and he had no intention of giving any support to a radical Liberal majority, whose aims he opposed.

Sensing that his reluctance to adopt a more self-assertive position could discredit his image as a liberal, Vicky arranged for the publication of her husband's letters in the foreign press which would place his opposition on record. On 11 June she asked Queen Victoria to publicize the Danzig speech in England, and sent her extracts from his correspondence, adding that other letters had been entrusted to Stockmar and the Grand Duke of Baden. Her campaign had no effect in Prussia, where the press edict forbade any publication of the letters; the circulation of rumours made Prussian liberals doubt the validity of the correspondence, and the furore soon died down.

In the long run, the Danzig incident did little to reassure liberals of Fritz's devotion to their cause. Bismarck was sure the Crown Princess had masterminded the entire episode to obtain publicity for her husband's actions and to acquaint public opinion with their philosophy. Embarrassed by the affair, Fritz begged the recipients of his letters not to show them to anyone. 'I will tell you what results I anticipate from your policy,' he wrote to Bismarck. 'You will go on quibbling with the Constitution until it loses all value in the eyes of the people. In that way you will on the one hand arouse anarchical movements that go beyond the bounds of the Constitution; while on the other hand, whether you intend it or not, you will pass from one venturesome interpretation to another until you are finally driven into an open breach of the Constitution. I regard those who lead his Majesty the King, my most gracious father, into such courses as the most dangerous advisers for Crown and Country.' 'Youth is hasty with words,' Bismarck scrawled in the margin.[14]

Yet he continued to try and convince his father that Bismarck and his unconstitutional policies were a liability to the monarchy, insisting that all constitutional conflict could be ended if Bismarck resigned and the King accepted the two-year service term. Angered at his son's persistence, the King told him he would obtain his military reforms through regular dissolutions of parliament if necessary until he had secured 'obedience'. Fritz also spoke to Bismarck, who shocked him by saying that a constitutional regime was 'untenable' in Prussia. Asked why he still bothered with the constitution at all, Bismarck said he would observe existing laws as long as he reasonably could.

The dilemma involved Vicky in much soul-searching with regard to her status in Prussia. She found it 'very disagreeable' to be seen by others as meddling and intriguing in politics, which she knew was not 'a ladies' profession' in Germany any more than it was in

England. How easy it would be, she knew, to choose a quiet life and live in peace with everybody, whose affection she would gain 'if I sought it by having no opinion of my own'; but she would not be 'a free-born Englishwoman' and her mother's child if she took the simpler option. It was still impossible for her to break free of her inheritance and the conviction that she had been sent to Prussia with a mission. She took heart from the fact that the aristocracy, who so disliked Queen Augusta, were at least still civil to her, 'though they looked upon me with jealousy as a stranger and as an English-woman,' and with her youthful optimism acknowledged that they saw that she was full of goodwill and wanted nothing more than to be friends with them.[15] Her optimism and good faith were to be sorely tested in the years ahead.

Fritz had been ordered to join his father at Gastein, where discussions were taking place with Emperor Franz Josef about the latter's suggestion of calling a conference of reigning German princes for the settlement of German affairs at Frankfurt. Efforts were being made to reach a compromise between Austria and Prussia, both struggling for supreme power in the future of the German Confederation. The King considered it his duty but his Minister wanted to prevent him, asking him bluntly if Austria was going to dictate to Prussia. Bismarck pleaded, cajoled, raged at his master, and eventually got his way with the excuse that Prussia's invitation had arrived so late that it was an insult. Fritz would also have welcomed Prussian participation at Frankfurt, knowing that the question of rivalry in the Confederation between his country and Austria could only be solved by either such a meeting, or armed conflict.

Despite King Wilhelm's absence the conference opened on 17 August, and Fritz felt that the honour of his family and state had been insulted; the proceedings had no right to open without Prussian participation. To Vicky such matters of personal pride were less important than the question of peaceful German co-existence, and she saw a chance of salvaging the situation in Queen Victoria's visit to Coburg to see the widow of Baron Stockmar. Though Fritz was at one with Bismarck in believing that Prussia ought to wrest the leadership of the German Confederation from Austria, and that unification should precede liberalization (unlike Vicky and the Prince Consort), he thought it was only right that his father should make every effort to co-operate with Austria. He and Vicky accepted the Queen's offer to try and persuade the King to go to Frankfurt. When Wilhelm paid her a courtesy call at the end of August, after Fritz and Vicky had returned home, she told him she favoured a rapprochement between Prussia and Austria. Primed carefully by Bismarck, the King told her that the Viennese ministry was out to ruin Prussia, and that Emperor Franz Josef was bent on increasing the influence of the Catholic church; as the two leading Protestant countries of Europe, Britain and Prussia should combine to restrain Austria. Realizing that his new Minister-President's influence made further argument useless, the Queen broke off the discussion. Without Wilhelm the Frankfurt conference achieved nothing.

After the cabinet voted to dissolve parliament on 2 September, Fritz asked his father whether he supported Bismarck's views on the future of government in Prussia, and reported to Vicky that the King believed there would be no more constitutions in twenty years' time. On asking him what would replace constitutions, the King said he did not know as he would probably not live long enough to find out, adding that the King of Prussia was never intended to be a weak figurehead in the face of a more powerful parliament. 'When I asked him how often he intended to dissolve parliament, he replied that dissolutions would continue until it became obedient, or until barricades were raised in the streets, or until he ascended the scaffold.'[16] It confirmed his son's worst fears; he was now positive his father's direction would lead to revolution, civil war, and the downfall of the monarchy.

The King's threat to suspend the constitution was forcing Fritz into a hostile stance towards the government and ministry. When he asked for permission to abstain from crown council meetings, indicating his intent to embark on a policy of passive resistance to the administration, the King refused, declaring he needed his son's support more than ever, and that refusal to attend crown council meetings indicated that he was under the influence of the King's enemies. The conversation ended with King William making a hollow threat to abdicate 'and you can see what you will do to Prussia with your ideas.'[17]

Fritz had more to say on the subject. Encouraged by Vicky, the British diplomat Robert Morier, and the privy counsellor in the ministry of justice, Heinrich von Friedberg, he wrote to the King that he would create difficulties in crown council meetings if forced to attend. The King passed his son's letter to Bismarck, who agreed that the Crown Prince's behaviour was the result of the influence of his liberal associates. Fritz had written that he could no longer consider himself a part of the ministry or an adviser to the king, in view of the government's unconstitutional actions.

Fritz wrote that same day to Bismarck telling him that he had given expression to his 'serious misgivings for the future', and that His Majesty knew he was 'a decided opponent of the Ministry'. Bismarck replied that he could 'only hope that your Royal Highness will one day find servants as faithful as I am to your father. I do not intend to be of the number.'[18] A few days later Fritz agreed to continue attending council sessions, on condition that he could express his opinions in writing to his father. Such a strategy was not without risk. Vicky learned that the King believed Fritz was expressing opinions inculcated in him by others, from whose adverse influences he should be extricated by any means possible. Meanwhile Baron Stockmar was warning Fritz that high-ranking members of the military élite still harboured the possibility of having him declared officially unfit to rule, and hoped to remove him and his line from the succession in favour of the more ideologically sound Prince Friedrich Karl and family.

This continual unpleasantness with his father made Fritz thankful for his happy home life, and he was never happier than when with Vicky and the children. Yet the continual treatment for Willy's left arm was a sore trial for the family. They agreed to electrical stimulus to try and shock the deformed muscles into movement, and to strapping his neck and shoulders into a cage-like contraption for an hour a day to correct the sideways tilt of the head, but the results were negligible. As one of the most maternal of women, Vicky was always distressed to see her eldest child being treated thus, and it was hard for her not to feel some sense of revulsion or even guilt at his deformity, especially when she looked at other children the same age with perfectly formed limbs. Despite his tantrums she and Fritz found him a lovable child, while Ditta and Henry were very quiet and shy with strangers, but in the security of their domestic circle they were cheerful and affectionate.

Vicky was equally happy in this domestic circle, especially as she never felt confident in the company of most of her in-laws, aware that they regarded her as a creature from another species. By the summer of 1863 she knew that the ladies of the Berlin court thought it 'a pity their future King had married one so plain and so unornamental for society.'[19] Her skin flushed red in the intense heat of the Berlin ballrooms, and she felt ill at ease at balls and social functions, where it was an effort to keep her eyes open through fatigue. Like her father she had always loved getting up early and going to bed at a sensible hour, and she found it difficult to stay awake until the small hours.

After autumn manoeuvres, the family left Potsdam at the end of September for a few weeks at Balmoral. Vicky was much amused at the sight of Fritz wearing the kilt, or a 'little skirt'.[20] Bertie invited them to Sandringham for his birthday celebrations on 9 November, and they arrived in Norfolk a few days in advance, having lingered on the journey south in order to compare the provincial art galleries with those in Germany. But on 6 November Fritz was summoned home for the opening of Parliament, due to take place three days later. He returned for the ceremony, and the King gave him permission not to continue attending council meetings on condition that he avoided any more opposition. Afterwards he travelled back to England, and on the journey he was told that King Frederik VII of Denmark had just died.

The problem of Schleswig-Holstein, both duchies of the German Confederation, had given rise to Palmerston's immortal quip that only three people had ever understood all the issues: the Prince Consort, now dead, a German professor, who had since gone mad, and he himself, who had regrettably forgotten all about it. On the accession of Prince Christian of Schleswig-Holstein-Sonderburg-Glucksburg to the Danish throne as King Christian IX, both duchies demanded their own government. Fritz, Augusta, and Queen Victoria all supported the claims of Duke Friedrich of Schleswig-Holstein ('Fritz Holstein'), married to the Queen's niece Adelaide of Hohenlohe-Langenburg. With the support of several other German states he issued a proclamation announcing that he had assumed government of both on the death of King Frederik. Denmark, on the other hand, intended to continue governing them itself.

Everyone was greatly preoccupied with the problem when Fritz rejoined Vicky and the children at Windsor. By the time Bertie and Alix arrived a few days later the family had foreseen trouble, for, as King Christian's eldest daughter Alix defiantly declared, 'the duchies belong to Papa'. They came into collision with Vicky and Fritz, and also with Fritz Holstein's mother-in-law Feodora, who was also staying at Windsor. On 18 November at breakfast there was a sharp difference of opinion between Fritz and the Queen. He argued that Britain had done Prussia a disservice by agreeing to the terms of the London Protocol of 1852, and that despite her German sympathies the Queen was too dependent on the will of her ministers.[21]

In her distress she poured out her heart to King Leopold, complaining that Fritz was 'very violent', that no respect was paid to her opinions now, and that it 'makes visits like Fritz and Vicky's *very painful* and *trying*.'[22] The King advised her that she should forbid any further mention of the matter in her presence. It was the most unpleasant visit Fritz and Vicky had yet paid to Britain, not just because of the family atmosphere but also as they feared war on a scale considerably beyond the family rows at Windsor and Sandringham. They knew Bismarck had no sympathy with the liberal Fritz Holstein, and characteristically the Minister-President kept silent to all but a few close associates. He intended to take the duchies for Prussia, which he admitted had no claim, but their amalgamation would give Prussia added prestige.

Though Fritz shared Bismarck's goal of a united Germany, with Prussia as leader, as a friend of Fritz Holstein from university days he would have been glad to see him assume undisputed rule of the territories. At the same time he had every understanding of Denmark's plight. As he had expected, Bismarck gave him no prior warning of events until the last minute; on 16 January 1864, with Austria's approval, he sent King Christian an ultimatum to evacuate and renounce all claim to the duchies within twenty-four hours. Opinion in the Diet of the German Confederation was almost as hostile to Prussia as it was in England, for Bismarck had acted without consulting the other states apart from Austria. He did not trust Fritz as he believed that, if the latter was told in advance, the news would be betrayed to Queen Victoria. 'It is hard that a frontier line should also be the line of demarcation between the interests of mother and daughter,' he had written to the King, 'but to forget the fact is always perilous to the state.'23 Prussia's future position as leader of the German states depended on subduing Austria, a policy which required Russian support, and Bismarck was eager to weaken links between Prussia and Britain's rival, Russia. One way to achieve this was to persist in his insinuations to the King of filial disloyalty on the part of the Crown Prince, the result being that from this time onwards there was an irrevocable decline in relations between the King on one hand and his son and daughter-in-law on the other. Henceforth, the King told Fritz, he would no longer be permitted to see government dispatches.

The King and Bismarck were still suspicious of Fritz after his contrary attitude regarding the Danzig affair, but he could hardly be kept at home while Prussia was at war, so he was sent to report to headquarters. Field-Marshal Wrangel had been appointed supreme commander of the allied armies of Prussia and Austria; though now eighty years of age and no longer capable of running a war, he was the only German officer who held a rank higher than the commander of the Austrian troops. Prince Friedrich Karl was commander of the Prussian forces.

The Danish forces were heavily outnumbered, and King Christian and his ministers hoped that England would come to their rescue in the event of war; Palmerston and Russell wished to do so, but Queen Victoria was as pro-German as ever, and Britain remained neutral. On 1 February Prussia and allied forces marched into Schleswig, and within a few days Fritz was promoted to joint command with Wrangel, whose evident senility he charitably excused on the grounds that the veteran officer was 'half crazy', his former energy having 'turned to obstinacy and stubbornness'. Depressed at Bismarck's hold on his father, Fritz prayed that God would give him enlightenment to see through the man 'who has proved to be Prussia's undoing.'[24] When the King bestowed on him the Order of the Red Eagle with Swords he was deeply touched by this paternal mark of favour, while writing to Duncker of his shame at being 'decorated after so little experience and active service, while as yet no officer has received any mark of distinction, although deserved by many.'[25] The men serving under him, he felt, would ask what honours were still left for really brave deeds on the field of battle.

Within a few days the Danish army abandoned its defences in Schleswig, allowing the Prussian army to advance and Fritz, bored with doing nothing, was granted permission to join the troops. While still a reluctant enemy of Denmark who never ceased to feel sympathy for King Christian and his family, he also resented being kept at headquarters for most of the time and felt his rightful place was at the battlefield. By April it was clear the Danes would soon be ready for peace, and an armistice was declared.

Vicky's division of loyalties between England and Prussia made her position increasingly painful. She had had a spate of angry letters from England; Queen Victoria admonished her with her hope that 'this dreadful war might have been prevented but you *all* (God forgive you for it) would have it.'[26] Bertie had condemned Prussia, saying that the war would 'be a stain for ever on Prussian history',[27] and in her anxiety Alix had given birth prematurely in January to a son, named Albert Victor. A visit to Vicky from her brother Affie had been spoilt by sarcastic comments from *The Times*, which reported the King's award of the Order of the Black Eagle to Queen Victoria's second son under the heading 'A very questionable honour'.[28] The Queen and her eldest daughter were equally incensed.

While she, like her husband, had never wanted war, Vicky was proud of her husband's role in the conflict and of Germany's victory, and angry at the 'continual meddling and interfering of England in other people's affairs' and unjust attacks on Prussia in the English press and parliament. As she wrote to Queen Victoria, the English would resent it 'if they were engaged in a war, to be dictated to in a pompous style, how they were to conduct it, indeed I am sure they would not stand such interference.'[29]

On 25 April a conference opened in London to discuss the war, with representation from all neutral and belligerent powers. An armistice was proposed, to last for six weeks from 11 May, and later that week Fritz returned home. Vicky was overjoyed to see him again, after the longest separation – over three months – they had yet known. During the war she had had to contend with her first taste of real unpopularity, especially when *The Times* chose to take King Wilhelm and his 'mischievous cabinet' to task, congratulating Crown Prince Friedrich Wilhelm on his principled stand on behalf of the Augustenburg claim, and on having a consort who shared his liberal views. Such articles were music to the ears of Bismarck and the military clique, who eagerly seized on her divided loyalties by spreading rumours that she was unhappy at the success of the allied troops; everything she said and did was at once criticized as being in imitation of England, therefore anti-Prussian. 'I feel as if I could smash the idiots; it is so spiteful and untrue', she wrote. 'I never was popular here, but since the war you can well imagine that my position has not improved owing to the English press.'[30]

On his return Fritz was appointed to the command of the Second Army Corps by the King, who received him with some indifference. He would have been proud of his son, had Bismarck not continually commented to him about the possible betrayal of state secrets his son could pass on to England. A few days' rest with Vicky elapsed before he began a tour of inspection, so he did not return to the front when the armistice expired in June, Prussian troops captured the island of Alsen, and the Danish cabinet sued for peace; negotiations opened at Vienna in July, and three months later a treaty was concluded. Denmark renounced her claims to Schleswig and Holstein, in favour of Prussia and Austria, a temporary measure which did not augur well for the future.

What Fritz and Vicky had dreaded from the beginning, and what Queen Augusta and the angry English press had foreseen, was true. Bismarck ignored Fritz Holstein in the peace negotiations; he had sent his country to war in order to seize the duchies for Prussia, and was already boasting to his confidantes that war against Austria was now only a question of time. Fritz felt no little revulsion at the part he had been forced to take in the campaign, fearing that apart from his wife, mother and mother-in-law, nobody would believe that he had not wantonly taken advantage of Denmark's military isolation, subsequent British neutrality, and Duke Friedrich's lack of influence at Berlin, in order to further his own country's territorial aims.

Vicky was pregnant again, but felt stronger than she had on the three previous occasions. For King Wilhelm's birthday in March she and Fritz had presented him with a sum of money to inaugurate a fund that would assist the families of dead or disabled soldiers. Her memories of meeting Florence Nightingale in England during the Crimean war, and her husband's experience on the front lines which made him well aware of the lack of proper medical attention for men on active service, made them both aware of how much work needed to be done. She undertook the task of helping to organize an army nursing corps, the kind of work she relished as it gave her a chance to be of use to her country.

There would be other calls on her time that summer, she assured Fritz while he was still at the front; they had 'many important books' to study. 'If you are pressed for time, I will summarize any books you won't have time to read. I'm ashamed to think how much I have yet to learn!'[31] The Prince Consort would indeed have been proud of his eldest daughter, never one to let slip any opportunity for self-improvement or to better her husband as well.

On 15 September 1864 Vicky gave birth to a third son, whom they named Sigismund at King Wilhelm's request. This was the first baby she was allowed to nurse herself, despite the disgust of Queen Victoria and Queen Augusta; to this could be attributed the intimacy with her five younger children throughout their lives that she never enjoyed with the three elder, who had been entrusted to wet nurses on Queen Augusta's orders. Before the birth she had wanted to ask Bertie and Alix to be godparents, but Queen Victoria advised that the time was not ripe for a reconciliation with the 'conquered party', so Emperor Franz Josef and Empress Elizabeth of Austria were asked instead.

After Sigi was christened, Fritz took Vicky for six weeks' holiday in Switzerland. On their way back they met the Waleses in Cologne, but Fritz had overlooked the fact that his uniform – which he wore as it never occurred to him to wear civilian clothes when meeting a fellow prince – was sporting the war decorations he had accepted with such reluctance. The Prince of Wales wrote afterwards, 'it was not pleasant to see him and his ADC always in Prussian uniform flaunting before our eyes a most objectionable ribbon which he received for his *deeds of valour???* against the unhappy Danes.'[32]

It was all the more painful for Fritz and Vicky as they privately agreed with Bertie's remark. On the King's orders, 18 December was declared a day of national thanksgiving for victory throughout Prussia; church bells pealed at regular intervals, special celebratory church services and military parades were held, decorations were awarded, and a dinner was given in the evening for all princes who had fought in the war, and members of the war cabinet. Fritz considered this show of triumphalism excessive, and he asked his father for permission not to attend. The angry King would not listen to him, but he made his protest all the same. He cut Bismarck dead at the dinner, and sat still when the other guests raised their glasses to toast the minister's health. The self-congratulatory atmosphere in Berlin, where the people basked in the reflected glory of their defeat of Denmark, irritated Vicky and Fritz. Victory over a smaller, considerably outnumbered foe was nothing to be proud of. Even more disturbingly, it showed that Bismarck's plan for a nation unified through war had a more direct if chauvinistic appeal for Prussia than the goal of a united Germany and constitutional monarchy which they forecast.

Fritz and Vicky wanted a place to live more informally, away from the trappings of state and prying servants, many of whom were chosen for the very purpose by Queen Augusta and Bismarck. Vicky found the village of Bornstädt by accident when she was out driving one day and her coachman took the wrong road from Berlin. The difference between the Prussian countryside and the tense atmosphere of the city impressed her with the same contrast between London and the Scottish Highlands which had struck her parents before buying their estate at Balmoral. Exploring the tangled wilderness, rough track sheltered by woodland, untrimmed grass and hedges, and dilapidated but strangely inviting humble cottages, she found a house for sale partly hidden by an avenue of poplars, with broken windows, flaking paint, and an untended garden. By Christmas 1863 she and Fritz had bought it, and in the following spring they had it converted into a farmhouse. He supervised the management of the land and the labour required to get it into shape, while she attended to the dairy, poultry-yard and garden. Fritz and Vicky bought the farm when they had only three children; by the time it was suitable for them as a residence, their family numbered five. Meanwhile Vicky had purchased two cows, a dairy had been installed, and the garden had been transformed into a playground with swings, seesaw, and a cricket field. Later they added chickens and ducks, and had a stable for the children's ponies built.

It did not take long for them to become thoroughly at home in the village. Time had stood still for the people who never undressed, tore food apart with their hands, and wrapped their babies in newspaper or rags before placing them on insect-ridden beds of damp straw. It was the kind of challenge Vicky relished, and she set about helping to show the villagers benefits of modern sanitation and hygiene. Soon she and Fritz knew nearly everyone, and it was not unusual to see them dressed as an English country squire and his wife, strolling along the roads or riding on horseback, always ready to stop and say good morning, or to enquire after the health of the sick.

Stories of the royal schoolmaster quickly passed into the realms of Prussian folklore. Fritz often visited the village school to listen to the children's lessons, sometimes taking the teacher's place. On one occasion, touching a medal, he asked a little girl to which kingdom it belonged. 'To the mineral kingdom,' she replied. 'And this?' he asked, pointing to a flower. 'To the vegetable kingdom.' 'And I myself: to what kingdom do I belong?' Back came the answer: 'to the kingdom of Heaven.'³³ Another morning, as he was talking to the youngsters and looking at their work, the master was handed a telegram telling him that his mother was seriously ill. 'Go at once, leave the school to me', Fritz told him, and carried on teaching his charges until a clergyman arrived to relieve him.³⁴

The writer Gustav zu Putlitz and his wife Elizabeth befriended Vicky and Fritz at this time, and were appointed Chamberlain and *Grande Maitresse* of the household. The former had first met Vicky when he was writing a history of the Neue Palais, and he was greatly impressed with her for being 'marvellously well read', admiring a drawing she had just done for one of her husband's military charities as 'conceived with real genius and most artistically executed. This young Princess has more than average gifts, and, besides, is more cultured than any woman I know of her age'. The next day he was writing with equal admiration of the way that 'It is astonishing that she not only reads, but commits everything to memory, and she discusses history like a historian, with excellent judgement and decision.' There could be no doubt of their happy marriage, he noted a few days later, of 'the perfect harmony of this union, in which the Crown Prince, notwithstanding the more brilliant qualities of the Princess, still preserves his simple and natural attitude and undeniable influence.'³⁵

Such glimpses of the couple at home showed that their marriage had remained the idyll that it was on the day of their wedding. 'The older I grow, the more I come to know of human beings, the more I thank God for having given me a wife like mine,' Fritz wrote at around this time. 'I trust that God will preserve our peace and domestic happiness. I ask for nothing else.'³⁶

Among others who enjoyed their hospitality at this time were Fritz Holstein and his brother Christian, both of whom had been deprived of their property and army commissions by Bismarck. Fritz had championed their cause as long as he could, arguing with his former friend Duncker who had not the courage to stand up to the Minister's wrath, believing that the creation of a new state of

Schleswig-Holstein under the Hereditary Prince's rule was the most satisfactory way of maintaining harmony between Prussia and Austria. Bismarck dismissed the Augustenburg claim by saying that the army had fought for Prussia, not for Duke Friedrich, and that to settle the duchies in his favour would encourage other pretenders. The convention of Gastein, signed in August 1865, agreed to the administration of Schleswig by Prussia, and that of Holstein by Austria – a temporary measure which augured badly for the future. Vicky was bitter at the way the Elbe Duchies and Fritz Holstein had been treated, writing to Queen Victoria how she wished that they and Prussia were rid of Bismarck. If her letter was opened by the post officials she would be accused of high treason – 'but I am as loyal as anyone as I love the King and would do anything to serve him.'[37]

Fritz and Vicky wanted to do something for this ill-treated family. Unlike his brother, Prince Christian was a bachelor and spent much of his time at Bornstädt playing with the children like an uncle or elder brother and sharing Fritz's cigars; their closeness in age (Christian was the elder by nine months) and his ability to speak fluent English endeared him to them. Although a good-natured soul, this bald, rather ugly and penniless Prince was hardly eligible by royal standards. Queen Victoria was anxious to find a husband for her third daughter Helena, an intelligent girl but plain and 'wanting in charm'.[38] Such meagre qualifications and her mother's insistence on keeping a married daughter in England limited her prospects, until Vicky suggested Christian. If the two liked each other, then he would presumably not object to living under the eye of a mother-in-law.

It was arranged that they should meet at Coburg in August. The anniversary of the Prince Consort's birth date had been chosen for the unveiling of a statue there to his memory. Though it was the first time that all nine brothers and sisters had been together since the wedding of the eldest in 1858, it was a joyless occasion. Fritz and Vicky felt uncomfortable as the terms of Gastein – signed a fortnight earlier – amounted to ill-disguised Prussian plunder, made all the worse as they were helpless to do anything about it. Bertie and Alix were still angry over the Danish defeat, and when introduced to

Prince Karl Bertie was outwardly civil but Alix defiantly tossed her head, refusing to speak to him. Fritz could not blame her, but such incidents did not endear him to his uncles, who constantly reminded him of his part in introducing a Danish princess into his wife's family. Then Queen Victoria was so incensed at the King's ignoring her letters that she would not call on him, or even visit Queen Augusta at Koblenz, let alone invite her to the unveiling. The latter was deeply offended at what she took to be a personal insult.

Christian and Helena realized that if they rejected this chance of marriage they would regret it, and despite Alix's injured pride at this partisanship of her father's rivals, it was not long before Queen Victoria announced their engagement. In Berlin Queen Augusta scoffed at the 'poor match', and Bismarck sneered at another ridiculous gesture of what he called the 'Anglo-Coburg faction'. When Vicky asked what her sister would like for a wedding present, their younger sister Louise mischievously suggested Bismarck's head on a charger.[39]

After Fritz's autumn manoeuvres he and Vicky visited England again, and on their way they stopped at Brussels to see King Leopold. Bedridden, pale and evidently dying but still mentally alert, he talked incessantly about family affairs and politics, expressed anger at Bismarck's policies, commented on the uneasy peace of Gastein, and remarked that he was glad he would not live long enough to see the results. Realizing sadly that they had seen him for the last time they continued to London, staying at the Prussian Embassy, before going with some trepidation to call on Bertie and Alix, who had become reconciled to the approaching marriage after pressure from the rest of the family.

King Leopold died on 10 December, within a week of what would have been his seventy-fifth birthday. He was the last surviving member of the triumvirate which had brought about the Coburg-Hohenzollern marriage. With the Prince Consort, Baron Stockmar and now King Leopold gone, Vicky and Fritz were more isolated than ever in Bismarck's Prussia. To whom, Fritz asked sadly, could they turn in future for wise and experienced counsel, especially in affairs of state?[40]

FIVE

'An era of reaction will ensue'

By the first few weeks of 1866 Vicky and Fritz were almost certain that another war, with Austria, was just a matter of time. Officially they knew nothing, Vicky told her mother; Fritz was 'kept *quite* out of it all, the King does not speak to him on the subject & the ministers *never communicate anything* to him.'[1] Yet they knew Bismarck intended to challenge Austria's status as the major European mainland power. He had already told Lord Augustus Loftus, British ambassador at Berlin, that it was his mission to force their neighbour and old ally 'into concessions or to war'. In February 1866 King Wilhelm informed his ministers that Austria had not kept her part of the Gastein convention, and Bismarck said that a struggle for power between Prussia and Austria was inevitable, as the latter was an obstacle to Prussia's mission to lead Germany.

In March 1866 Loftus assured the King that the British ministers were prepared to use their good offices towards a peaceful solution to any differences between Prussia and Austria. The King asked Fritz to write to Queen Victoria, accepting any offer of mediation her government might make. Believing that war was as good as forestalled, Fritz did so with delight, while Vicky assured her mother that she could be 'the means of averting a Européan conflagration.'[2] This did not suit Bismarck, who told Loftus that as Austria was the party which threatened to disturb the peace, the British government and ministers should address themselves to Vienna. Bismarck further persuaded the King that Emperor Franz Josef's wish to make the duchies independent contravened Prussian policy and also the Gastein convention. He was so persuasive that the King, bristling at Austria's perfidy, wanted war at once, and Bismarck had to restrain him; Prussia was not yet ready.

Knowing that Bismarck wielded more power than his sovereign, the Foreign Secretary, Lord Clarendon, insisted that the British government could do nothing; it was up to the Queen, if she wished, to use her influence. While the pacifist liberal majority in the *Landtag* suggested a European conference, Fritz wrote despondently to the Duke of Saxe-Coburg that 'Fratricidal is the expression I employ to designate Bismarck's resolve of forcing a war with Austria upon us.'[3] Two days later Queen Victoria informed Fritz that, much as she regretted the likelihood of war between Austria and Prussia, she would consider it even worse if her government was party to 'so gross a violation of all the principles on which we pride ourselves in England, as the violent annexation of the duchies to Prussia against the known feelings and wishes of the People.'[4]

Meanwhile in April Count Guido Usedom, Prussian Ambassador in Florence, negotiated an alliance with Italy by which the latter would join Prussia if war broke out between Austria and Prussia within three months, and in return she would receive possession of the province of Venetia, which was still under Habsburg domination though historically regarded as part of Italy. Bismarck had to act quickly, as the treaty effectively destroyed the German Confederation, the constitution of which forbade any member to ally itself with a foreign power against another. If he did not strike at once, Prussia would be taken to task for flouting the Confederation's peaceful co-existence.

On the morning of 12 April Vicky went to Potsdam for her confinement, expected in a week, at the Neue Palais. Her labour began on the journey, and the train could not accelerate as another was immediately ahead on the same line. She was taken from the carriage in a state of collapse by her ladies and hurried into the palace, giving birth to a daughter hours later. Princess Frederica Amelia Wilhelmina Victoria (to be known as Victoria, or 'Moretta' in the family), was christened on 24 May, at a gloomy ceremony in the Friedenskirche at Potsdam. On the next day Fritz was due to leave to assume command of the Second Army in Silesia.

It was clear that the war would divide the family more thoroughly than the Danish conflict had done; already their German relations were taking sides. Austria's allies included the Grand Duke of Hesse and his nephew Louis, Vicky's brother-in-law, the blind King Georg of Hanover and his family. On Prussia's side was Louis's brother Henry, who had served with the Prussian army for several years, and commanded the Second Lancers. The Duke of Saxe-Coburg prudently remained neutral.

The day after Fritz left, twenty-one-months old Sigi became ill. Vicky initially thought his fretfulness was caused by teething troubles, but within twenty-four hours he was too weak to stand. Dr Wegner and his colleagues had gone with the army to the front, and all she could do was consult an inexperienced local junior practitioner who either failed to diagnose that the disease was meningitis, or else could do nothing to alleviate the symptoms of a disease which generally proved fatal. Sigi's convulsions became increasingly severe and he died in agony on 18 June.

Deprived of her husband's company during one of the most harrowing experiences a mother could ever know, Vicky was left to face this tragedy with only the other children and her servants for company, and she was shattered by grief. For once the King and Queen were deeply moved, and showed a degree of tenderness which she had never known from them before. Her anguish at the loss of the 'little sunbeam in the house',[5] the sight of his toys scattered around the cot, his clothes which she had lovingly made, the memories of his helpless struggle as he screamed for his distracted mother to soothe him, had touched even Queen Augusta. She had been fond of the child, and she left for the battlefront so she could give the heartbreaking news to Fritz in person. King Wilhelm granted him leave to return home for the funeral but he gently declined, saying that as he was in the service of the fatherland he would never forgive himself if they were attacked while he was absent from his post.[6] In her torment Vicky found this stoic denial hard to accept, acknowledging with some bitterness: 'In you, of course, the soldier is uppermost.'[7] She prepared an anteroom of the Freedom Church in Potsdam with cushions, carpets, pictures and flowers for the funeral, which she attended in a state of deep shock, remaining dry-eyed and composed as if turned to stone.

A few days later she took the other children with her to the small town of Heringsdorf on the Baltic, wishing to get far away from court for a while. In the worst moments of her misery she turned to writing letters to Queen Victoria for solace, apologizing unreservedly for 'wearying' her mother with her sorrow. The Queen was sympathetic until Vicky wrote that she would give up 'house & home, future & all'[8] to have her youngest son back, only to be told firmly that she should not tempt Providence.

At length she found an outlet for her feelings in making a waxen image of her dead son which she placed in his crib. Beside it she left his shoes, silver rattle and ball, as if just thrown aside by his hand. For several years she kept this shrine as a testament to the tragedy in a small locked room in the Neue Palais, which only family and a few select friends were allowed to see.

On 27 June the Silesian army won a victory over the Austrian forces, and the following week the combined forces of Moltke, chief of staff and the army of the Elbe, under Prince Friedrich Karl, met the Austrian troops near the town of Königgrätz. Fritz was summoned to bring his troops at once for an all-out attack. Until his arrival soon after midday, victory hung in the balance; by the evening over 40,000 Austrians were dead, wounded or taken prisoner, and the rest of the army was in retreat, while the Prussian forces lost less than 10,000. After the fighting, Fritz came face to face with his father who awarded him the Order *Pour le Mérite*, an honour usually conferred only for personal gallantry on the field of battle. It was the first decoration he felt he had truly earned, but it made no difference to his feelings at the carnage around them. 'War is an appalling thing,' he wrote in his diary that evening, 'and the man who brings it about with a stroke of his pen at the "green table", little reeks what he is conjuring with.'[9]

The conflict was now effectively over, and Fritz waited at his headquarters for the council of war, called for 23 July. At first the King wanted to follow Austrian troops to Vienna and annihilate them there if necessary, and when told this was impracticable, he insisted that Prussia's victory must mean territorial gain. He could not see Bismarck's view that it would be folly to antagonize the

Austrian empire unduly by depriving her of land, in case it was needed to help fight France or some other power in future. Bismarck had merely intended to expel Austria from the German Confederation, leaving Prussia as the undisputed superior power, and when he saw the King threatening to wreck his plans he stormed out of the council chamber. The situation was retrieved by Fritz, who assured them that he for one had never wanted war in the first place, was ready to support any plan for peace, and persuaded the King to 'bite into this sour apple and accept a disgraceful peace.'[10]

After the preliminaries of peace were signed on 26 July Fritz returned home, breaking his journey at the Friedenskirche in Potsdam, where his youngest daughter had been christened, and his son lay buried. Victories could not compensate for the loss of a child, he wrote; 'in the midst of great events, the more sharply does such a piercing grief wound a father's heart.'[11] Vicky was still at Heringsdorf, and he joined them in the woods nearby, as she watched their children playing under the summer sun. Peace was formally signed at Prague on 22 August, by which Prussia formally annexed Schleswig, Holstein, the kingdom of Hanover, and the landgraviate of Hesse-Homburg.

After three months Vicky's grief at the death of their youngest son was beginning to abate, thanks in no small measure to Queen Victoria's insistence that she should snap out of it and count her blessings. In the exultation of victory she put aside her mourning dresses, which she would normally have worn for a year, in order to look suitably regal for the return of the Prussian army to Berlin. For all her hatred of war she could not help taking some pride in Prussia's success, or at least her husband's part in it. The present leadership under Bismarck, they still told themselves, was a temporary setback, but in the next reign a more enlightened regime would prevail.

In October Fritz went to St Petersburg to represent Prussia at the wedding of the Tsarevich, later Tsar Alexander III, to Princess Dagmar of Denmark. Vicky had her reservations about his going; she feared gloomily that her brothers had no 'feeling of companionship' for Fritz, as his tastes, occupations and interests were so different to theirs.[12] Yet the brothers-in-law got on much better than

Fritz had dared to hope. Bertie had stopped in Berlin on his way to visit Vicky, and she found him very friendly and conciliatory; he had seen through her emotional letters to Queen Victoria, with their angry condemnations of Bismarck in one line and glowing praise for Prussian troops in the next. At the palace of Tsarskoe-Selo Bertie found in Fritz the same gentle, war-abhorring fellow who had acted as his best man, and whose medal-flaunting at Cologne the previous year had been no more than tactless oversight.

Fritz's success with one fellow-heir did not attend his meeting with the other. After the wedding he drove with the Tsarevich through the streets of St Petersburg. The latter, he noted, 'never said a single sensible word, even when he did open his mouth.'[13] Alexander was by nature a suspicious character who did not yet know his guest well enough to be aware of his relationship with Bismarck, against whom like his bride he bore a grudge for the conquest of Denmark. However Fritz immediately disarmed the bride, telling her that it must be very unpleasant for her to see him at her wedding in the light of recent events.

By early the following year the possibility of conflict was looming once more, with Luxembourg the centre of controversy. After the war the French ambassador to Prussia, Count Benedetti, had asked Prussia to agree to French annexation of Belgium and Luxembourg as the price of France's neutrality. King Wilhelm and Bismarck rejected the demand for Belgium, as to acquiesce in such a claim would incur British hostility. Luxembourg was a grand duchy under the sovereignty of the King of Holland, while belonging to the North German Confederation created by the treaties signed by the pro-Austrian states after the war, with the King of Prussia in control of all the armed forces. To Emperor Napoleon it would be a strategic addition to France, at a time when the Prussians had achieved victory in two short successive wars and were challenging the French for European supremacy. The people of Luxembourg did not regard themselves as Germans though the territory was used as a Prussian fortress, and King William III of Holland would probably not be averse to renouncing his sovereignty over it in return for the settlement of his debts. Bismarck informed Benedetti that he was prepared to be 'obliging' on the matter, but his prevarication provoked the French into an unfriendly attitude towards Prussia.

Vicky and Fritz feared that another war would be the result. In March 1867 the French put pressure on King William III to cede Luxembourg to France, but he was reluctant to do so without Prussian consent. German nationalists appealed to the government to prevent the cession of any German-speaking territory to the French, and Bismarck declared that his government would be seriously discredited if it agreed to such a move. To Vicky and Fritz, Bismarck was right for once. People were in 'a wonderful state of excitement' about Luxembourg, Vicky wrote, and she considered anything was preferable to giving France any part of Germany. 'Should there be a war against France – which would be a dreadful calamity on the one side – the unity of Germany would be effected at once.'[14] A couple of weeks later, she reiterated that the aggression came from France. If peace could not be upheld, she thought it would be the lesser of two evils if armed conflict broke out now rather than later, 'horrible as it is. A war with France will be a very different thing from a war with Austria but if our honour is at stake – for the sake of Germany we must not hang back.'[15]

With the new German Confederation in its infancy, Bismarck was not ready for another war, and in May a European conference in London agreed to withdrawal of the Prussian garrison, and the affirmation of Luxembourg's neutrality and independence. France was left with a feeling of humiliation and a bitter distrust of Bismarck. Nevertheless peace was cemented, temporarily at least, by a gathering of royalties in Paris at the international exposition in May. Though the Prussian royal family had nearly cancelled their visit because of the Luxembourg crisis, they were persuaded to reconsider and Fritz, Vicky, King Wilhelm and Queen Augusta duly attended, joining guests including the Prince of Wales, his brother Alfred, Duke of Edinburgh, their sister Alice and her husband Louis, Emperor Franz Josef and Tsar Alexander II.

France's furtive alliances with Italy and the Luxembourg affair had engendered considerable suspicion in Prussia, and much as Fritz liked the company of Napoleon and Eugenie on a personal level, he found it difficult to trust them. Though Vicky was equally obliged to try and separate political loyalties from personal friendship, she was quickly put at her ease by the attentions of her hosts, their charm and the trouble they took in order to entertain their guests. She was especially touched when Napoleon and Eugenie talked to her about her parents, and the Emperor diplomatically told her that the Prince Consort was the most distinguished and the most remarkable man he had ever known.

However she sank into a mood of intense depression as the first anniversary of Sigi's tragic death came closer. A combination of this, the early weeks of a sixth pregnancy, and her abhorrence of late nights and suffocating ballrooms, all proved too much for her. She had stopped dancing when her son died, and shared the other guests' appetite for endless social functions even less than usual. One evening, just before another ball, she begged Fritz to be allowed to go home. With a heavy heart he asked the King, who retorted that she would have to wait another few days. Defiantly she ordered her maids to pack and left for Germany that night, leaving Fritz to face his father's wrath alone. He returned to Berlin with the King the day before the anniversary of his little son's death.

A few days later the gathering at Paris was overshadowed by the grim news that Napoleon's puppet Mexican empire had fallen and his protégé Emperor Maximilian, brother of Franz Josef, had been captured and shot by rebels. The Empress Carlota, formerly Princess Charlotte, daughter of the late King Leopold of the Belgians and a second cousin of Vicky, had spent the previous few months in Europe begging for armed intervention to try and save him, but with the strain she had suffered complete mental collapse, and was destined to spend the rest of her sixty years confined in a castle near Brussels. There had been moments when Vicky similarly dreaded going the same way, as her mother had done after the Prince Consort's death. That somebody like Charlotte, who had always seemed so calm and self-possessed, could lose her reason and be condemned to living a wasted life, was a frightening reminder of what might strike at any time.

107

Fritz had played a major role on Prussia's behalf in the first two wars, and was much loved and respected by the officers and men who had fought under him. His words of comfort to the wounded and thanks to his troops after each battle made his genuine interest in their well-being self-evident, and while his kindly, diffident manner may have been less assertive than that of his brusque, impatient cousin Friedrich Karl, it made him more popular. As a war hero who was first in line to the throne, it was only natural that he should be given some recognition at home during the years of peace as part of his preparation for kingship. However Bismarck had other ideas, preferring to send him abroad on various ceremonial duties, so he was rarely at home. At first Vicky and Fritz were pleased, as it widened the circles in which his value and talents would be appreciated. In due course it became apparent that this was an attempt to banish him from Prussia as his presence was a constant criticism of Bismarck's reactionary policies, and it was also an officially-approved way of keeping husband and wife apart. It was clear that Fritz's stand at Danzig was no mere passing phase, and after the war of 1866 it was noticeable that the Crown Prince of Prussia was conspicuous by his absence from the political limelight. Apart from his military duties and regular attendance at crown council meetings, his only official function was as his father's representative on politically inconsequential missions abroad.

Bismarck knew it was mainly Vicky's influence that prevented him from making a disciple of her husband, despite the fact that in some ways, particularly their respect for monarchical power, Fritz and Bismarck had more in common with each other than he did with Vicky. His subtle campaign of vilification against her was partly his means of revenge, partly his way of destroying what little respect her in-laws still had for her. She was well aware of this, complaining to Queen Victoria that their children were 'universally pitied for having the great misfortune of having me for their Mama with my "*unglücklichen englischen Ideen*" [unfortunate English ideas] and "*unpreussischen Gesinnugen*" [un-Prussian views]'.[16]

By degrees they found themselves gradually isolated from their most trusted friends in Prussia, those whom next to her Bismarck most feared. These included Morier, Prince Hohenzollern (still well-respected despite his resignation as Minister-President in 1862), and Baron Roggenbach, the Liberal Prussian representative at Frankfurt. Spies were planted in the Neue Palais; when a vacancy appeared in the household, Bismarck and his crony Moritz Busch filled the position with someone instructed to watch their employers carefully, and to report back on anything they saw or heard that might be of interest. By the time of the Paris exposition two such trained 'servants' were established in the accounts department, thus giving Bismarck the key to details of Fritz and Vicky's domestic expenditure. The other staff reported obligingly on who visited the palace and Fritz had to stop inviting Morier, the only alternative being to risk his expulsion from Prussia on some trumped-up charge of interference. He was still welcome at Bornstädt, where he came regularly with discretion, warning Fritz and Vicky to take great care in all they did at the palace, in all they said to each other unless sure they were alone and nobody was listening at the door, and in not writing anything remotely inappropriate even in a 'private' diary except in cipher. Vicky had sometimes found her desk smelling of tobacco, or with the lock broken, and knew that dirty work was afoot.

Vicky gave birth to their youngest son on 10 February 1868, her mother's wedding anniversary, and named him Waldemar. Overjoyed with this fourth son, she was soon longing to become pregnant again, writing to Fritz that 'All the pain of labour is nothing compared to the happiness of having such a dear little creature to hold & to nurse oneself.'[17]

In April Fritz went to Rome for the wedding of Crown Prince Umberto of Italy to Princess Margharita of Naples. He was treated to an enthusiastic reception, and greeted everywhere with cries of *'Evviva Prussia, l'angelo protettore d'Italia!'*, while the press made much of his constant smile and martial bearing. After defeat in 1866 Austria had ceded Venetia to Italy, and a grateful King Victor Emmanuel conferred upon Fritz the Grand Cross of the Military Order of Merit of Savoy in recognition of his services to Italian unity. The wedding was followed by a court ball, where Princess Margharita was dancing with a banker's son. When he accidentally stepped on her gown and tore the trimming, gasps of horror through the ballroom turned to astonishment as Fritz instantly produced a case from his coat pocket, took out a pair of scissors, knelt down and cut off the torn strip of lace. The Princess held out her hand to take it back, but instead he pressed it to his heart, folded it and replaced it in his pocket with the scissors. 'He is a true knight,' murmured the amazed onlookers, but a Stuttgart press reporter was less poetic: 'These Prussians are sharp fellows, always armed, and ready for everything.'[18]

Meanwhile Vicky and her sister Alice were staying at the home of the Duke of Coburg in Gotha, an occasion marred by Vicky's ill-health. Since her marriage she had suffered numerous minor upsets on a regular basis, but a severe bout of illness at this time left her with a lasting legacy. After an attack of 'severe neuralgic headache' and excruciating pain, especially in the nerve above her eye, she was advised to take quinine as a remedy, but this produced a severe rash which turned her face bright red. Her ears, eyelids and nose were so swollen that for a few days she went temporarily deaf, her eyes were almost completely shut, and she could only breathe with difficulty. Well aware of how unsightly her 'fire-red shapeless mass' of a face looked, she felt obliged to hide herself from view until the worst of the trouble had subsided.[19]

From this time onwards the neuralgia, violent headaches and recurrent pains in her back, side and limbs persisted regularly. Sometimes she needed morphine injections to deaden the pain, and her eyes were so inflamed that she had to wear blue-tinted glasses. Extremes of temperature, excessive standing or sitting in overheated ballrooms, exposure to gaslight in the theatre, and walking outside with a cold wind blowing in her face, were liable to bring on or exacerbate these symptoms which sometimes left her at her wits' end. Only many years after her death did the possibility emerge that she had inherited the excruciatingly uncomfortable though not life-threatening condition of porphyria from which her great-grandfather King George III had suffered so severely. In her case the complaint was perhaps likewise responsible for affecting her mental reason and impairing her judgement to some degree.

In January 1869 Willy celebrated his tenth birthday, was awarded the Order of the Black Eagle and appointed Lieutenant in the First Regiment of Guards. Photographs of him standing proudly in his uniform showed his left arm looking almost normal, a tribute to the work of the tailor who made the left sleeve slightly shorter than the right, and to the boy's tenacity in trying his best to overcome the handicap. By this time it was clear that all the treatment to which he had been subjected as a small boy had been in vain. He could not run fast, climb trees, or cut his food with normal cutlery. Because of his distorted sense of balance, the arduous business of learning to ride, a necessity for a future King of Prussia, had initially terrified him as he struggled to stay in the saddle.

A disastrous choice of tutor for Willy and Henry, Georg Hinzpeter, appointed in 1866, exacerbated the problem. This stern, humourless disciplinarian had little understanding of children; his principles as a governor were based on what he termed Prussian simplicity, which Fritz and Vicky believed would stop 'that terrible Prussian pride and ambition'. While he condemned personal pride, he constantly held up to his charges the example of their country and her superiority to all others, at a time when Bismarck was making a mockery of the principles of democratic government and advancing her prestige with the sword. The boys spent twelve hours a day at their lessons, with breaks only for meals and physical exercise. For breakfast they ate dry bread, and when entertaining visitors for tea they had to offer their guests cakes without taking any themselves. Henry apparently suffered no lasting ill-effects, but the spartan regime left its mark on Willy.

Already Vicky knew she was having problems with her children. Like Queen Victoria she was candid to the point of bluntness about them, partly from a desire to encourage them to strive for greater things, partly to discourage vanity. Nevertheless she created a deeper bond with the five younger children, those whom she was allowed to nurse herself. Unhappily the three elder ones seemed to sense their mother's disappointment, or her continual fault-finding where they were concerned, and grew up to resent her indulgent attitude towards their smaller siblings. As their father was often absent, she

111

became the dominant influence in their formative years. In her letters to her mother Charlotte was criticized as 'stupid and backward', while Henry was 'slow and plodding'. Though Queen Victoria was no stranger to the art of finding or magnifying faults in most of her own children, she counselled patience, assuring Vicky they would surely turn out far better than she feared.

Vicky always insisted on an active role in helping to prepare them for their future life and education. In 1866 she asked Queen Victoria for copies of memoranda written by her father and Baron Stockmar to use in setting up a similar educational guide to that used at Buckingham Palace. She felt that Charlotte's French governess was exceeding her station; 'I cannot and will not abandon all right of interfering with the children's education and must reserve to myself to judge of what they are to learn & who is to teach them.'[20]

In September 1869 Fritz was chosen to represent Prussia at the opening of the Suez canal. Emperor Franz Josef, Emperor Napoleon and Empress Eugenie would be there as well, and for Bismarck it was a good way of disguising any future intentions he might have entertained with a view to threatening to declare war on France. Emperor Franz Josef, he knew, had been on Fritz's conscience since the war of 1866, and in the event of a Franco-German conflict, it would suit his purposes for Habsburg and Hohenzollern to have an informal reconciliation. Both men got on very well together, and the Austrian Emperor knew better than to bear the Crown Prince any malice for merely discharging his duty. Another acquaintance of Fritz during his time in north Africa, according to rumour, was a Spanish courtesan, Dolores Cada. It was said that evidence of syphilitic infection soon appeared and was discreetly treated by the Khedive's physician.[21] Nevertheless this skeleton in the cupboard would return to haunt him some eighteen years later.*

Meanwhile Vicky took a holiday from Berlin and stayed in Cannes, taking Willy and Henry. They were joined by her sister

* See below, p. 197.

Alice, at twenty-six already prone to chronic rheumatism and neuralgia, and they spent a pleasant few weeks in each others' company. Always self-deprecating about her personal appearance, Vicky had convinced herself – or so her letters to Queen Victoria suggested – that she was the ugly one and her sad-faced, hollow-cheeked sister was much the prettier. This may have been a way of trying to get Alice back into the Queen's good books, for both sisters had incurred her wrath by their 'awful and disgusting' preference for nursing their babies themselves instead of handing them over to wet-nurses. Moreover Alice had been tactless or brave enough to speak out against Helena's marriage to Christian, as she thought 'Lenchen' was being sacrificed to the selfish whims of their mother, adamant on keeping at least one married daughter nearby at her constant beck and call. Vicky was mildly jealous of King Wilhelm's obvious preference for Alice, convinced her father-in-law thought she was ugly and a bore in comparison. The King's obvious preference may have been born from a desire to irritate Queen Augusta, who called Alice an atheist for daring to question the infallibility of the Bible and showing an interest in the teachings of free-thinkers who challenged the issue.

Ever since the treaty of Prague Vicky and Fritz had lived in continual dread of a third war; they suspected Bismarck was biding his time, allowing the North German Confederation and its mutual alliance to mature before drawing the sword against France. A pretext was not long in coming. In 1868 the childless Queen Isabella of Spain had abdicated, and the Prime Minister Marshal Prim recommended Leopold, a younger son of Prince Hohenzollern, as her successor. After the Prince discussed his son's candidature with a few friends, including Fritz, he wanted nothing to do with such a potentially unstable throne in a country of which they knew nothing. Negotiations between the Spanish and Prussian governments had remained secret, and on Leopold's refusal in April 1870 Fritz thought the affair was closed.

He reckoned without Bismarck, who saw how to pick a quarrel with France through skilful manipulation of the matter. To

Napoleon and his advisers, the idea of a Hohenzollern on the Spanish throne would be blatant encirclement. Prussia had demonstrated her military prowess twice in the past six years, and Prince Leopold's brother Karl had been elected Prince of Roumania in 1866. Like Fritz, King Wilhelm initially opposed the candidature for a similar reason; it did not suit the dignity of his family to accept a throne after the previous monarch had been deposed.

Fritz and Vicky were at Potsdam, where Vicky had given birth to a third daughter Sophie, on 14 June, when they heard that Leopold had accepted the throne after all. They were not surprised to hear that negotiations had been reopened several days previously; the King and his statesman had let the news become public knowledge without bothering to inform their Crown Prince. Their shock was nothing to that of the government in Paris, who demanded that Leopold must renounce the throne again. Wearily Fritz told Vicky that this could only end in mobilization; Vicky told him not to give up hope so easily; he should go and face the King, and demand to be kept informed. When he went to Berlin he found Bismarck, who pretended to take Fritz into his confidence, saying he hoped the business could be settled amicably. Fritz did not share Vicky's acute perception; Bismarck was mild and ostensibly communicative when matters were playing into his hands and his schemes seemed to be working, hysterical if they were not. If Vicky had been present she would have known better than to take him at face value, but Fritz was deceived and returned happily to the Neue Palais. The next thing he heard was what he had hoped for; Leopold had withdrawn his acceptance again. Fritz was confident that this was the end of it but Vicky, suffering from post-natal depression and taught by bitter experience not to be too optimistic, thought otherwise. She dreaded the prospect of France, confident of military superiority, making capital from the issue by declaring war; like Fritz she thought Prussia was outnumbered in terms of troops and not ready to fight.

Not for some time did Fritz realize that he had been tricked into believing that Bismarck did not want war. His presence at Berlin would have been a sign that he was indulging in subterfuge to spark off the war for which he was waiting. That he was at Varzin, supervising the autumn harvest and entertaining guests, meant that either he had laid the snare and was waiting for France to walk into it, or the air was clear and everyone could look forward to peace after all. Fritz was one of the many who believed the latter.

Against his better judgment, Napoleon and his government sent the King a telegram demanding that Leopold's candidature for the Spanish throne should not be renewed. From Ems Wilhelm dictated a politely-worded message that he could give no guarantee one way or the other. Bismarck received it for approval while dining with Roon and Moltke, and thought it too conciliatory. Setting to work with his pen he deleted about two-thirds of it; what was left read as an abrupt snub. On receiving this, the famous 'Ems telegram', the French government felt grossly insulted; and on 15 July France declared war. So well had Bismarck played his role that Fritz and Vicky were not alone in believing Napoleon to be the aggressor.

When Fritz called on Bismarck a couple of days later, the latter told him that there was no way of avoiding war; Prussian honour was at stake. When the King, reluctant for a full-scale campaign against France, talked at the war council of partial mobilization, he persuaded his father that this would not be enough. After the meeting he walked out gravely to the crowds assembled around the station at Wildpark, and publicly announced the result to an enthusiastic reception. Three days later, he noted in his diary: 'General enthusiasm: Germany rises like one man, and will restore its unity.'[22]

Fritz had faith in Prussia's ability to organize her soldiers to advantage in battle, but Vicky believed the odds were fearfully against them, and wondered how many of the women would be mourning the loss of a husband or son by Christmas. Maybe England would come to the rescue, but much as Queen Victoria appreciated her German family connections, she still had a corner in her heart for Napoleon and Eugenie. Moreover, the Prussia of the 1850s that Prince Albert had seen as the way towards an united liberal Germany had been replaced by a sabre-rattling kingdom in which liberalism was no longer the dominant force. While France was the apparent aggressor, Lord Loftus and Lord Bloomfield, present and former British ministers in Berlin, had warned Lord Clarendon at the Foreign Office of Bismarck's lack of scruples in his pursuit of German unity, and that it would be all too tempting to lay blame on the French.

Fritz and Vicky hoped that Britain might send troops to fight alongside Germany against France. The rest of the family, wrote Vicky, felt that England 'would have had it in her power to prevent this awful war, had she in concert with Russia, Austria and Italy, declared she would take arms against the aggressor'.[23] She was concerned lest public opinion in Germany would criticize her as England, it was said, had sided with the French against them and had 'interpreted her neutrality to the exclusive benefit of France'. It would be glorious, she wrote to Queen Victoria, if England helped them to victory 'and if our nations stood once more as in the greatest days of old, side by side in the field of honour.' While she admitted that Emperor Napoleon was 'not the scourge of Europe his uncle was', that she knew he would rather be at peace, and that she had strong personal regard for him and Eugenie, who had always shown them kindness, 'one must really admit that they have behaved ill in every way'.[24]

On Sunday 24 July Sophie was christened in the Friedenskirche. What should have been a happy occasion was overshadowed by 'anxious faces and tearful eyes, and a gloom and foreshadowing of all the misery in store'.[25] The men in their uniforms and high boots were an uncomfortable reminder of the battlefields they would soon witness, and the King trembled so much that he had to ask the stony-faced Queen Augusta to hold their grandchild. Fritz had been given command of the Bavarian and Württemberg troops, and asked the respective Kings to stand as godparents.

On the Monday husband and wife took Communion together in the chapel, and early next morning Fritz took his leave. Having agreed with Vicky that they would spare each other a formal parting, he left a farewell note. He was in command of the Third Army, the others being under General von Steinmetz and Prince Friedrich Karl, with the King in supreme command, and General von Blumenthal his Chief of Staff. On 30 July he established his first headquarters at Speyer, about a hundred miles from the French border.

Within a week they had reached France, and won victories at Weissenberg and Wörth. At headquarters after the second battle he poured out his heart to his friend Gustav Freytag, who had accompanied him as an official chronicler of the campaign. He detested 'this butchery', had 'never longed for war laurels, and would willingly have left such fame to others without envying them.'[26] Thankfully the butchery was to be of short duration. At the end of August the German forces won a decisive battle at Sedan, near the frontier of neutral Belgium. Emperor Napoleon and his commanders surrendered on 1 September and three days later a republic was proclaimed in Paris, but the new French leaders vowed to fight until the Germans were defeated.

Contrary to general expectations, the victor had been determined within one month of fighting, but Fritz's sense of triumph was shortlived. Like Vicky, he believed in the superiority of the hardworking Prussians to the licentious French, but he could not forget how often he had enjoyed French hospitality at its finest. Soon after the surrender he talked privately with Napoleon, and learnt that he had never wanted war in the first place; contrary to popular belief he was not the real aggressor. It had never occurred to Fritz that declaration of hostilities had been provoked by Bismarck's trickery. Eager to ensure that the former sovereign was treated well, he appealed to King Wilhelm to ask him to hand over his sword in private, and let him retire to the late King's castle at Bellevue, promising him that he could join his wife and son in England after the war.

In Berlin and Windsor, reaction was less charitable. Carried away by Prussian success, Vicky's expressions of regret for Emperor Napoleon, who 'brought his fall upon himself', were tempered with uncharacteristically priggish judgments. 'May we all learn what frivolity, conceit and immorality lead to!'[27] Queen Victoria called the Emperor's fall a 'judgment from heaven' and retribution on a guilty government and vainglorious nation, 'the fulfilment of beloved

Papa's most earnest wishes!'[28] Vicky was pleased that the Prussian character was 'now appreciated and seen in its true light, its superiority acknowledged with pleasure and pride', and regretted the harm it had done to Bertie, Affie, 'and to the young and brilliant aristocracy of London!'[29]

Vicky and her children had left Berlin for Homburg near the French border, where barracks had been put at her disposal to organize a military hospital. Visiting the hospital every day, she was a model of efficiency, insisting that there was more to medical care than covering the wounded with filthy rags to keep them warm; the rags were to be burnt, wounds were to be properly dressed, walls and floors of the wards were to be scrubbed thoroughly with disinfectant. Wounded German and French soldiers were resigned to their fate as they were brought in to die on the floors of makeshift huts. Her concern for their plight deeply touched them as they saw that here was somebody who genuinely cared for their condition and was prepared to do something about it, and they clung to her hands and skirts as she went past, mouthing words of gratitude that made it hard for her not to give way to tears in front of them.

She wrote to Fritz in the few hours she could spare and he sent her his war diary, in which he recorded the campaign from personal experience, combining factual accounts and his personal thoughts.* As she received each instalment she read it, mentally following every movement and route as far as her knowledge of France allowed, consulting a map when necessary. It angered her when the German newspapers reported each victory without once mentioning his name. She knew he would not care as long as his army received due recognition, but she could not but feel hurt when his homeland

---

* In addition to the version published in Germany in 1926 and in English translation a year later, there are three manuscript versions in the Geheimes Preussisches Staatsarchiv, Merseburg. While most of the entries are in Fritz's own handwriting, there are some additions and passages in other hands, including significant comments indicating sympathy with progressive, as opposed to constitutional, liberalism, written by Vicky. See Kollander, 93–5.

Christening of Victoria, Princess Royal, 10 February 1841, lithograph after a portrait by Charles Robert Leslie. Queen Victoria and Prince Albert are on the right; those on the left include the Duchess of Kent, King Leopold of the Belgians, and Queen Adelaide, after whom the Princess was given her second name.

Victoria, Princess Royal, with Prince Albert's greyhound Eos, lithograph after a portrait by Edwin Landseer, 1841.

Prince Friedrich Wilhelm of Prussia, by Franz Xaver Winterhalter, 1851. By gracious permission of Her Majesty Queen Elizabeth II © 2000.

Victoria, Princess Royal, engraving after a portrait by Franz Xaver Winterhalter, 1856.

Prince Wilhelm of Prussia, by Franz
Xaver Winterhalter, 1848. By gracious
permission of Her Majesty Queen
Elizabeth II © 2000.

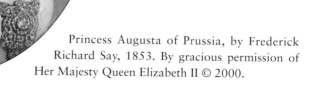

Princess Augusta of Prussia, by Frederick
Richard Say, 1853. By gracious permission of
Her Majesty Queen Elizabeth II © 2000.

The Coronation of Wilhelm I as King of Prussia, 18 October 1861, by George Housman Thomas. The Crown Princess is paying homage to the King. By gracious permission of Her Majesty Queen Elizabeth II © 2000.

Prince Friedrich Wilhelm of Prussia and Victoria, Princess Royal, from a medal commemorating their wedding. By kind permission of the British Museum.

Queen Victoria, the Prince Consort, and their children, from a montage of *carte de visite* photographs, *c.* 1860. The Crown Princess of Prussia is second from left. By kind permission of Mary Evans Picture Library.

Prince Henry, Prince Wilhelm, Princess Charlotte and Princess Victoria of Prussia, August 1870. By gracious permission of Her Majesty Queen Elizabeth II © 2000.

Crown Prince Friedrich Wilhelm of Prussia at Wörth, August 1870, lithograph after a painting by Wilhelm Camphausen.

Friedrich, Grand Duke of Baden.

'Proclamation of the German Empire at Versailles, 18 January 1871', by Anton von Werner. Emperor Wilhelm is flanked by Crown Prince Friedrich Wilhelm and Friedrich, Grand Duke of Baden, with Bismarck standing below the dais on the right. By kind permission of Mary Evans Picture Library.

Prince Friedrich Karl of Prussia.

Princess Sophie, Prince Waldemar, Princess Victoria and Princess Margaret of Prussia, photograph by G. Churchill, June 1878. By gracious permission of Her Majesty Queen Elizabeth II © 2000.

Count Götz von Seckendorff, photograph by Reichard & Lindner, *c.* 1877. By gracious permission of Her Majesty Queen Elizabeth II © 2000.

Crown Prince Friedrich Wilhelm, *c.* 1880.

Dr Morell Mackenzie, *c.* 1887.

Crown Princess
Friedrich Wilhelm at
Flete, Devon, with
members of the Mildmay
family, photograph by
Lady Mildmay,
27 August 1887.

Crown Prince Friedrich
Wilhelm at Queen
Victoria's Jubilee
procession, London,
21 June 1887.

Kaiser Friedrich III and
Bismarck, by Karl Rohling,
1888. By kind permission of
Mary Evans Picture Library.

THE INHARMONIOUS BISMARCK.

'The inharmonious
Bismarck', cartoon by
Linley Sambourne, from
Punch, 21 April 1888. The
Empress Victoria and
Bismarck are 'out of tune'
over the proposal that her
daughter Victoria should
marry Alexander, former
Prince of Bulgaria.

Empress Frederick with Princess Sophie of Prussia and Crown Prince Constantine of Greece (standing), Princesses Victoria and Margaret of Prussia (seated), photograph by W. Hoffert, September 1888. By gracious permission of Her Majesty Queen Elizabeth II © 2000.

Presentation by Queen Victoria of Colours to the 2nd Battalion Cameron Highlanders, Balmoral, photograph by Milne, 29 October 1898. Empress Frederick is seated in the carriage beside her mother. By gracious permission of Her Majesty Queen Elizabeth II © 2000.

Kaiser Wilhelm II.

Charlotte, Hereditary Princess of Saxe-
Meiningen.

Empress Augusta Victoria (Dona).

Empress Frederick and her family at Friedrichshof, photograph by Voigt, 24 May 1900. Back row, left to right: Princess Henry of Prussia; Crown Princess Sophie of Greece; Charlotte, Hereditary Princess of Saxe-Meiningen; Empress Augusta Victoria; Empress Frederick; Princess Adolf of Schaumburg-Lippe; Princess Friedrich Karl of Hesse. Centre

row: Prince Alexander, Princess Helen, and Prince Paul of Greece. Seated at front: Prince Adolf of Schaumburg-Lippe; Prince Friedrich Karl of Hesse; Prince Henry of Prussia; Kaiser Wilhelm II; Crown Prince Constantine of Greece; Prince Albert of Schleswig-Holstein (son of Empress Frederick's sister Helena); Ernest, Grand Duke of Hesse.

Empress Frederick, from a mourning card.

chose to ignore him, especially as the English press repeatedly praised his heroic virtues and leadership. It was in these pages that he noted, a few days after Sedan, that her presence in the hospitals was much appreciated, and how the doctors declared themselves astonished at her wide range of knowledge.

Not everybody appreciated this new broom sweeping clean. 'To overcome the prejudice of doctors and patients against fresh air is really almost impossible,' she wrote in despair to Queen Victoria. 'We have not one nurse or dresser here yet, only people from the town, who are dirty, ignorant and useless in the extreme, but we have sent for some better help which we shall have soon.'[30] Soon this hard-working, energetic figure was too popular for the liking of others. Her position in Germany had been made no easier by alleged remarks of Bertie in London to the French and Austrian ambassadors in London at dinner, of his hopes that Prussia would be defeated. Such comments were passed on to the court at Berlin by Count Bernstorff, the Prussian ambassador in London, who had never liked the Prince of Wales and had doubtless grossly distorted his words if not made up the story altogether. The Prince assured the Prime Minister, Gladstone, in writing that such statements were without foundation, but the damage was done.[31] In October Queen Augusta came to Homburg. Vicky felt sorry for her, as her well-known French sympathies had made her unpopular, but it irritated her that the Queen was nominal head of the hospital and ambulance services in Germany and took so little interest in them, continuing with her social life despite the war. Queen Augusta was jealous of Vicky's popularity, and it was surely no coincidence when the latter received an angry letter a few days later from King Wilhelm, ordering her back to Berlin on the grounds that he had not given her permission to go to Homburg with the children, and that she obviously did not understand her duties as Crown Princess. Back home for a much-needed rest, her temper cooled as she drew up plans for modernizing hospitals and nursing homes in peacetime.

The siege of Paris had begun on 19 September. French armies at Toul and Strasbourg surrendered the following week, and by the end of October the fortress of Metz had capitulated after 70 days.

Orléans capitulated early in December, leaving Paris as the last remaining bastion of resistance against the invaders.

Now at headquarters on the outskirts of Versailles, Fritz insisted that Paris should be starved into surrender rather than bombarded, as it was more humane and less costly in terms of German men and artillery. Even if such a campaign did end successfully, it would still result in disproportionately heavy losses. Moltke and Blumenthal agreed; Roon was the only officer to share Bismarck's view. Being a politician and not a soldier, the Count wanted to solve the matter the quick way – shell the city so it would surrender within a few days. It came as a surprise to find that he was outnumbered. Even before he had Moltke's and Blumenthal's support, Fritz clung to his preference for no bombardment. It shattered Bismarck's conviction that the Crown Prince was easily swayed once away from his wife. Public opinion in Berlin strongly favoured an all-out attack on the capital, some agreeing with Countess Bismarck's suggestion of shooting down every French civilian, adults, children and babies alike. On 28 November Fritz noted in his diary that she had told everyone he was responsible for delaying the bombardment. He admitted that he did not intend to open fire 'till in the opinion of professional gunners and experts the necessary ammunition each single siege gun requires for an effective uninterrupted bombardment is there on the spot.'[32]

The Count and Countess were about to get their own back. In Berlin it was said that he was delaying action not for technical considerations but on 'petticoat orders'; the two Queens, Augusta and Victoria, urged by the Crown Princess, would not allow it. For a short time the mutual loneliness of Vicky and Augusta during the war had brought them closer together, and this new friendship added fuel to the fire. It was Vicky who was attacked most of all, partly as the Bismarcks saw more to be gained in a vendetta directed towards Prussia's future Queen than against the present one, and partly because of England's neutrality. As anti-French hysteria grew in Berlin, so did the whispering campaign against Vicky, and by December Fritz was exasperated at the continued vilification of his wife. Still his troops were not ready to carry out a bombardment of Paris, and he would not yield to 'the war drones, who follow the course of the war without responsibility or knowledge'[33] with no idea what they were talking about.

Paris endured the siege stoically. The aristocracy and wealthy middle-classes had to make few sacrifices, so the poor suffered most, their houses demolished so the bricks could be used for barricades, the homeless sitting on pavements in the howling wind and rain, clutching their possessions and huddling together, desperate to keep warm. Soldiers cut down the avenues of trees in an attempt to slow the German advance. Fritz shuddered to think of the deprivations that innocent civilians, particularly women and children, suffered because of a war they could not help. As an example to the troops, he and the King confined themselves largely to a diet of dry bread and cheese, with very little meat.

Meanwhile the equally pressing consideration of German unity was occupying Fritz's mind. He regularly thought of his late mentors, the Prince Consort, King Leopold and Baron Stockmar, and their plans for a free German imperial state under a monarchical head to 'march at the forefront of civilisation and be in a position to develop and bring to bear all noble ideals of the modern world.'[34] At the same time representatives of four South German states, Bavaria, Württemberg, Baden and Hesse, were discussing an alliance after the war, possibly under a reorganized German Confederation. Soon after they had approached Bismarck for a discussion which settled nothing, Fritz asked him for his views on an imperial Germany. Bismarck pointed out that most of the states were agreeable but King Ludwig II of Bavaria was reluctant to let Prussia take the initiative, and without Bavarian approval Württemberg would also withhold consent. When Fritz suggested that any states which resisted might be compelled, Bismarck snapped that he had no right to say so.

Fritz knew he was not bothered by Ludwig's obstinacy, so much as by the North German Confederation Parliament or *Reichstag*. He had recently spoken to the leaders who knew that in their Crown Prince was a champion not only of empire, but also of majority rule, free elections, and more constitutional monarchy. If the *Reichstag* took the initiative in unifying Germany, its authority and power would be considerably enhanced. Bismarck knew that if he did not act soon, his political enemies at home in Prussia would be in the ascendant and his own career would be jeopardised. As successive British ministers at the Berlin Embassy had suspected, he intended to unite Germany at the right moment, as long as he could do it in a way that would increase his own authority. The moment was now, before the next *Reichstag* meeting. After Fritz had gone, with angry taunts of *Kaiserwahnsinn* (Emperor-madness) ringing in his ears, Bismarck set to work. Loath to admit the superiority of Hohenzollerns over Wittelsbachs King Ludwig remained obdurate, until the Count dangled before him the prospect of a healthy sum from the *Welfenfonds*, and persuaded him to sign the letter drafted for him inviting King Wilhelm to assume the imperial crown. The King thus believed the creation of the Empire to be at the request of the German princes, not the people. Even Fritz was taken in for a while, and thought that Ludwig had written the letter of his own free will.

On 4 January 1871 Bismarck goaded the King into giving the order for the bombardment of Paris to begin. 'What good to us is all power, all martial glory and renown, if hatred and mistrust meet us at every turn, if every step we advance in our development is a subject for suspicion and grudging?' Fritz wrote in his diary. 'Bismarck has made us great and powerful, but he has robbed us of our friends, the sympathies of the world, and – our conscience.'[35] For all the superiority of German artillery the bombardment was a comparative failure; only 97 Frenchmen were killed, 278 wounded, and 1,400 buildings damaged for an expenditure of 12,000 shells; the several hundred Prussian gunners lost to French counter-battery fire made their enemy's losses appear trifling. Once fire had been opened on the city, Bismarck felt that military matters as well as political decisions should be his responsibility, much to the disgust of Moltke. To prevent them from falling out completely Fritz's mediation skills were soon called for.

The bombardment entered its third week on the same day as the proclamation of the Empire, which took place in the Hall of Mirrors at Versailles. Fritz tried in vain to impress upon his father that the elevation of three German princes to the rank of King by the first

Napoleon, sixty years earlier, made it necessary for him to accept the rank of Kaiser in order to assert his superiority. The old man grumbled at having to 'bid farewell to the old Prussia, to which alone he clung and would always cling.'[36] He was not even allowed his own way over the title, which he wanted to be 'Kaiser of Germany'; Fritz and Bismarck recommended 'German Kaiser', or 'Kaiser in Germany', which emphasized the merging of Prussia into something greater, and would be more acceptable to the other German princes.

Both men were in a thoroughly bad temper when proceedings began shortly after midday on 18 January as the new Emperor entered the hall, filled with a crowd of princes, officers and deputations from army regiments. Mounting the dais decorated with brightly-coloured regimental banners, he addressed the throng brokenly before handing over to Bismarck, who read the imperial proclamation in an expressionless voice. The Grand Duke of Baden tried to inject some enthusiasm into the ceremonies as he stood on the dais requesting three cheers for His Majesty the Kaiser, the father-in-law who stood crossly beside him. Afterwards the sovereign stumped out without even glancing at Bismarck.

For Fritz the pageantry of the proceedings so befitting the new imperial era had been spoilt by the bad atmosphere caused by their ungracious demeanour. Moreover he had been defeated in his aim to help the *Reichstag* in presenting unity as a popular cause, as he had hoped. The Prince Consort, he wrote to Vicky some time later, would have been impressed by such changes, but 'would not have approved of the methods whereby unification was achieved any more than you and I.'[37]

On 28 January an armistice of three weeks was arranged between Bismarck and the French Foreign Minister Jules Favre, extended twice to allow peace negotiations to be completed. France had to cede the greater part of Alsace and Lorraine, including the fortress of Metz, and pay an indemnity of five million marks. Fritz and the Grand Duke of Baden protested that such humiliation would leave the country thirsting for revenge, but Bismarck and Moltke insisted that the enemy's spirit must be broken, and the King was greedy for the spoils denied him after their victory over Austria in 1866.

Back at Berlin, an exhausted Vicky contemplated the changes and took stock of her situation. 25 January, her thirteenth wedding anniversary, was the first she and her husband had spent apart. In a mood of gloom she cast her mind back to the birth of her first child twelve years earlier, and how the first years of his life were so unhappy for her; 'I fought against the disappointment & the gnawing worry; for his arm has embittered my whole life – & I never really felt delight at having him! It was *wrong* & ungrateful, & I have in fact got over it . . .' She admitted that she was proud of him, though she could by no means consider him a genius or an interesting character, but at least she could hope he would become 'a pure, faithful, true person, who delights in the *good* & the *beautiful* & understands the spirit of his time.'[38] Perhaps she could see in her heart of hearts that he would be found wanting on almost every count. Her work for the hospitals had taken her away from her sons and she was anxious at losing contact with them. What worried her even more was the prolonged absence of their father. Willy and Henry were high-spirited boys, Willy was becoming particularly wilful, and they needed their father's firm control.

However she could console herself with the knowledge that his return home was in sight, and only the thought of seeing his family again made Fritz endure the gloating formality of a triumphal march into Paris on 1 March. Yet he could see hope for the future. 'A noble task lies before our Government, if it is firmly resolved to strive earnestly for the internal development of the Empire on liberal lines in accord with the spirit of the age, and by so doing give the world a guarantee for lasting peace.'[39] On 17 March he set foot on Prussian soil again at Wildpark station. As he and Vicky drove back to the Unter den Linden in an open carriage, waving to the cheering crowds who lined his route with cries of '*Unser Fritz*', he was pleased to be at home again after the longest separation they had yet endured – and were ever to know – which had seemed more like eight years than eight months. It was an unforgettable moment as they stepped out of the vehicle and he set eyes again on his children, assembled on the palace threshold to welcome their conquering father who was the toast of the city. Still the crowds cheered, to break into a deafening roar when a window opened to reveal the smiling family of eight, Fritz fondly holding nine-month-old Sophie in his arms.

In London the Foreign Secretary Lord Granville had written to Queen Victoria that the Crown Prince had 'distinguished himself not only by his military success, but by his humanity, his moderation and his large political views', while his friendship, 'in spite of the atmosphere with which he has been surrounded, is invaluable for the future.'[40] However endless festivities at home to commemorate the victory, and the formalities of day-to-day business, denied him the rest he needed. The first imperial *Reichstag* was opened on 21 March with Bismarck raised to the rank of Prince. To Augusta, victory celebrations meant more court balls and drawing-rooms, at which she insisted that Fritz and Vicky should take part and accompany her. Her 'orders' were peppered with bitter attacks on the pro-French sympathies of England, and particularly on a speech made by Queen Victoria at the opening of Parliament in February referring to the belligerent powers as 'two great and brave nations', which she saw as a snub for Germany.

On 16 June the victorious army entered Berlin through the Brandenburg Gate, an occasion for more waving of flags and handkerchiefs, cascades of flowers and wreaths. The procession held a sinister note for Vicky as she rode through the gate beside Fritz, resplendent with his new Field-Marshal's baton. When she turned round and saw Willy, following on his small dappled pony she was alarmed at the look of pride on his face, basking in the knowledge that one day this victorious heritage would be his. He seemed to look up to his grandfather the Kaiser as the living embodiment of all this glory, rather than his father whose active participation in the war and intense desire for German unity in the face of prevarication from others had done far more to make it possible.

Even at the time, Vicky had had her reservations about the new era that her husband had greeted so enthusiastically, seeing confusion everywhere. 'Our political judgement, our interest in social progress and in the progressive development of our own country has diminished because of the war!' she wrote. 'I fear that an era of reaction will ensue – I can already see its dark shadows hovering over us!'[41]

SIX

'Malice is rampant'

Vicky and Fritz's sojourn during the summer of 1871 at Osborne was their first visit to England for nearly three years, since they had spent Christmas 1868 there. It was a relief to escape from the martial atmosphere of Berlin, and see for themselves that the general anti-German feeling in England was not directed at them personally. When Berlin commemorated the first anniversary of victory at Sedan in September 1871, they refused to join in the official celebrations and boycotted the church services. They maintained that the real heroic deeds had occurred on the battlefield and that to take part in the celebrations would only be adding to Bismarck's self-glorification, but their principled refusal to take part in such humbug, as they saw it, cost them support from other members of the family and public.

Angered by their visit to England, the Kaiser vented his displeasure on them by initially refusing permission to take the children to Wilhelmshöhe in Kassel, away from Potsdam, when a smallpox epidemic was raging in Berlin and three hundred children died within ten days. Potsdam, he retorted, was perfectly healthy, and they would stay there unless he received an official written statement to the contrary from the court doctor. 'Just think of Fritz at forty being treated like a boy of six',[1] Vicky complained to Queen Victoria. To ensure he was not disobeyed, the Kaiser sent a general to the palace as guard and virtual gaoler. Having made his point, he relented and let them go to Kassel, but not on grounds of health, 'a ridiculous excuse'. They spent several weeks there until all danger of infection was gone, but Fritz was furious with his father for imposing such petty restrictions.

Vicky was pregnant again, and deeply hurt when Empress Augusta chose to break the news to Queen Victoria herself. To add

126

to her discomfort her old friend Countess Blücher, who had helped her through previous confinements, had recently died. She felt more than usually wretched and fearful of the consequences, but Queen Victoria bluntly told her that she hoped she (Vicky) would be satisfied, '& not go on exhausting your *health* & strength so precious to *all* you belong to & so necessary to your husband & children & to your adopted country.'[2] The Empress then promised that she would be with Vicky for her confinement, asking her at the same time if she would help her secure an invitation to visit Queen Victoria in England. When she received an invitation for early May, she exasperated her daughter-in-law and the Queen by asking if it could be altered to June, and then left the heavily-pregnant Vicky, going to England in mid-April instead.

Fortunately Vicky gave birth to a fourth daughter without complications on 22 April 1872, named Margaret in honour of Crown Princess Margharita of Italy, one of the godparents. By the time of the baby's christening her head was covered in short hair and she was nicknamed Mossy; the name stuck to her throughout her life. Vicky was mildly disappointed that this eighth child was a girl, as the patriot in her made her feel she owed Germany another son. However she was disinclined to go through a ninth confinement, and Mossy remained the baby of the family.

By this time Vicky had recognized that the youngest children would always be the ones closest to her. Like her mother, she had learnt from bitter experience that it only brought disappointment to expect too much of her sons and daughters. Where their upbringing was involved, she fretted about the difficulty of doing the right thing for them as a parent; 'I am often so *despondent* & think with *such* a heavy heart about the future of the 3 eldest!'[3]

With fewer military duties in peacetime, Fritz found a new role as a patron of the arts and appointment as Protector of Public Museums, with special responsibility for raising the standard of the royal museums and galleries and overseeing the acquisition of new exhibits. Now Prussia was no longer a small military kingdom, but the centre of a new imperial power, it had to take its place alongside the cultural centres of Dresden and Munich, and compete with other countries in the arts as well as in industrial and commercial expansion. Every report to the minister of education on museums was to be initially submitted to him, and he was to see a copy of every order from the ministry. Vicky was in her element, helping to discharge a function so close to one of her father's passions, and she and Fritz relished regular visits to studios of painters and sculptors at home and abroad. Anton von Werner, who had accompanied him on the Franco-Prussian campaign and painted the official group portrait of the proclamation ceremony at Versailles, owed his position as a leading historical artist and his presidency of the Fine Arts Academy to Fritz's patronage, while the painter Adolf von Menzel and the sculptor Reinhold Begas also came to know their Crown Prince and Princess well and appreciate their keen interest in their work. At the same time Fritz was foremost in instigating and encouraging new excavations at Olympia in Greece and Pergamon in Asia Minor, which eventually resulted in the exhibition of the life-sized Greek temple and Babylonian victory walk at the Pergamon museum in Berlin.

Another of his schemes to bear fruit was the Hohenzollern Museum. It was inspired by a visit before his marriage to the Rosenbørg Castle, Copenhagen, a museum containing souvenirs of the Danish monarchy, and he wanted to establish a similar collection in Berlin commemorating his own dynasty. Portraits, weapons, furniture and similar items, accompanied by captions and explanations, all found their place in a new museum opened on 22 March 1877, the Kaiser's eightieth birthday.

Politically Vicky and Fritz had grounds for optimism during the first few years of empire, regarded as Prussia's 'liberal era'. The National Liberals comprised the majority party in the *Reichstag*, the Prussian cabinet included three liberal ministers, and they pursued a policy of free trade which ushered in several years of economic prosperity. Despite liberal setbacks during the crisis which brought Bismarck to power, they had made gains in the late 1860s and early 1870s, with the constitution intact and unification achieved. With an elderly Kaiser and Bismarck in uncertain health, liberals looked forward to the day when politicians of their stamp would hold the highest offices of state. While recent advances promised further progressive reforms, they were divided as to the benefits of an increase in parliamentary power. The Crown Prince, and liberals such as Heinrich von Treitschke, Heinrich von Sybel, and Rudolf Haym, saw the foundation of the empire as the fulfilment of the liberal programme, and questioned the desirability of transferring English institutions to Germany. Other National Liberals and Progressives hoped the future course of liberal reform would see the formation of a government responsible to parliament that would control the budget of the military, the strongest support of the monarchy.

Meanwhile Fritz supported the ministry's efforts to combat certain forces in the empire, especially the Roman Catholic church in Germany. He was at one with Bismarck and the liberal majority in thinking that the German Catholics owed more allegiance to Rome than to the imperial government, and they wanted to restrict the power of an apparently anti-national and potentially disruptive spirit in the new empire. Hostility toward Catholics increased after the founding in Prussia in 1870 of the Catholic Centre Party, which had become the second largest party in the *Reichstag* within a year. Bismarck thought that German Catholics, supported by their counterparts in Austria and France, could compromise imperial unity and undermine the Protestant majority in Germany, while the liberals opposed the Roman Catholic church's restraints upon individual freedom. The anti-Catholic campaign, the *Kulturkampf*, or cultural struggle between modernity and medievalism, took the form of measures designed to combat what they saw as a Catholic threat, such as a law eliminating ecclesiastical supervision in schools, and the disbanding of an anti-liberal Jesuit order. It reached its height in May 1873 with anti-Catholic legislation in Prussia, the 'May Laws', placing restrictions on the training and employment of priests and on the church's disciplinary powers. By supporting these measures the liberals believed their support of the *Kulturkampf* would ultimately increase the power of the *Reichstag* against Bismarck's autocratic policies in other fields.

As he had long advocated the liberal ideal of a secular state, Fritz supported these measures, seeing in the *Kulturkampf* the realization of schemes that he himself had proposed earlier to control Catholic influence in Germany. He had previously tried to alert his father and Bismarck to what he saw as Rome's attempts to increase its clerical authority in Germany; a few years earlier he had discussed a plan with Friedberg, the Minister of Justice, to grant the German Catholic church a status similar to that of the Hungarian Catholic church, which had looser ties with Rome. The scheme found them at one with Bismarck, intent on bringing the German Catholic church under state control so it might serve as a unifying force in the empire. *Kulturkampf* legislation resembled Fritz's goals so closely that the British ambassador to Germany, Odo Russell, suspected Bismarck's support of the campaign was part of a plan to make himself indispensable to the future Kaiser.

As a tireless advocate of greater religious freedom for Catholics, Vicky took issue with her husband's views on the subject. Reproached by her mother for not sharing the 'fervent Protestantism' of herself, the Prince Consort and Fritz, Vicky defended her own tolerance; 'if other people are not of my way of thinking I can regret it, and think them difficult to understand but I do not blame them.'[4]

By the late 1870s many supporters of the *Kulturkampf*, including Bismarck, saw it as a failure. German Catholics' hostility to the government was increasing, as did the power of the Centre Party in the *Reichstag*. Some liberals also turned against the struggle as the discriminatory nature of such legislation conflicted with their endorsement of individual liberty. Fritz did not share their view, telling the Liberal leader Bamberger that deputies to the *Reichstag* from the Centre Party were not Germans but 'aliens' whose influence was intolerable. While he regretted some of the discriminatory legislation of the *Kulturkampf*, he believed that since the struggle had been undertaken, they needed to see it through, and he did not believe that German Catholics were turning against the monarchy.

Fritz's endorsement of Bismarck's policies during the early 1870s suggested that the Chancellor would be retained in office after Kaiser Wilhelm's death. In November 1872 after a visit to Dresden to celebrate the golden wedding of the King and Queen of Saxony he intended to go directly from the festivities to join Vicky and the children in Switzerland, but on the journey he fell ill with an intestinal complaint. After a slow convalescence, most of which was spent at Karlsruhe with the Grand Duke and Duchess of Baden, he went for a cure at Wiesbaden. The right-wing *Rheinische Kurier* chose this moment to report that the Crown Prince had warned his wife that the physicians told him his illness was dangerous; his father was old, their eldest son was still a minor, and it was possible that she might be called upon to act as Regent for a time. In such a case, she had to promise her husband 'to do nothing without Prince Bismarck, whose counsels have raised our House to undreamed-of power and greatness.'[5]

Some liberals looked askance at this rapprochement between their heir and the Chancellor, fearing that the latter was exaggerating such a threat in order to increase the power of his political office. Despite Vicky's mistrust of Bismarck, by the end of the decade even she was convinced that his services would be indispensable during her husband's coming reign, as she supported his foreign policy. As she told Queen Victoria, while she thought him 'a misfortune for Germany and for the development of liberties, our trade &c. and certainly a danger for the Crown', she believed he was 'entirely for England, and has a sincere wish to be well with England, and that England's power should on all occasions rise superior to Russia's.'[6]

It was ironic that while Fritz and Bismarck broadly agreed in several of their aims for government policy in the imperial era, the Chancellor did not hesitate to instigate many of the unpleasant stories about Fritz and Vicky. It suited him to portray the heir, a reluctant warrior but a war hero for all that, an intelligent ruler waiting in the wings despite a self-deprecating demeanour and lack of confidence in himself, as a weakling dominated by his more forceful wife who, he asserted, had the interests of her native England above all at heart. His spite toward anyone who ever opposed him robbed Fritz of his rightful reputation as a military commander. Many in Germany shared the opinion of Baron Hugo von Reischach, a Hussar who served under all three German Emperors, who spoke of him as 'the leader in two wars', thought

131

him a superior general to his more famous cousin Friedrich Karl, and as dedicated to the army as his father. Regrettably such verdicts counted less than that of Bismarck, ever ready to distort the Crown Prince's mistrust of the arrogant militarism of contemporary Prussia.

While Fritz may have disappointed some of the more progressive liberals and radicals, his own wife among them, by his caution and respect for the power of the crown, in some ways he was ahead of his time. With his respect for a free press, he surprised some of the authorities in class-conscious Berlin by receiving reporters and editors at the palace and making a point of seeking them out to talk to at official functions. He openly favoured the advancement of women and supported a petition, sent to the *Reichstag* in 1872, advocating that they should be allowed to pursue careers in such professions as the postal, telegraphic and railway services, bastions of male bureaucracy. Only his support enabled Vicky to start the Victoria Lyceum, a place where girls, still barred from universities, could attend scholarly lectures on an equal level with men. She gave him advice and support and kept up his spirits when he became depressed. In an aggressively patriarchal society where wives were expected to limit their activities to *Kinder, Küche und Kirche* (children, kitchen and church), this partnership left them vulnerable to Bismarck's scorn.

In April 1873, a few weeks after his return from Wiesbaden, Fritz and Vicky were invited to the International Exhibition at Vienna, where they met the painter Heinrich von Angeli. After seeing his portraits in the exhibition Fritz and Vicky visited Angeli in his studio and invited him to Potsdam, thus aiding the start of his career as the foremost portrait painter to the royal European courts in succession to the dying Franz Xaver Winterhalter, and also an enduring friendship between the Austrian and his patrons. He came to the Neue Palais most years from 1873 onwards to paint and instruct his sitters, and as a trusted companion who enjoyed the company of the continent's most enlightened heir and his consort, comparing their palace to the house of a private citizen, where the hosts and children made up a 'simple and charming family picture'. He was impressed by Fritz's quiet character, 'never speaking a word more than is absolutely necessary in family conversation,'[7] and noted that he never mentioned military or political topics at home.

After leaving Vienna in May they had a brief holiday at Venice, Milan and near the Italian lakes, before returning to Potsdam to prepare for the reception of the Shah of Persia, then touring the Western world like a travelling circus complete with a suite of ministers, attendants and a harem. On arrival he lived up to his eccentric reputation, and despite their initial doubts Fritz and Vicky were quite taken with him. He had no sense of time, and kept everybody waiting nearly an hour before appearing at a military inspection and other functions arranged in his honour. Unable to manage a knife and fork, he tore food apart with his bare hands at meals, spitting it out after chewing so he could examine the remains. Most of the family found him undignified and a great bore; the papers marked his visit with disparaging reports and anecdotes, though his admiration for England and everything English, and dislike of Russia, probably did much to colour his reception at court.

In January 1874 Queen Victoria's second son Alfred, Duke of Edinburgh, married Marie, the only surviving daughter of Tsar Alexander II, and Vicky and Fritz were among the royal guests invited to St Petersburg. It was Vicky's first visit to Russia, and she did not like the country, deciding she was '*profoundly thankful*' she did not have to live there; 'over the whole of Russia there seems to me to hang a dull, heavy, silent melancholy *very* depressing to the spirits!'[8] Nevertheless she got on well with the Tsar, who presented her with a glittering diamond and ruby bracelet as a memento of the occasion. Several months after their return Bismarck suggested that she had gone with the purpose of persuading the Tsar to conclude an Anglo-Russian alliance against Germany, and a grateful Tsar had presented her with the jewellery for this very reason. Though Emperor Wilhelm had the sense to exclaim that he did not believe it for a moment, he still regretted that he had allowed his daughter-in-law to accompany her husband to St Petersburg.[9] The whispering campaign against her was so firmly established among the Anglophobes and anti-liberal court circles that many others accepted the slander without question.

The ever more oppressive atmosphere of Berlin drove husband and wife increasingly to Bornstädt, away from spiteful gossip and the all-pervading aura of the Chancellor, to the joys of country life and friendly villagers who formed their impressions of the couple not on gossip and calumny but on what they saw at first-hand. Vicky always preferred fresh air and found court functions increasingly difficult to endure. She had never managed to master her overwhelming shyness, found it difficult to make small talk and much preferred good conversation on the wide range of subjects which interested her to the malicious gossip that other German princesses relished.

Her children were always welcomed by their English grandmother on visits to Windsor, Osborne and Balmoral. The younger ones loved these holidays almost as much as their mother did, and she had particularly high hopes for Waldie, in whom she saw something of the Prince Consort with his love of animals and interest in science and geology. Of all Queen Victoria's grandchildren, he was the most keen when it came to looking for minerals and fossils on the Isle of Wight. When they were there he proudly collected fragments of fossilized coniferous wood, ammonite, and an iguanadon's tooth, which Vicky carefully labelled and deposited in the museum at the Swiss Cottage where she had played and learned to cook during childhood. Yet it was on one of their English visits that the little imp gave Queen Victoria a nasty fright. Working in her room one evening she looked up from her papers to see the beady eyes of a small crocodile leering at her, and her screams brought the whole household running. Waldie had let his pet crocodile 'Bob' out of its box, and order was not restored until he rescued the wandering pachyderm, helpless with laughter as he did so.

Vicky was touched that the Queen never forgot her grand-children's birthdays, marking the occasions with gifts of ponies, or family heirlooms for the future such as candlesticks, silver plate or jewellery. The Emperor and Empress ignored their birthdays, so Queen Victoria's thoughtfulness was appreciated all the more. Emperor Wilhelm displayed more fondness to them than the increasingly distant Empress, but he was a thrifty soul and his family obligations stopped short of sending presents.

The Queen did not always show the same affection at this time for the children's parents, and on several of their visits to England after 1871 they were reduced to staying at the Prussian Embassy, or at Sandringham. Fritz, she informed her private secretary Sir Henry Ponsonby in 1874, was 'rather weak & to a certain extent obstinate not *conceited* but absurdly proud, as all his family are, thinking no family higher or greater than the Hohenzollerns.'[10] Nine years later, writing to her granddaughter Victoria, Alice's eldest child, she complained that he and Vicky were '*not* pleasant in *Germany*', but 'high & mighty there'.[11] That her son-in-law and daughter were destined to succeed to an imperial throne while she was a mere Queen was sufficient cause for jealousy, even after her declaration as Empress of India in 1876.

The happy family circle was not destined to remain so much longer; almost imperceptibly, the forces that would set Willy against them were at work. In January 1873 ex-Emperor Napoleon died in exile at Chislehurst in Kent. Remembering the happy times she had known at the glittering French court, and touched by his pathetic downfall and disease-racked last years, Vicky was deeply upset. Willy found her emotional reaction hard to understand, as he recalled how desperate she had been when his father had gone to war against France. He asked Hinzpeter, whose careful choice of words made his charge believe that his mother was committing treason by mourning one of Germany's most notorious enemies. The idea took root in the impressionable boy's mind, and over the next few years he took all his confidential problems to the governor, whom he regarded as his best friend. This pleased Hinzpeter as, like many other German men with old-fashioned views, he disliked Vicky because she was a woman whose brains made him feel inferior.

It was sad that Willy felt unable to talk to his father, as they had been close to each other in the past. Like his brother-in-law Bertie, Fritz took to heart the differences which had prevented him from enjoying an easy relationship with his own father, and with this in mind he had wanted a good relationship with his sons from the start. But another of Bismarck's schemes had borne fruit; in sending Fritz on representative missions around Europe and beyond, he was keeping him away from his son. The less Willy saw of his father, the more he would look upon him as a stranger as he grew up, and in due course this would make it easier for the Chancellor to turn him against his parents and their politics. It would also foster the impression that the Crown Prince was an ineffectual father, completely ruled by his wife when it came to bringing up the boy.

Vicky would never deny that she was certainly a demanding parent. Raised by a perfectionist father who had sent her to Prussia to produce a generation of reformers, she saw it as her duty to bring up the future Kaiser in the same image, with qualities she had been taught as necessary for moral and political leadership. Taught never to be satisfied with herself, she would not give up trying to encourage her own children, particularly the eldest and most important, in a similar fashion. She worried endlessly about their health and childhood illnesses, particularly Willy, who like his father was always susceptible to colds and nasal infections. In his case, the damage to his arm, shoulder and left ear had weakened his immunity to such complaints.

It need hardly be said that the experience of her first confinement had left her with a lasting mistrust of German doctors. This scepticism with regards to their abilities had been compounded when Sigi's meningitis went unrecognized until it was too late, and from that time onwards, whenever she was in England she consulted English doctors. Back at home in Berlin and Potsdam, she always watched out for things the German doctors might not notice. Unlike their Hohenzollern cousins, Vicky and Fritz's children were small and thin. She was always sensitive to any criticism of them, particularly of Willy's deformed arm, and was outraged when Fritz's cousin, the loud-mouthed Friedrich Karl, said openly that a one-armed man should never be King of Prussia.[12]

Vicky and Fritz's children lived a happy, homely existence as youngsters, which had more in common with the childhood life of Queen Victoria's children than those of the average Prussian prince and princess of the age. The family spent winters in Berlin, summers in Potsdam, and took family holidays further afield, usually England, in July or August. Like Vicky, her children always keenly anticipated their annual departure for the country. In Potsdam the children rode on horseback with their mother most mornings, and on holidays went for long walks with their father. When he was at home he took his sons rowing or swimming, and when they were old enough all three went hunting together.

The children always had breakfast with their parents. In later years, the younger ones always came into their parents' room promptly at 7 a.m. and sat on their bed having tea and toast. Princess Victoria later looked back fondly on this part of her life, during which her mother never neglected them even though she always seemed to be active and busy. 'Every moment that she could spare away from the various duties which devolved upon her was spent with us. She carefully supervised and watched our upbringing both in the nursery and the schoolroom.'[13] Poultney Bigelow, the son of an American diplomat and one of Willy's playmates, thought that no parents could have shown more interest in their children than the Crown Prince and Princess. Willy's parents were usually there with 'a smile and kind word'[14] when their children ate supper, though the Crown Princess had a sharp eye for napkins not properly tucked in or any lapse in nursery manners.

Fritz's university education had seemed little short of revolutionary in the 1840s, and a proposal to send Willy to the Kassel *Gymnasium* (grammar school) in 1874 for three years also astonished the court. Contrary to popular belief, the idea was not Vicky's but that of Hinzpeter, who wanted to bring the boys further under his control and therefore take them away from their parents, suggesting it in such a way that she soon believed it to be of her making. She agreed that it would surely prevent 'that terrible Prussian pride' from ensnaring Willy; he must not grow up with the idea that he was of 'a different flesh and blood to the poor, the peasants and working classes and servants'.[15] The Kaiser complained that as the boy was his eventual heir, he should have been consulted first. He wanted Willy to stay in Berlin, to appear at manoeuvres and reviews as his father had done at the same age, and to be in the public eye as much as possible – just what Fritz and Vicky did not want. Yet it had been an error of judgment to keep the plan to themselves, and not let the Kaiser know until so near the time. Vicky did herself a disservice by not admitting that it had been Hinzpeter's idea in the first place, since the old man had the same unbounded faith in the governor that she did. Either the thought of defying her father-in-law for the sake of what she believed to be right for her son carried her away, or else she knew Wilhelm to be so completely under Bismarck's influence that he would not believe her if she denied all responsibility. The Empress took their part, which only hardened her husband's opposition.

Willy's confirmation on 1 September 1874 at the Friedenskirche took place after an argument between Vicky and the Emperor. Her eyes were red and she made a great effort to keep herself from trembling as she watched her son calmly listening to long tedious addresses, and answering the forty prepared questions without hesitation or embarrassment. Henry was also going to school in preparation for a career in the navy, and later that week she and Fritz saw the boys leave home, to stay at Schloss Wilhelmshöhe under Hinzpeter's surveillance and attend their schools as day pupils.

In April and May 1875 Vicky and Fritz enjoyed a short spring holiday in Italy. They visited King Victor Emmanuel and Crown Prince Umberto, and Vicky's artistic talent throve under the guidance of Anton von Werner, staying in Venice at the time. It was a rude shock for them when they returned to Berlin in May to find Germany apparently on the verge of war again.

France had recovered quickly from the recent conflict, paying off her indemnity by September 1873, eighteen months before the date specified in the Frankfurt treaty. The subsequent departure of the last German soldier from occupied territory was soon followed by reorganization of the French army, and representatives of every political party in the country were talking of revenge. When Bismarck learnt that the government in Paris was purchasing thousands of cavalry horses from German stables, he published a decree suspending the export of any more. Shortly afterwards a meeting between King Victor Emmanuel of Italy and Emperor Franz Josef at Venice gave rise to rumours that an Austro-Italian-French coalition was being hatched, and Bismarck's recent anti-Catholic legislation made the supposed alliance look like a threat to Germany. In April 1875 the *Kölnische Zeitung* published an article commenting on the threat to European peace posed by the French army and the Venetian encounter. Two more right-wing papers took up the theme, and stock exchanges all over the continent were shaken by the scare. The Grand Duchess of Baden drew the Kaiser's attention to these articles and he wrote in some anxiety to Bismarck, who disclaimed any connection with the panic. Everything was calm by the time Vicky and Fritz came home, but after previous experiences they knew better than to place trust where it did not belong. In June Bismarck assured Fritz eloquently that 'he had never wished for war nor intended it' and blamed the alarm on the press. He wished he could believe the Chancellor, but as Vicky said, 'as long as he lives we cannot ever feel safe or comfortable'.[16] Kaiser Wilhelm wrote personally to Queen Victoria, assuring her that any thoughts of war had been entirely a fabrication by the newspapers, particularly *The Times*.

The affair cast a shadow over Fritz's activities during the summer, including a visit to Vienna for the funeral of ex-Austrian Emperor Ferdinand, his opening of a horticultural exhibition at Koln, and another round of army inspections. He was sufficiently soured for once to complain about having to dash 'from one (German state) to the other by rail, like a State messenger' when he wrote to Prince Carol of Roumania that autumn. He was willing to fulfil his duties, 'but there are limits, especially when one is no longer as young as one was'.[17] His hollow existence as a representative at Bismarck's beck and call was beginning to make him feel old and weary before his time. Even allowing for his delicate health, for him to complain of feeling his age at forty-four, when his father had ascended the throne in his sixties and showed no sign of relinquishing it on the threshold of eighty, was disturbing. In a mood of depression at this time he told Hinzpeter that he felt he would never rule; the succession would skip a generation.[18]

In the following year another war scare came from the Balkans. When Slav nationalists rioted in Bosnia and Herzegovina in the summer of 1875, ministers representing members of the *Dreikaiserbund* agreed to fight if necessary in order to put down the revolt. Russia particularly favoured armed intervention, and the alliance would probably draw Germany and Austria into any ensuing conflict. With outward calm Fritz braved himself for the order to mobilize in a war he dreaded far more than the previous campaigns. The Slavs and Turks were dangerous enemies who thought nothing of stabbing their opponents in the back and torturing rather than taking prisoners; and, worst of all, it could have brought him face to face with British soldiers. Disraeli, his foreign minister Lord Salisbury and the British government distrusted Bismarck as much as they did Russia, whose threatened expansion in the Balkans would be at the expense of British trade routes to India and the far east.

Willy's education at Kassel was not an unqualified success. His regular placing as tenth in a class of seventeen did not cure his passion for boasting, and far from treating him as one of them, his fellow-pupils looked up to their eventual ruler and flattered him endlessly. Moreover he had gone there with misgivings about the liberal notions of his parents. To him Bismarck was a hero whose policies of blood and iron had made Germany great; liberalism, so it seemed, had contributed nothing to the birth of the Empire. His history lessons had reinforced his faith in the Chancellor, and Hinzpeter had contributed his share by encouraging him to speak out. The boy had found fault with everything – the headmaster, the curriculum, the 'lack of Germanism' – largely for its own sake.

When it came to persuading her adolescent son as to the merits of her opinions, Vicky could be her own worst enemy. Her constant descriptions of herself as an Englishwoman and a free-born Briton did nothing to help her, particularly when she regularly used such phrases in letters to Willy. England, she told him, was 'the freest, the most progressive advanced, & liberal & the most developed race in the world, also the *richest*, she clearly is more suited than any *other* to civilize other countries!'[19] Hinzpeter warned her against this trumpeting of English superiority, but she failed to see that the end result was bound to be a defiant reaction.

For the time being, however, the volcano lay dormant, and nobody was more eager to help fight Willy's battles than his parents. He was to come of age on 27 January 1877 and enter the First Regiment of Guards as a lieutenant, wearing the highest decorations that Russia, Austria and Italy could offer him. Britain stayed aloof at first, and not without reason. Queen Victoria had invited him to stay at Windsor during the previous autumn, and was so un-impressed with his demeanour that she decided to send him only the Grand Commandership of the Bath. A sulking Willy bullied Vicky into pressing her mother to send the Order of the Garter instead, the best that she could bestow. The examples of the other countries were on his side, as was precedent; his grandfather had awarded the Queen's three elder sons – the Prince of Wales, the Duke of Edinburgh, and Arthur, Duke of Connaught – the Black Eagle. Lamely Vicky wrote that he would be satisfied with the Bath, but the nation would not. The Queen saw through this excuse, but hesitated to provoke a family quarrel and reluctantly gave her grandson the Garter. After receiving his Guards commission, he followed in his father's footsteps and went to study at Bonn, reading eight subjects, including history, science, philosophy and art.

Ditta was no less of a worry. As a child she had often been naughty and backward. She had got her mother into trouble with Queen Victoria at Balmoral by refusing to shake hands with the Highland servant John Brown: 'Mama says I ought not to be too familiar with servants.'[20] Nor did she improve as she grew up, largely due to the Empress Augusta who petted and encouraged her by the sly method of not discouraging her spiteful remarks against her parents. At sixteen she was a typical Hohenzollern princess of the mould so dreaded by Vicky on her arrival in Prussia; vain, discontented, with an insatiable appetite for malicious gossip and all-night socialising.

In April 1877, shortly after she and Henry were confirmed, the Kaiser announced her engagement at a family dinner to the Hereditary Prince Bernhard of Saxe-Meiningen, son of Fritz's childhood friend. He and Vicky were very pleased about the betrothal, and relieved to see her gain her independence, but

Catherine Radziwill saw that the foolish and frivolous girl could not have been in love with anyone at the time; she was only marrying in order to escape a family life that was becoming irksome.[21] Bernhard was a college friend of Willy, and in the spring all three were riding on the switchback railway in the Pfaueninsel, the royal pleasure-park on the Isle of Peacocks in the river Havel at Berlin, where Fritz had often played as a small boy. Bernard was standing behind her when Willy accelerated the controls for a joke. Terrified, Ditta held on to her brother's friend, and imagined that she was in love with him.

A few weeks after the engagement was made public, Fritz and Vicky went to Kiel to see Henry enter the German navy on board the training ship *Niobe*. Henry was not measuring up to the standards required of him. The previous year, Vicky had complained of his being lazy and difficult to teach, slow, indifferent, and never reading a book unless made to. 'He gives a great deal of trouble, and as his character is so weak, I often fear he will be led away when he grows older – to many a thing which is not right'.[22] Perhaps a few months on board ship, she and Fritz hoped, would be the making of him.

Before the end of April war had at last broken out between Russia and Turkey in the Balkans. Fritz and Vicky had hoped for peace throughout the year – 'there has really been enough war!' – but the latter's fears that 'the Russians will have their own way, and that they only mean to wait until spring comes, and brings them a more convenient opportunity for fighting' were soon realized.[23] Despite Bismarck's pro-Russian policy, he was restrained from intervention largely through the Emperor's reluctance to see his country at war again. Fritz took great interest in the course of the fighting as his cousin Carol of Roumania, who had been his orderly officer during the Danish war, was at the Russian front. In January 1878 the Turkish army was forced to surrender, and it was to a background of fragile peace that Fritz turned his attention once more to the immediate family circle.

Royalties from all over Europe including his brothers-in-law from England, the Prince of Wales and the Duke of Connaught, came to Berlin in February for a double wedding on the 18th; that of Ditta and Bernhard, and of Prince Friedrich Karl's second daughter

Elizabeth to the son of the Grand Duke of Oldenburg. It was an exhausting ceremony lasting for over six hours, but according to her uncle Bertie Ditta, looking 'like a fresh little rose'[24] in her silver moiré train, emerged from it all with the vitality of her seemingly ageless grandparents. Fritz and Vicky were surprised by the grace and lack of emotion their daughter showed at the signing of the register and the endless *Fackeltanz* or bridal torch dance. The excessive solemnity of the programme was lightened for them not so much by the bride's outward calm as by Bertie's presence. Having visited the court of Berlin more often than the rest of his relations except Alice (who was too ill to come this time), he saw much of the wearying atmosphere in which his brother-in-law and sister had to live. His cheerful manner and compliments to even the sourest of the German princesses made him an immediate success with everyone, and the Kaiser was flattered by the way in which his son's guest had a good word for everything and everyone.

The following month the Sultan of Turkey concluded peace at San Stefano, by which a large amount of territory was ceded to Russia. In Britain Disraeli and Salisbury insisted that Europe would not recognise the treaty as it stood, and on the initiative of the Austrian Foreign Minister Julius Andrassy a congress at Berlin, under Bismarck's presidency, was summoned to discuss the Eastern problem. For once the Kaiser had to suggest that his son and daughter-in-law might like to accept an invitation from Queen Victoria to go and stay in England. Like his Chancellor he was normally impatient with them for visiting as often as they did, but Bismarck had been incensed by improving relations between Vicky and his master. The Crown Princess, he asserted, whose hatred of the Russians was well-known, would undoubtedly use her influence to stir Disraeli into making some sort of trouble when he arrived, and he asked the King to send her out of the country before the Congress opened.

With mixed feelings Fritz and Vicky left for England, staying with Bertie and Alix at Marlborough House and then at Hatfield House, Hertfordshire, with Lord Salisbury, whose other guests included Prince and Princess Christian and Disraeli. On the next day, 2 June,

Count Münster, German Ambassador in London, handed Salisbury Bismarck's official invitation to Britain to take part in the Berlin Congress. A few hours later their peace of mind was shattered when a servant came from Hatfield to bring news from Germany of a serious attempt on the Kaiser's life.

During the previous month Max Hödel, a plumber's employee, had fired at the Kaiser as he was driving in an open carriage through Berlin with the Grand Duchess of Baden, but he was unhurt. Three weeks later Karl Nobiling, a Doctor of Economics with suspected socialist sympathies, shot at him from the upper window of an inn overlooking the street. This time he was severely wounded; bullets penetrated his helmet and went into his neck, back and arm. With blood pouring down his face he was hastily rushed back to the Schloss, and over thirty grains of shot were removed from his body. The surgeon Dr Langenbeck was amazed that he had survived such a vicious attack, and doubted he would last the night.

Fritz and Vicky reached Calais shortly before midnight, within hours of the outrage, and they stepped onto the yacht with the gloomy news that the old man's life was despaired of. Fritz was 'in floods of tears', while Vicky retained her composure; when asked why, by her shocked lady-in-waiting, she replied that it was necessary for her husband. On returning to Berlin they found the Empress similarly 'calm and natural', and certainly in a better frame of mind than those around her who had evidently 'lost their heads'.[25] As they drew nearer to Berlin, where anxious men and women were expecting the imminent proclamation of their second Kaiser, Fritz prayed that his father would be saved. Though he had long awaited his accession, the last thing he wished to do was to inherit it by the hand of an assassin. Besides, he and Vicky had heard rumours of anarchist plots to kill them all, and she had personally received threatening letters saying that she would be shot as well if she appeared in public.[26]

On the day after their return Fritz was commissioned to take temporary control of the government. The wounded Kaiser had insisted that his son could only represent him and was to rule according to his own principles, not to the Crown Prince's, and shortly after regaining consciousness he had signed a bill ensuring that affairs of state would continue as before. When Fritz met Bismarck to discuss the form of these representative functions, Bismarck presented him with a document, *Stellvertreter Urkunde*, reflecting these conditions and thus denying him a decisive role in important matters of state, even as his father's deputy. It was clear that his decisions would be subject to approval of, or either ignored by, the Chancellor, who would take notice of Fritz's opinions on domestic and foreign policy only if they suited him. Unlike the regency of 1858 to which Wilhelm had been appointed as a result of his brother's illness, Fritz was empowered to act just as a deputy until his father's return to health. It placed a new strain on relations between both men during the Emperor's convalescence, as Fritz knew that Bismarck was taking no chances and ensuring he would have no influence on state affairs.

Vicky saw this in a positive light; because of political unrest after the two assassination attempts, she knew repressive measures would be undertaken to restore order, and as they were bound to be unpopular, she thought it as well that Fritz should not be considered responsible for them. It was better for it to be known that he was powerless to oppose conservative policies enacted during his regency.

When Bismarck dissolved the *Reichstag*, during the ensuing election campaign the government press made much of the responsibility of the Social Democrats and their alleged left liberal allies for both assassination attempts. The conservatives gained seats at the expense of the liberal and progressive parties, which gave Bismarck a comfortable passage for his anti-socialist bill in the autumn. Though rejected by the centre and progressive parties, it was passed comfortably by the conservatives and national liberals. Its provisions included outlawing of the Social Democratic Party, to which Hödel had belonged, its meetings and assemblies forbidden, and socialists found guilty of breaking the law exiled. To Vicky it was part of a growing reactionary trend in German politics which violated liberal principles of equality before the law and freedom of assembly, though to Fritz socialism was an unhealthy movement to be eradicated.

The Congress of Berlin opened on 13 June, to revise the unsatisfactory peace terms imposed by Russia on Turkey at the treaty of San Stefano, and was dissolved a month later. Fritz took no part beyond welcoming foreign representatives to the city and addressing them at the gala dinner on the opening night. Though not consulted about negotiations at the conference table, there was little doubt that he approved of Russia's aims of territorial expansion being thwarted, chiefly due to Disraeli's and Andrassy's protection of their own national interests; England took possession of the island of Cyprus, and Austria was permitted to occupy Bosnia and Herzegovina.

Nobiling was in prison awaiting trial, and died a few weeks later of wounds self-inflicted before his arrest, but Hödel had already been arraigned and sentenced to death. According to Prussian law, executions had to be ratified by the sovereign before being carried out. The Kaiser had always opposed the death penalty and commuted such sentences passed to him for approval to life imprisonment. After the verdict on Hödel, gossips suggested that if the Crown Prince spared him, it would be due to the influence of his consort who wanted to encourage future attempts on her father-in-law so that she and her husband could come to the throne sooner. Like his father Fritz was reluctant to sanction a death sentence, but the popular view was that it would be foolish to show leniency in such a case, especially as one attempt had so nearly succeeded and it seemed the time for stern measures. After a prolonged period of soul-searching he signed the death warrant on 8 August. General von Albedyll, head of the military cabinet, saw how much Fritz took the matter to heart, and believed he could not sleep on the night of the execution. He was obviously relieved on hearing it was all over, and pleased with a letter from his father thanking him for having spared him the ordeal. Hödel went unrepentantly to the scaffold, crying 'Bravo for the Commune!'[27] before the executioner's act silenced him.

When the Kaiser attended a military review at Kassel in September it was evident that he was recovering. He still trembled but was looking much fitter, as he appeared on horseback in public for the first time since June, and in a matter of weeks he was restored to full health. On 5 December Fritz relinquished the hollow regency and the Kaiser returned to Berlin, sobered by the thought that 'this trial' had been imposed on him in his own capital and by a fellow-Prussian, but apparently none the worse.

It was believed that Fritz would be given some special position in the government in recognition of his recent duties, but this proved to be unfounded. The day after stepping down, he received a formal letter of thanks from his 'affectionate father', which was impersonal enough to be published in the papers. Wilhelm was certainly grateful to his son for having deputised for him, and had it been in his power perhaps he would have tried to give him something more substantial in return. Yet the shock of his attack had weakened what little resistance to Bismarck the infirmity of old age had left him, and he no longer had the stamina to argue privately with his Chancellor. Far from attempting to disagree with him, as he frequently had before, he was more than ever in the statesman's clutches. Soon after the end of the regency he became convinced that Germany had been unfairly treated at the Congress, and that Fritz was responsible. He did not realize that his son had played no part, and when a guest at one of the Empress's parties pointed out that Bismarck alone was to blame for what had taken place, he retorted that his Chancellor was only human. 'It was but natural that he should try and make himself pleasant to the Crown Prince.'[28]

After the Emperor resumed his duties, Bismarck revived a plan which had been mentioned the previous year, to make Fritz *Statthalter* or governor of Alsace-Lorraine. His motives for doing so were questionable. Some thought it an honest effort by the Chancellor to provide him with some official government duty, though others, including Fritz and Vicky themselves, saw it as a gesture to remove him from Berlin to prevent him from interfering with the conservative programme. Since 1871 the provinces had been governed by a dictatorship from Berlin, but after a few years the conservatives in the *Reichstag* felt that they should be granted some independence in the hope of uniting them more firmly to the empire. The question of appointing an officer to govern them, answerable only to the Emperor, was raised, and the Crown Prince was the obvious choice. When advised by more sympathetic sources that most of his decisions as *Statthalter* would be subject to Bismarck's approval, and he would not have a free hand in filling the posts in his administration of the province, Fritz refused the post.

In November 1878 diphtheria struck the Grand Ducal family of Hesse, claiming the life of Alice's youngest daughter May. Just as the rest were recovering, Alice herself died four weeks later, on 14 December, the anniversary of the Prince Consort's death. Vicky and Fritz were both forbidden by the Kaiser to attend the funeral for fear of infection. Maliciously the Empress commented at a tea-party a week later that it was just as well for Alice's children that she had died because 'like all English Princesses, she was a complete atheist'[29] – a spiteful judgment on her friendship with the controversial theologian David Strauss.

In March 1879 Fritz and Vicky went to England to attend the wedding of Louise, daughter of Friedrich Karl, to the Duke of Connaught. The bride's father distinguished himself by his bad behaviour to his son-in-law's family, complained that his daughter's house did not have enough rooms, and told everyone that he had confidently expected his previous visit to England to be his last.

Within a day or two of returning to Berlin, Fritz and Vicky were watching the younger children rehearsing a pantomime one afternoon when Waldie complained of a sore throat. He was the most appealing of their three sons, and gave promise of being everything the others were not. Although the Prince, Friedrich Karl, never cared much for his nephew and niece, even he admitted that Waldie was 'the most delightful boy'[30] he had ever seen. Yet for all his love of practical jokes and often unruly behaviour, he was a thin, undersized child who had inherited his father's delicate health. A cold broke down his resistance to the dreaded diphtheria which had killed his aunt and cousin, ominous white patches appeared on his throat, and he could hardly swallow or close his mouth as his tonsils were so swollen. Vicky washed him with hot vinegar and water, changed his linen and clothes and put them all into a pail of carbolic water, wearing a mackintosh over her own clothes and spraying herself with carbolic acid before returning to the others to prevent the spread of infection. Tragically it was all to no avail and on 27 March he died.

This second untimely death was the worst tragedy that Fritz and Vicky had yet to suffer. When they lost Sigi, Vicky had told Catherine Radziwill that to lose a child was not just a dreadful sorrow, but an unnatural one too – 'we don't bring our babies into the world in order to survive them!'[31] Waldie's birth had filled the gap left by his dead brother. Now they were distraught with grief. Not generally given to extravagant displays of emotion, Fritz threw himself on the small coffin at the funeral before Waldie was laid to rest beside the brother he had never known. Even the birth of a first grandchild, Charlotte's and Bernhard's daughter Feodora, born on 12 May, brought them no solace. Though he appeared outwardly indifferent, Willy was moved by the effect on his parents. The 'distress and silent desperation', he wrote to Georg II, Duke of Saxe-Meiningen, were hard to describe; 'my poor father has grown old overnight and is so unhappy that he is almost apathetic to everything that happens around him. Mama has shown superhuman strength of character outwardly, but all too often she breaks down in her infinite sorrow.'[32]

'Ours is indeed a grief which must last a lifetime,' Vicky wrote to Lord Napier. 'We can hardly realise yet that we have the lost the darling boy who was our pride and delight, who seemed to grow daily in health and strength, in intelligence and vigour of character. We had fondly hoped he would grow up to be of use to his country, and his family – we had planned and dreamt of a bright and useful future for him – of all that we dare not think now and will not repine, but the wrench is too terrible and Life can never be the same again. He is missed every hour of the day, and the House has lost half its life.'[33]

To Carol of Roumania, Fritz wrote that with Waldie's death life had 'lost what remaining joy it still had to offer us, and we can only gather satisfaction from the execution of our tasks and duties.'[34] A combination of grief at the death of his youngest son, and the effect of years of frustration and the experience of a hollow regency, had given him little encouragement for the future. In a bleak mood of despair in May, he told Vicky that he considered himself henceforth 'retired from political life'.[35] Depression with having 'been unable to take the reins during the best years of my manhood' had disheartened him, and the death of Waldie had been what he called the final blow.[36]

Vicky writhed with agonised fury when she read that an Orthodox Protestant minister, on hearing of their bereavement, remarked that he hoped it was a trial sent by God to humiliate her.[37] She struggled through the next few weeks in shock, with hormonal upsets followed by giddiness, rheumatism and neuralgia. Dr Wegner recommended that she should spend the winter in a warmer climate, though Vicky feared that the Empress would never consent as it coincided with the social season. Soon there were more disquieting symptoms – noises in her head, uncontrollable shaking in her hands, and fear of imminent suffocation. In July she and Fritz agreed that it was essential for her to go away for the winter, to Styria and Italy. The Kaiser and Empress were strongly against the idea, and demanded she present her father-in-law with a medical certificate before he would approve what he scathingly called a 'bathing trip'.

Physically and mentally Vicky was at a low ebb. Years of spending winters in unhealthy overheated palaces, attempts on the Kaiser's life and rumours of threats on her and her husband, and above all her two recent bereavements, had brought her to the verge of a complete nervous breakdown, and she insisted she would probably not survive another winter in the city. As for wanting to get away for a few months, she told Fritz bitterly, his parents, particularly the Empress, treated her 'as if I were committing a *crime*!!!'[38] Yet she and Fritz stood firm, and on 1 September she and her court marshal Count Seckendorff travelled to Styria in Southern Austria. The local physicians diagnosed anaemia, debilitating rheumatism and severe depression. She did not return to Germany for nearly nine months.

For the first few days she was in the grip of deep depression at years of cumulative tragedies. When Queen Victoria suggested that so long an absence from all her 'associations' would be painful, she assured her mother that this would not be the case. The whole social and political atmosphere at Berlin had become intolerable for her. 'Liberty, independence exist not and we have simply to obey, and have every sort of galling interference in our own home. The spirit of espionage, malevolence, and jealousy and malice is rampant and there are many wicked people whose harmful influence cripple and hinder one at every step one takes. . . . All this has worn away gradually a deal of my courage and a deal of my strength'.[39]

On 15 September, which would have been Sigi's fifteenth birthday, she was filled with a sense of desolation and longing for her two youngest sons. As if her father's death and her eldest son's arm 'were not sufficient misfortune for us'.[40] Willy visited her in Venice in October and Fritz joined them a few days later for a series of walks and excursions. They hoped the growing estrangement between Vicky and Willy might heal, but he was unprepared to sympathize with her growing homesickness for England and aversion to their home at Prussia – 'You know that I have nothing at Berlin to make my Life there anything but odious!'[41] In a twenty-eight-page letter she poured out her misery to her son – her mental and physical anxiety and fatigue, and her homesickness which she could forget in Italy but not in Berlin. It was an emotional cry for help which she might well have read through in a calmer frame of mind and torn up. But Willy took exception to her complaints about her lack of freedom of speech at Berlin, and the 'very dangerous' web of lies and espionage at the courts of Berlin and Potsdam. Her constructive suggestions for the betterment of Berlin, such as providing parks, gardens and squares, more schools and hospitals, more attention to housing for the poor, opportunities for art, and the improvement of museums, carried no weight with him. She ended by telling him to burn the letter, a plea which obviously fell on deaf ears.

He never answered it, finding it embarrassing or disloyal if not both. For her thirty-ninth birthday a fortnight later he wrote her a distant note of about four lines promising that he would congratulate her 'properly' in a day or two; he had no time that day as he was going hunting. This promised letter never arrived and she was furious, believing he could not be bothered to write. Charlotte readily took her side and tried her utmost to make peace, saddened at her brother's cold-heartedness but suggesting to Vicky in mitigation that it was the fault of Hinzpeter who had done so much to 'destroy his gentler emotions' and turn him against his mother.

Willy had suffered intermittently for the best part of two years with a serious infection in his right ear. One specialist who examined him found a chronic abscess and a perforated eardrum, and another warned that there was a grave risk to his mental health if not his life if it should spread to the brain. Having lost one son through meningitis, the parents spent an anxious few months dreading the death of the other one from a similar disease. Prolonged periods of rest and care on Willy's part effected a temporary cure, though he was warned that the condition could recur.

When Vicky returned to Berlin in May 1880, she was not surprised to find that nothing had changed for the better. 'How the usual frigidness and bitterness of the people here pains me when one comes back', she wrote to her mother.[42] Though she was a little stronger in spirit after her long absence and better prepared to confront the challenges of a hostile environment, those around them, not least her husband, were aware that after the death of Waldie she would never be the same woman again. Even at the end of the year, she could still write to her friend Countess Marie Dönhoff that when she looked at her other children round the Christmas tree 'I bitterly miss the two dear boys that were my pride and joy.'[43] She had become more brittle, suffered increasingly from mood swings, was more vulnerable to depression, and less ready to accept opposition. With a husband who was gradually losing self-confidence, it was not an encouraging outlook for either of them. Yet for the moment they both had each other, and remained as devoted as ever – the one consolation they would have in the increasingly tragic times ahead.

SEVEN

'He complains about his wasted life'

Vicky and Fritz were keen to see their eldest son suitably and happily married. During his university days they had encouraged Willy's visits to his aunt Alice, her husband Louis and their children, hoping the homely atmosphere of Darmstadt would be a good influence on him and counteract the fawning, military ambience of Berlin. By the age of nineteen he had become besotted with their second daughter Elizabeth ('Ella'), and during the last months of her short life Alice thought the young couple would be well-matched. She made no effort to dispel any impression among the rest of the family that a betrothal might soon follow.

Nevertheless Ella and her sisters did not take to their restless, showy cousin, and she had as good as pledged herself to her distant Romanov kinsman, Grand Duke Serge of Russia. Unlike her sister, Vicky felt such a marriage between first cousins was inadvisable as Alice's younger son, the haemophiliac 'Frittie', had bled to death after what should have only been a minor fall, and the risk that any children of a marriage between the future German Emperor and Ella might suffer from the same condition was too great.* She had hoped for some time that he might instead marry one of the daughters of their old friend Duke Friedrich of Holstein, the nieces of Prince and Princess Christian, and granddaughters of Queen Victoria's late half-sister Feodora. Once he became aware that a betrothal with Ella

---

* Vicky knew it would bode ill for the future of the German Empire if her grandsons in direct succession to the throne should suffer from the bleeding disease. In view of the marriage of Alice's daughter Alix to the future Tsar Nicholas II of Russia in 1894 and the consequences of their only son Alexis's haemophilia, her caution was thoroughly vindicated.

153

could never be, he started paying court to the Duke's daughter Princess Augusta Victoria of Schleswig-Holstein-Sonderburg-Augustenburg, 'Dona', a plain, pious but even-tempered young woman three months older than himself.

Dona was not considered particularly aristocratic, rich or pretty, and Kaiser Wilhelm threatened to forbid the match until Bismarck withdrew his objections after her father's death from cancer in January 1880. On personal grounds the Chancellor approved of this simple, unambitious woman, whose evident lack of cleverness placed her in a different class from the regrettable tradition of intelligent Hohenzollern consorts. When she and Willy were betrothed in February, the news was received coldly in Berlin, partly for reasons of lineage, and partly as the late Duke's claim to the duchies of Schleswig and Holstein, which had been dismissed by Bismarck after the war of 1864, was but a recent memory. Vicky knew the Berliners might not consider her grand enough, but as they made plain their dislike for everything foreign so much, she expected they would be pleased enough with a Princess bred, born and educated in Germany; 'and more spite, ill-will, backbiting and criticism of the unkindest sort, she never can have to endure – than I have gone through for twenty-two years.'[1]

Willy's sister Charlotte thought her brother too cold-hearted and incapable of being in love with anyone except himself. She found Dona silent, uncommunicative, very shy and a poor figure beside her more lively sister Caroline Matilda ('Calma'), and also thought her brother-in-law Ernest of Saxe-Meiningen was in love with Dona and had hoped to marry her. She and Bernhard told Fritz with concern that Willy was 'strangely cool' about Dona, gave no sign of any affection for her or enthusiasm about the betrothal. Fritz shared her doubts, and felt Willy was 'not truly committed' to the marriage.

Nevertheless Vicky saw the betrothal as an alliance between their dynasty and the Augustenbergs and a kind of atonement for past wrongs, and they admired him for his determination to marry Dona in the face of public disapproval. University and barracks life had given him too many airs and graces, and they were sure the domesticity of married life would cure him of this. Vicky approved of her mild temperament, writing to her mother, 'I am so delighted that you think Victoria [Dona] so gentle and amiable and sweet'.[2] Maybe she did not foresee that it would take more than a good-natured disposition to act as a restraining influence on this eldest son. Meanwhile Charlotte was still not reconciled to her brother's marriage. Vicky was disturbed by her hostile attitude and her apparent stirring up of feelings against Dona, and at length Fritz told her firmly that it boded ill for family unity if she kept her brother and sister-in-law at arm's length instead of welcoming them. She was not the only one, for the ever-irascible Prince Karl and his son Friedrich Karl dismissed Dona as a *parvenu* and called the marriage a danger to the dynasty.

The wedding took place on 27 February 1881 at a ceremony which, said Vicky, was 'exhausting, suffocating and interminable as all the Berlin state weddings are.'[3] She and Fritz were quite 'knocked up' by the end, and they never ceased to marvel at how the Kaiser and Empress retained their vitality throughout. However she admitted that the bride 'looked charming and everyone was taken with her sweetness and grace.'[4]

Two weeks later Tsar Alexander II was assassinated and Fritz was sent to the funeral, despite anonymous letters that he and Vicky had received assuring him that if he went he would be the next victim. Even the Prince of Wales, who was going as well, urged him to resist the order. He had heard from his sister-in-law Marie, now Tsarina, that the family were living in a state of virtual police siege to protect them from the wave of street-fighting, stone-throwing and terrorist threats that had followed. Thanks to strict security the obsequies passed off without incident, as Vicky had been more confident than her husband that they would – as she wrote to Queen Victoria, 'there could be no object in attempting the life of so many Foreigners at once.'[5]

At least Fritz and Vicky could take continued pleasure in his official capacity as a patron of the arts. After the Hohenzollern Museum was opened he accepted the patronage of the German Anthropological Society, under the presidency of the pathologist and Progressive Liberal member of the *Reichstag*, Professor Rudolf von

Virchow. The society's collections rapidly increased under his encouragement and the guidance of his old tutor Ernst Curtius, and he helped persuade the ministry to finance excavations in Greece and Asia Minor, as well as play a part in plans for their display in the Berlin *Volkervunde* (Ethnographical Museum). His proudest achievement was the *Kunstgewerbe* (Arts and Crafts Museum), inspired largely by the Victoria and Albert Museum at Kensington, which he and Vicky often visited when they were in England. It had started in 1867 as a small collection of industrial arts, to which they added their own collection of tapestries and porcelain after the Franco-Prussian war, and Queen Victoria presented a large consignment of rare Indian vases, ivories and lacquer articles from the Kensington museum. Opened on 21 November 1881, Vicky's birthday, the ceremony was followed by a party for the architects, advisers and scholars who had contributed to its success.

In the 1881 elections the Progressives won an impressive victory at the expense of National Liberals and Free Conservatives. After Gladstone's decisive Liberal victory in Britain the previous year, Vicky was encouraged by what looked like an increasingly democratic movement sweeping both countries, and made plain her enthusiasm for Gladstone, her mother's *bête noire*, but Fritz was more cautious. He wondered if the British election results were a reflection of increasing British radicalism, but was reassured by Roggenbach and Stockmar that liberal victory owed less to revolutionary fervour than to support from the depressed agricultural population who hoped the Liberals would take more heed of their difficulties than the outgoing Tories.

After the elections Bismarck launched a campaign to break the growing strength of the Progressive party, partly to support his own power base and partly as he feared that continued electoral victories of the Progressives might accelerate a German republic. Gladstone and the English radicals, he averred, were impatient for the reign of Kaiser Friedrich who would surely encourage comparable democratization in Germany. As Chancellor he did not intend Germany to be ruled 'after the English fashion' and in January 1882 he issued a royal rescript against parliamentary government, signed by Kaiser Wilhelm as King of Prussia, proclaiming the sovereign's right to personal control over the politics of members of his government, and stating that government officials could be dismissed from their posts if they did not hold aloof 'from all agitation' against the ministry. In England the *Morning Post* dismissed it as resembling one of King Charles I's messages to the Long Parliament. Vicky was furious when Bismarck declared that the Crown Prince approved of the measure, though he had been horrified to read of it in the papers. To alienate the heir's political supporters and tarnish his image with the public, articles appeared in the press asserting the heir's satisfaction with Bismarck's policies. As Vicky said, it was calculated to spread the impression that the Crown Prince would approve of everything that the government did 'were it not for his English wife'.[6] The papers suggested that progressive liberals, under the reign of Kaiser Friedrich, would pursue a disastrous foreign policy and an anti-Russian alliance, precipitating the possibility of war with Russia, and electors were advised to vote for right-wing parties in the interests of peace and stability.

After being weakened by losses in the elections of 1882 the Progressive party aligned with the Secession Party, a breakaway grouping of former National Liberals, to form the *Deutsche-Freisinnige Partei* (German Free-Thinking Party). Among its leaders were Eugen Richter, Ludwig von Bamberger and Max von Forckenbeck, all personal friends of Fritz. In their words it was committed to the preservation of constitutional parliamentary order, the right to free speech and free elections, and increasing the power of the *Reichstag* in financial matters and regulation of church laws. To Vicky it gave promise of dismantling many of Bismarck's more reactionary policies, while Fritz had reservations, perceiving its objectives at odds with his belief in constitutional liberalism and acceptance of a stronger parliament. Nevertheless with Vicky's encouragement he sent a telegram to Bamberger congratulating him on the creation of the *Deutsche-Freisinnige Partei*. It became known as the *Kronprinzen Partei* or Crown Prince's party, and the telegram gave the impression that he supported their goals. The National

Liberal leaders were uneasy with his apparent support for such left-wing policies, and wondered if he still had the energy or commitment to compromise between them and his own ideas for a liberal Germany. Bismarck continued to suspect the dismantling of his conservative policies in the next reign under a 'Gladstone ministry', seeing the new grouping as a powerful opposition to his conservative-liberal minority alliance and as vocal supporters of the Crown Prince. The Chancellor's security, he considered, depended on driving a wedge between the new coalition and the heir to the throne.

Fritz's Court Marshal (or Chamberlain) Karl von Normann arranged a discreet consultation in his own apartments between his master and Eugen Richter, but nothing could remain secret from Bismarck for long, and Normann was dismissed on a trumped-up charge of having plotted an attack on the Chancellor's position with the Crown Princess and Empress, and thus coming between the Emperor and his people. He was transferred as Minister to Oldenburg, and replaced in the household by Count Hugo von Radolinski, a devoted adherent of Bismarck. Fritz was powerless to do anything but assure Normann that once he was Emperor he would recall him. Once installed, Radolinski made it his mission to get rid of the Crown Princess's Chamberlain, the faithful Count Götz von Seckendorff, who shared her political outlook and a love of sketching and painting. Despite a vicious campaign to undermine his integrity, Seckendorff retained his position in the household.

Bismarck's suspicions about the Crown Princess's political orientation were shared by Queen Victoria, who looked askance at her daughter's enthusiasm for Gladstone and his fellow Liberals in England, telling her she was 'such an extraordinary Radical that you even appear a republican at heart'.[7] During the election campaign of 1884 Bismarck was keen to exploit any differences in the *Deutsche-Freisinnige Partei* ranks. The party was divided on Bismarck's social welfare legislation, on the renewal of anti-socialist legislation, and over Bismarck's intention to acquire German colonies in Africa. While Fritz endorsed a colonial policy for patriotic reasons he was concerned at its implications for Anglo-German relations, whereas Vicky firmly opposed it, seeing it as Bismarck's means to gain support for other conservative policies. The Germans were always reproaching the English for their anti-German prejudices, she maintained, while they forgot that they themselves had 'many more and much more deeply-seated ones about other countries, especially England! They imagine England is jealous of Germany's attempting to have colonies. . . . This colonial sugar plum may easily turn into a bitter almond, and the beginning seems to me sad enough if it cannot be obtained without an estrangement between England and Germany.'[8]

On 25 January 1883 Vicky and Fritz celebrated their silver wedding. Gifts poured in from corporations and guilds throughout Germany, including paintings and sculpture by living artists, ivory and ebony cabinets, and from the *Reichstag* a magnificent carved oak dining-room suite. Collections were made nationally and in Berlin amounting to over one thousand marks, and presented to them by an official deputation for distribution to charities of their choice. A large sum went towards founding a children's hospital in Vicky's name.

Yet the occasion was marred by more family arguments. Vicky had requested a *tableau vivant*, like those in which she had eagerly participated as a girl to entertain her parents on anniversaries, and a Venetian ball to follow. They were both postponed for a few days by the sudden death of Fritz's uncle Karl, and when they took place Dona spoilt matters; representing the Queen of Love who was to offer her parents-in-law a bouquet of flowers with a few words of thanksgiving as they sat on a dais between the Kaiser and Empress, she wore a tight dress which showed up her pregnant figure, her pallid face, and bright scarlet arms. For the ball she refused to wear a dress Vicky had given her, to show that she did not take kindly to what she considered to be her mother-in-law's interference. At the performance she missed a vital cue, and was effortlessly upstaged by Ditta who, true to form, did not attempt to conceal her disdain of the sister-in-law whom she found slow and stupid, and had accepted as one of the family with the utmost reluctance.

Always sensitive to the feelings of others especially where family was concerned, Vicky had done her best to develop a more welcoming relationship with Dona than she had experienced in her early days of marriage from Augusta and her other in-laws, but her efforts were gracelessly rebuffed. She encouraged Dona to buy some attractive dresses instead of the unbecoming garments she usually chose, and to wear tight underclothes to restore her figure after the birth of her first son Wilhelm in May 1882. Dona replied coldly that there was no point in getting her shape back only to lose it again, as her husband intended to safeguard the imperial succession, a cruel remark to make to a woman who had lost two of her sons. Her mother-in-law, Dona knew, had a reputation for supposedly managing other people's lives; she herself was not going to be dictated to.

If Dona was a disappointment to Vicky and Fritz, her husband was becoming downright incorrigible. With marriage increased his sickening air of self-importance, his admiration of Bismarck, and his taunts that his parents were 'not German enough'. On the rare occasions when he visited his parents, it was usually with an enormous suite which made it impossible for them to talk to him alone. Though Ditta (who was now usually known as 'Charly' to her own generation, if not to her parents) led the life of a social butterfly at the head of Berlin's 'smart young things', thinking of little but gossip, fine clothes and fashionable dinner parties, she had every sympathy with her parents and tried to reconcile them with her brother, whose childish and egotistical manner she resented. In March 1882 she was distressed by 'a number of *appalling* scenes' between Willy and their parents, owing to the former's lack of consideration towards his mother, and she was 'so beside myself at Papa's appearance, he was literally ill with rage!'[9] Even though Dona worshipped her husband, she was not above making similar occasional complaints in private about his immature behaviour.

Already convinced to some extent that his life no longer seemed to have any real purpose where Germany was concerned, Fritz was increasingly upset at being shut out by the close bond between Willy and the old Kaiser, and the sly way in which they made arrangements with each other behind his back. Regretting his son's cold-heartedness and vanity, he had been astonished by his evident lack of feeling at the time of Dona's father's death, though whether it was out of embarrassment at showing his feelings or whether because the death of the man to whose daughter he was about to become betrothed meant nothing to him, nobody could understand. Now Fritz was angered by his lack of common courtesy, notably his refusal to reply to friendly letters and telegrams. Matters came to a head during a father-and-son exchange in November 1883 when Fritz had a long discussion with him, asking how he could justify his inconsiderate behaviour? Willy told his father he had shown quite openly for a long time that he could not stand him. Taxed with the accusation that he kept everything from his parents, he defended himself by saying that his mother was always very outspoken when he tried to express his opinions on political matters which were contrary to her own.[10] Vicky was grieved by 'his boundless egoism and his heartlessness', and while she acknowledged that their opinions and views were totally different and probably always would be, all she asked for was 'a bit of love & gratitude for all that I have suffered & done for him!'[11]

These arguments came just after Fritz had been asked to visit King Alfonso XII of Spain, and he wanted Willy to accompany him. He was furious when Willy wrote to the Kaiser, requesting he should not be allowed to go as such a trip could not be reconciled with his duties at home as a newly appointed battalion commander. The reason was that Willy did not want to be overshadowed by his father, whom he knew was more popular in other European countries than him. To Fritz's despair, his father and Bismarck forbade Vicky to accompany him in order to prevent her from 'causing mischief' at the court of Madrid.

However King Alfonso and Queen Christina were the most gracious of hosts in their efforts to entertain him, though as an animal lover he would rather have foregone the 'repulsive spectacle' of a bullfight ordered in his honour; 'If I had not been officially obliged to stay there, I would gladly have departed at the end of the first victim.'[12] He inspected the troops and barracks, paid several evening visits to the theatre, and was most impressed with the museums; 'I employ these leisure moments in the contemplation of treasures that I shall probably never see again in my life.'[13] At the Prado he particularly enjoyed the masterpieces of the Italian and Spanish schools, particularly those of his favourite artist Velasquez, and the displays of armoury in the royal palace, the unique collection of Gobelin tapestries, and the Escorial, which he considered essential 'in order to appreciate the past glories of Spain.'[14] Yet the occasion would have given him far more pleasure had either his art-loving wife, or an amenable, courteous son and heir, been by his side.

Vicky was increasingly worried by the way that frustrated years of waiting and a perpetual *Weltschmerz* (world-weariness) were telling on Fritz. His winter illnesses left him progressively weaker, he lost weight and looked pale. Observers were alarmed by his increasing depression and lack of interest in what he would do during his coming reign. Albrecht von Stosch, his close friend from military campaigns and adviser and a man who shared his cautious liberalism though too conservative for Vicky, thought him low and out of spirits, an old man before his time. 'Strength not exercised dies away; he keeps aloof from activity and influence.'[15] Three years later Professor Geffcken, a close friend of Vicky and Fritz, was saddened to find him increasingly pessimistic and bitter; 'he complains about his wasted life, and I believe that the reason he feels this way is because he does not work.'[16] He paid little attention to affairs of state, was convinced that his day had passed, and felt he had become a mere parade horse, only fit for receiving foreign dignitaries.

In 1851 Prince Alexander of Hesse had married a lady-in-waiting of his sister Marie, then the wife of the Tsarevich, and was dismissed from the Russian army. Granted the title of Prince Battenberg, he and his wife had four sons and a daughter. The eldest, Louis, married Victoria of Hesse, Alice's eldest daughter in April 1884, and Fritz and Vicky were among wedding guests at Darmstadt. Also there was Beatrice, Vicky's youngest sister, who fell in love with the third son, Henry. Though Queen Victoria had initially hoped to keep this daughter in perpetual spinsterhood as her lifelong unofficial secretary and helpmeet, after her initial disapproval she consented to their betrothal, and stood her ground defiantly against those in Berlin who looked down on the Battenbergs.

In Berlin Vicky was her only champion; Fritz was inclined to disagree with her and take his father's view; nothing the Queen said could alter the fact that Henry was only a minor German prince. For this his mother-in-law took him to task – fancy Fritz speaking of Henry 'as not being of Geblut (stock), a little like about animals.' How, she asked angrily, could Empress Augusta object, when the father of her son-in-law was the son of 'a very bad woman'? If one enquired too deeply into the background of all the royal and princely families on the continent, 'many black spots would be found', and fresh blood had to be infused occasionally, or the race would degenerate physically and morally. Her most withering attack was reserved for Willy and Dona. As for the latter, 'poor little insignificant Princess, raised entirely by your kindness to the position she is in – I have no words'; she had initially been ill-received in Berlin as a future Empress as the Augustenburgs were hardly of more noble birth than the Battenbergs. If the Queen of England thought someone good enough for her daughter, 'what have other people got to say?'[17]

They might have said nothing had it not been for the likelihood of a Battenberg-Hohenzollern marriage. In 1878 the Balkan state of Bulgaria was created by the terms of the Berlin congress, under the rule of Henry's elder brother Alexander ('Sandro'). Under his liberal uncle Tsar Alexander II in Russia his position was relatively safe, but the Tsar's assassination brought his son, Alexander III, no admirer of Sandro, to the throne, and his mild dislike soon turned to implacable hatred of the young ruler. Then while on a tour of Europe in 1883, this handsome bachelor was presented to Fritz and Vicky at Potsdam. Meeting his hosts' eldest unmarried daughter Victoria, whom Lady Ponsonby called 'a kind of wild, Scandinavian woman, with much of her mother's impetuosity and her eldest brother's eccentricity',[18] he decided he had found a wife. Perhaps he was not so much in love, rather looking for a pretty, well-connected consort who would provide him with sons and thereby help him to secure his position.

He came along at the right time to fit into the equation, as for once Vicky's matchmaking instincts let her get totally carried away. She had evolved a plan whereby England, Germany, Austria and Italy would unite to help and support Bulgaria, helping her to act as a barrier to Russian progress towards Constantinople. Should Russia consider war against such an alliance, the coalition would have to ensure that Bulgaria, Roumania, Serbia, Turkey and Greece did not help her, and that these countries should reach a 'secret agreement' with the others, who would try and isolate Russia and France from any other alliances, 'but then live as far as possible in a peaceful & good relationship with them.' Spain and Portugal had to be regarded as potential members of the alliance, so they would not go to the assistance of France. Germany, she felt, could do much to guide the Orient towards civilization, and invest considerable capital there in partnership with England.[19] Two years later she had not given up hope of this grand design, which would help to create 'a new order in Europe', with their three younger daughters wearing the crowns of Greece, Bulgaria and Roumania; German Protestant princesses 'would not have a bad mission there, – & Germany would gain a decisive influence!'[20] This audacious scheme could hardly be taken seriously; one can only suppose that her extreme frustration with her and Fritz's life on the margins of German history provoked her into such ideas, but even so she must have realized that it was sheer fantasy.

Bismarck immediately vetoed any serious consideration of a Battenberg-Hohenzollern alliance for political reasons. It was to Germany's advantage not to be involved in the Orient, and thus avoid difficulties with Russia and Turkey. He believed Gladstone did not want a Europe with friendly Russo-German relations, and that as the English-born Crown Princess was known to be an admirer of Gladstone, he was quite prepared to expose her to the press as the agent of a foreign power. If the marriage took place he would resign.

Willy, and friends of his in government and military circles, may have thought the Crown Princess's passionate partisanship of Sandro was nothing more and nothing less than a way of finding a spiritual son of hers, but little attention should be paid to such gossip. While she and Willy were clearly estranged almost beyond the point of no return, and while Henry was a disappointment, any suggestion that she should have seen Sandro as a younger reincarnation of the Prince Consort, or another Waldemar to replace her promising, much-mourned youngest son, was wild exaggeration. Only a little more feasible was Willy's declaration that his father, on becoming Emperor, meant to appoint Sandro *Statthalter* of Alsace-Lorraine, a position which he had no right to offer to anybody other than the German Crown Prince. Before he let the Battenberger assume such a post, Willy asserted, he would put a bullet through his head.[21] It was ironic as Willy had known and liked Sandro during his days at the Kassel Gymnasium, and there had been a possibility at one stage of Sandro marrying Dona's sister Calma.

Fritz did not approve of the marriage proposal. He knew Sandro's hold on power was precarious, and he wanted a better fate for his daughter than as the wife of an exiled ex-sovereign prince. At first he forbade Vicky to encourage the match any further. His pride may have been genuinely insulted at the idea of the son of a morganatic marriage becoming his son-in-law, and he was probably also anxious to avoid another family row as he knew his parents were united in their opposition. To him it was a 'monstrous idea' and a weight on his mind, and he told Vicky that Sandro ought to 'keep away until we are in a position to see our way more clearly.'[22] Vicky told Queen Victoria, who passed on the information to Victoria of Hesse, that Moretta was 'violently in love with Sandro; says she never cared for anyone else, or ever will marry any one else; – that she will wait any time for him & has refused to look at any other Princes who might be good partis for her. Uncle F[ritz] was very angry & tried to put it out of her head – but he did not succeed & she is more than ever anxious abt. it.'[23]

He might have persuaded his wife and daughter gently into seeing the affair in a more realistic light had it not been for the reactions of

Bismarck and Queen Victoria. Sandro's interview with the Kaiser, asking for the hand of his granddaughter, ended violently with Wilhelm, recalling his family's opposition to Elise Radziwill, trembling with anger and the Prince threatening to leave Bulgaria if thwarted. On the other hand Bismarck, who would not countenance any match that might provoke Russia, suggested cynically that the young man would do better to marry a millionairess; his throne would be safer if he could strengthen his position by bribery. When Sandro accepted an invitation to Balmoral a few months later, Queen Victoria was delighted with him. His stubborn resistance to Russia won her admiration, but she was equally taken with his good looks and compared him to 'beloved Papa' in letters to her children. With her mother on her side, and with Bismarck advocating bribery and corruption, Vicky championed him as a son-in-law more strongly than ever.

Fritz was extremely fond of his three younger daughters, but Moretta's statement in her memoirs, written in the late 1920s, that her engagement was approved of by both her parents at this stage,[24] was probably no more than an understandable desire to avoid reopening old wounds. For once it is almost impossible to refute the charge in this case that he was influenced by Vicky somewhat against his own judgment, too bowed down by the blows of the passing years to quarrel with anyone, let alone the wife who had been his mainstay for nearly thirty often difficult years, with whom he was still ardently in love. The Prince of Wales's approval of Sandro as a husband for his niece weakened his resistance even further. He liked and admired Sandro as a person, and had it not been for the *mésalliance* factor he would have thought him most suitable for Moretta. At length Vicky's persuasion, Moretta's heartfelt letters and Bertie's endorsement reconciled him to the morganatic element, but he knew it would be folly to encourage the betrothal in the face of combined opposition from his father and Bismarck. If and when he was Kaiser it would be a different matter, but as Crown Prince there was little they could do but wait. Bismarck saw advantages in Moretta entering the Roman Catholic church and marrying Crown Prince Carlos of Portugal, who might have been a King in waiting but was ugly and extremely fat. Neither Moretta nor her mother considered the Portuguese throne a model of stability.*

Willy and Dona readily joined Bismarck in condemning the match, while Ditta loyally took her mother's side. She felt ashamed that Willy should behave so badly to their Grandma in England, who had 'always been kindness itself to him since his birth'.[25] Henry shared Wilhelm's view in that such a match was not right for the dignity of the Hohenzollerns, but as he was in love with his cousin Irene, whose eldest sister Victoria was married to Sandro's eldest brother Louis, he found himself in a dilemma.

It was clear that Bismarck intended to prevent Moretta from marrying Sandro. When Queen Victoria sanctioned the marriages of his brothers into her brood and gave her support to this one as well, the Chancellor declared that it was her intention to bring about a permanent estrangement between Germany and Russia to British advantage. Moreover, he scoffed that with her fondness for match-making, and being unaccustomed to contradiction, she would probably arrive at Potsdam with the parson in her travelling bag and the bridegroom in her trunk to perform the wedding on the spot.

When the Prince of Wales visited Berlin, Bismarck told him that the affections of princesses counted for nothing when weighed in the balance against national political interests. For once he had an ally in Empress Augusta, who had wanted Ella of Hesse to marry her grandson Prince Friedrich of Baden, but when Ella pledged herself to Grand Duke Serge of Russia Queen Victoria was blamed. When the latter ardently championed the Sandro–Moretta romance, Augusta regarded it as an insult to herself and her family; her old friend was deliberately encouraging the marriage of a Prussian princess to a morganatically-born prince while 'plucking the finest fruits', the

---

* Their apprehensions were justified. Carlos became King of Portugal in 1889 and was assassinated with his elder son and heir in 1908. His younger son, Manuel, ascended the throne but was deposed and the country became a republic two years later.

Romanovs, for her beloved Hessian relations. That the Queen was the grandmother of Moretta just as much as of Ella, and vehemently opposed the latter's engagement on acount of her distrust of Russia, seemingly counted for nothing. Then when the *Almanach de Gotha*, the directory of royal and noble status and genealogy, suddenly demoted the Battenbergs from Part I to Part II, containing the lesser aristocracy (including the Bismarcks, to add insult to injury), the Queen was furious, believing the Empress to be responsible. The Empress warned Vicky and Fritz separately that the marriage must never come about, calling it a 'pointless project' that must be abandoned.

Meanwhile Vicky and Moretta, braving the Empress's wrath, watched events in Bulgaria with ill-disguised admiration for her ruler. During the autumn of 1885 he repulsed a Serbian invasion of his territory, supported by Austria-Hungary, at the battle of Slivnitza, and Vicky sent him a twenty-eight-page letter of congratulation. Frustrated by her refusal to give in, Bismarck and his cronies whispered it was really she and not Moretta who was in love with the Battenberg prince. It was certainly easier for them to attack her than Queen Victoria, who applauded Sandro just as vigorously in her own way, compared him to the Prince Consort, and never missed an opportunity of inviting him to stay with her. Nevertheless she foresaw Russian jealousy at his success and knew that the Tsar's patience was wearing dangerously thin.

By April 1886 Sandro's position was increasingly tenuous. The popularity he had won after his victory the previous year was strongly resented at St Petersburg, and only one thing might save his position, immediate marriage to a suitably-connected princess. It was not to be. One August morning a gang of Russian officers burst into his palace at Sofia, forced him at gunpoint to sign a hastily-improvised deed of abdication, and sent him under arrest to the Austrian frontier. Public opinion in Bulgaria demanded his return a week later, but he had had enough. He sent a conciliatory telegram to Tsar Alexander III which was treated with contempt, and after receiving further threats he ratified his deed of abdication.

Though furious with Russia, Vicky admitted that the dignity of his departure was 'an honourable one for him and his people and he can lay down his crown of thorns with a clear conscience'.[26] 'His *noble* character and rare abilities, and his gallant conduct indeed deserve praise and admiration, as his hard fate must call forth sympathy,' she wrote to Lord Napier. 'Seldom did so much injustice and ingratitude fall to any man's share. He did his duty from first to last, and deserves the approval of all honest men and good soldiers.'[27]

Vicky felt more and more ill at ease in the atmosphere of Berlin. She, Fritz and their three younger daughters regularly visited Italy, where they enjoyed the lakes and mountains of the north, Venice, Florence and the Riviera. Returning to the capital in the autumn of 1885, she wrote to Countess Dönhoff how bitterly she felt the contrast 'when I come back to the heavy dull stiffness, to the cold ugliness of north Germany and the neighbourhood of Berlin! The moral atmosphere of the Court, the political and official world seems to *suffocate* me!'[28]

In 1884 Fritz told Bismarck that he intended to include some of the National Liberals, including their leader Johannes Miquel, in his government when he came to the throne, and he would be glad to have Bismarck retain the Chancellorship. Bismarck said he had no objection to the Crown Prince attempting to govern with the National Liberals, but if he wanted to go further towards the left, he would soon be rushing headlong down the slope to republicanism.[29] He was concerned about reports from other ministers and members of the *Reichstag* suggesting the Crown Prince no longer had the stamina to resist any attempts his strong-willed wife might have about attempting to bring the *Deutsch-Freisinnige Partei* to power when they were Emperor and Empress. Some of her letters to Fritz underlined a fervent belief that the damage done by Bismarck could be rectified if the Chancellor relinquished control over domestic policy to the party's leaders. She readily conceded that Bismarck remained the man for 'exceptional circumstances'; his 'power, energy, clear-headedness [and] genial courage' had accomplished much for them during foreign policy crises, but domestic policy required other qualities which could be found in the progressive left, who unlike him had 'the insight and the drive to improve and dignify the situation' and were committed to 'bringing out the best in human nature'. They would foster the development of what she saw as right for Germany; a strong government that could protect the country from danger abroad with a good and strong army, an efficient but small navy; most important of all, they would have nothing to do with absolutism or imperialism on one hand, or 'the development of a workers' state' on the other.[30]

If Fritz felt that she was pandering to extreme radical or leftist elements, he did not argue with her. Whether this was because he accepted her judgment without question, or because he simply did not have the vigour to argue with her, is debatable. But some of those around them, mainly Bismarck's supporters (or men who owed their advancement to him), readily believed the latter, and blamed her for undermining her husband's self-confidence. Baron Friedrich von Holstein of the Foreign Office, a recluse whose office safe was known as the 'Poison Cupboard' because of its wealth of incriminating secrets about anyone of importance in contemporary life, was no admirer of the Crown Prince or Princess. He felt that the Crown Prince's character grew weaker by the year, in inverse proportion to the increase of her influence, and said he could not believe that he would ever assert his own will in opposition to hers. Gustav von Sommerfeld complained that the heir was 'not a man at all, he has no ideas of his own, unless she allows him.'[31] Radolinski told Holstein and others that when the Crown Prince ascended the throne, his wife would be Emperor in all but name. Holstein thought he might be persuaded to renounce his place in the succession, as he was 'already a prey to misgivings both on foreign affairs [England] and on domestic policy'.[32] If there was a struggle for the throne his son Wilhelm, who possessed greater determination of character and was an 'ardent soldier, anti-democratic, anti-English'[33] would surely be the people's choice as well as that of the ministers.

Bismarck knew the Crown Princess would prevent her husband from renouncing the throne while his father was alive, but if a political crisis was to occur during his reign or could be conveniently contrived for the purpose, he might consider abdication. Some were prepared to suggest that when Kaiser Wilhelm died, the Crown Princess should not be permitted to become Empress, but forced to flee or be banished from Germany, or even imprisoned, presumably on a trumped-up charge of being an agent of a foreign power. Others, led by Waldersee, Deputy Chief of General Staff, demanded that the Crown Prince should be asked or forced to renounce his place in the succession so that his son would become his grandfather's heir.

Prince Wilhelm declared openly that his mother had always remained an Englishwoman at heart, and was credited with being the inspiration for the idea of having his parents forcibly separated. Holstein knew that Bismarck would never propose such a medieval idea, but Wilhelm might, as he was said to be 'heartless, fiercely determined, obstinate and cunning, and moreover penetrated with the idea that every personal consideration should be subordinated to the interests of the state. The Crown Prince is afraid of his son already'.[34] While Bismarck had the grace to keep aloof from such squalid machinations, he spoke to the *Reichstag* in March 1885 of the disastrous consequences which dynastic interests could have on state policy, and the dangers of such ties with international relations, a theme to which he had referred shortly after coming to power many years earlier. His reference to the French revolution and the fate of Marie Antoinette were analogies interpreted as a warning to the Crown Princess. A year later, Waldersee made it evident that if the *Reichstag* and ministers were prepared to accept any proposals for greater democracy by Emperor Friedrich and his wife in the next reign, the military was not. Democracy was anathema to the Prussian army, whose privileged status would be threatened. In tones redolent of the controversy which had reared its head in the early days of King Wilhelm's reign and his obstinacy over the military reforms, the army would not stop at intervening with the intention of overthrowing Kaiser Friedrich and placing Prince Wilhelm on the throne to 'restore kingship to its rightful position'.[35]

By 1885 Kaiser Wilhelm was becoming ever more frail with kidney disorders, blood loss, and minor strokes. That summer the

Chancellor was called to the Neue Palais and asked if he would be willing to remain in office after His Majesty's death. He replied that he would, on two conditions: no parliamentary government, and no foreign influence in politics. To these, so it is said, Fritz wholeheartedly agreed.

While there is no doubt that the meeting took place, Bismarck's reminiscences form the only record of what took place. They can hardly be accepted at face value, as they were distorted by lies and personal spite, with the tone coloured by what he or his sycophantic assistant Lothar Bucher, to whom much of the work was dictated, wished the world to remember of him. Yet Fritz knew it would be impossible to dismiss his father's chief statesman on his accession, and the best he could do was to wait until they clashed, then rely on the support of the radicals and the *Freisinnige* to press for his resignation. Moreover, as Catherine Radziwill suggested, he would not have accepted such conditions without strongly resenting the reference to 'foreign influence', an obvious slight to Vicky;[36] Bismarck was one of the last people from whom he would have tolerated such disrespect. Maybe the Chancellor intended to safeguard his position in the event of Fritz's sudden accession, because he knew the Crown Prince to be a man of his word;[37] and for him to accept the conditions offered would be consistent with the view that he was weary of his aimless life and had little hope for the future.

Vicky wrote to Friedberg that the Emperor and Bismarck had 'created a unique and wondrous structure', though it had its weaknesses, and her husband would retain the best qualities of the old empire but give the German people the kind of education that would prepare them to make their own political judgments. Her husband's reign would retain and build on everything that had made Prussia great; his reign would emphasize military power, industriousness, order, cultural development and prosperity. As central government could not be expected to do everything, the new administration would initiate transition to a new political order in which the administrative powers held by the central assembly would gradually be transferred to the people. New social legislation would inspire trust among the working classes, so there would be no need for them to have to live with socialist agitation. 'The strong hand of a Prince Bismarck will no doubt be capable of building these bridges that will safely enable us to cross into a new era that will crown his lifetime achievements,' she wrote. Perhaps, she added, if he would see her more often, he would realize that she was not 'the disruptive and dangerous person' that she was considered to be.[38]

Bismarck was not the sworn foe of the Crown Prince and Princess that posterity has often suggested. Much as they opposed some of his methods, they respected much of what he had done for Germany, while he found in them some of the fundamental qualities lacking in the Emperor and Empress. The Crown Prince, he told his press chief Moritz Busch, was 'more human, so to speak, more upright and modest' than his father, while the Crown Princess was 'unaffected and sincere, which her mother-in-law is not . . . she is honourable and has no great pretensions.'[39]

Bismarck agreed to meet Fritz and Vicky in July 1885, and on the way Radolinski joined him at Wildpark Station. He told Radolinski what he intended to say to the Crown Prince and Princess, in other words he would express his disapproval of the 'English influence' the Crown Princess had brought to Germany and of the Battenberg marriage, and stress the advantages of marrying Princess Victoria into the Portuguese royal family. He knew Radolinski would repeat this to her, and when he did she was so angry that she could hardly bring herself to speak to Bismarck more than necessary. Meanwhile Bismarck met Fritz alone, with nobody to weigh in to support him. Yet posterity only has Bismarck's version of events, and has only his word for it when he says that the Crown Prince simply pursed his lips and tacitly agreed with all he said.

At about this time Fritz also drafted proclamations to be issued to his Chancellor and his people on accession. These were done with several advisers including Stosch, Friedberg, Roggenbach and Geffcken. The two latter wished to see Bismarck's influence limited during the next reign, whereas the two others preferred to retain the status quo. These proclamations included a commitment to keeping the Chancellor's policies within constitutional bounds.

Though long since retired and in failing health, Baron Ernest von Stockmar remained a trusted friend and mentor to Vicky and Fritz, as a link with the early days of their marriage, and perhaps the only man in Germany outside their immediate family whom they could really trust. On 6 May 1886 he died after a long illness, and though not unexpected, it was a great shock to them both. 'It seems to me as if we have practically been orphaned,' Fritz wrote to his wife; '& as if everything is becoming desolate and empty all around us!'[40]

Another perpetual source of anxiety to Vicky and Fritz was Bismarck's attention to their eldest son, whom he was treating as if he was already Crown Prince. Fritz suddenly found himself replaced as Prussia's royal representative abroad, as unlike his son he was not a supporter of the *Dreikaiserbund* which he regarded as a reactionary alliance behind the times. Willy was sent to Russia to represent the Kaiser at the Tsarevich Nicholas's coming-of-age celebrations, though Fritz had assumed that he would be asked first to represent his father. When the Kaiser's court chamberlain congratulated Vicky at a family dinner on her son's appointment, she was thoroughly put out and asked the Kaiser, who replied with some embarrassment that he had only made his mind up that morning. When she asked why neither she nor her husband had been notified before other members of the court, he lost his temper, told her he had good reasons, and would put up with no interference. During the dinner, guests saw her eyes were filled with tears.

The visit came at a sensitive time, for the protests of Fritz and Vicky that the former should be going instead of his son coincided with the coup in Bulgaria which overthrew Sandro. Vicky received a cypher telegram from Queen Victoria urging them both to be resolute and demand that Fritz should insist on going. Vicky had second thoughts after the Bulgarian news and decided it might look like cowardice or at least tacit approval if he was to meet the Tsar, but she still keenly felt it was an insult for Fritz to be passed over.

Willy assumed that the court at St Petersburg cared little for his parents in view of their pro-Battenbergs attitude. His mother completely ruled his father, he assured the Tsar, and his uncle, the Prince of Wales, was not to be trusted. He was unaware of Tsar

Alexander's respect for family life and, remarkably, his warm regard for Bertie, his brother-in-law. The Tsar never forgave Willy for such unfilial talk and cold-shouldered him for the rest of his visit, later dismissing him as '*Un garçon mal élevé et de mauvaise foi.*'* Initially he was convinced that his visit had been a great success, but soon afterwards he began to feel that the Tsar was not the personal friend or German ally that he had supposed. He also distrusted the menacing, arrogant tone in Russian officers he had not seen in his first visit, and it took little persuasion from the clique at court and the military to revise his previously friendly opinions about Russia.

In the autumn of 1886 Bismarck arranged for Willy to enter the Foreign Office at Berlin for some experience in international affairs. That the young man had no enthusiasm or ability for hard work, and preferred to act the part of a well-informed prince for show, was of no account; the Chancellor needed to drive a wedge between Wilhelm and the damaging influence of Waldersee and his hawkish Potsdam guards officers. Fritz wrote to Bismarck, protesting that the appointment was dangerous 'in view of his tendency towards overbearingness and self-conceit.'[41] He thought it vital that his son should learn more about the domestic affairs of his own country first before concerning himself with foreign policy, all the more given his propensity for over-hasty and highly impetuous judgement. Bismarck took refuge in pointing out that the plan was endorsed by the Kaiser, who told Herbert Bismarck that his grandson was extraordinarily mature, unlike his son with his 'regrettable political views' and his refusal to talk to him, the Kaiser, about politics. The latter, who was still quite resolute and argumentative for his age, made it plain that his own son was to be regarded as of no account, even though he was heir to the throne.

Bismarck's aim to use the young prince's foreign office experience as a counterweight against the pernicious influence of Waldersee was wise, for as the aged Moltke's deputy, Waldersee had long been convinced that conflict against France or Russia or both was vital to

---

* A badly brought-up and disloyal boy.

175

German interests, with only an elderly Kaiser and Chancellor as the main obstacles. Though Bismarck did not want war, Waldersee maintained, he thought he was trying to create discord between England and Russia, especially in the aftermath of the Bulgaria crisis; and that once Kaiser Wilhelm was dead, Tsar Alexander III would feel less inhibited about opposing Germany because of Frederick's well-known English sympathies. On Frederick's accession, there was every chance that war between Germany and Russia would soon follow. If Germany was to instigate a preventive war with France, it would be best to strike at once while Kaiser Wilhelm was still alive, as the special bond of trust between him and the Tsar would be a sure guarantee of Russian neutrality. A preventive war by Germany and Austria against France and perhaps Russia might escalate into conflagration on a wider scale, but in Waldersee's estimation the risk was worth taking; to wait too long would put Germany at a disadvantage.

Vicky and Fritz suspected a major clash of arms was quite possible, with French hostility the most likely cause, this time complicated by Anglo-French rivalry for the control of Egypt. France's refusal to cooperate with European intervention in North Africa left Britain to defend her interests alone, and President Grévy's government threatened to induce Germany to promise neutrality in the event of Anglo-French conflict. If Germany agreed then France would guarantee her support, but if Bismarck refused then the French government would accept Russia's offers of an alliance. Fritz and Vicky considered it unlikely as Bismarck still apparently distrusted France, but they knew that as long as Germany did not give the French a formal declaration granting her a free hand towards England she would not move a step. They therefore felt that England should take 'some energetic step in Egypt to her own advantage' in order to assert her superiority and control.[42]

An initiative for an Anglo-German alliance came from Herbert Bismarck, who believed that England would be a more reliable ally than the heterogeneous, weak Austro-Hungarian empire, and had come close to convincing his father of such a necessity. Such a proposition brought the Bismarcks closer to the outlook of the Crown

Prince and Princess, though they were more sympathetic to the cause of Austria and thoroughly anti-Russian. Vicky was particularly outraged by Russia's 'barbaric' behaviour in Bulgaria, and in a letter to Queen Victoria she endorsed a quadruple alliance between England, Italy, Austria-Hungary and Turkey as a sure guarantee of peace. If these powers were to form a coalition in concert with Germany, Russia would probably give up her designs on Bulgaria and Constantinople, and never risk a war against such opposition.

In November 1886 Queen Victoria was warned by Morier, then ambassador in St Petersburg, that Bismarck was urging Russia to occupy Bulgaria in order to secure for himself a free hand against France, and she wondered if it was true. Vicky thought it unlikely that Bismarck would plan a pre-emptive strike against France alone. It would be in his, and Germany's, best interests to take Russia and France on simultaneously, as she would surely have England, Austria, Italy, Turkey and the Danube countries on her side. If conflict was to erupt over the Orient, Germany would probably not have to go to war at all, or would do so by joining forces with the other Powers, which would make the situation much easier. Fritz was pleased that they had managed to keep Russia from continuing to threaten Bulgaria, a matter which 'made the Tsar foam with rage at Bismarck'.[43]

Fritz was advised by the military attaché from Paris, Karl von Villaume, on a visit to Berlin, that the French did not want war and were shocked at Russia's behaviour, though General Boulanger, the French war minister who was keen for immediate revenge on Germany, did not share their views. At a meeting in January 1887 Fritz spoke to Bismarck, who exaggerated Boulanger's threat to peace. He drew attention to France's renewed purchase of horses and building materials for the construction of barracks near the frontier fortresses, and spoke in vague terms of hopes for an 'understanding' with England and Italy. Fritz warned Queen Victoria that Boulanger was likely to be appointed as Minister President in France, and if so he was expected to 'venture to attempt a desperate coup in order to gratify his ambition & vanity as a second Napoleon. Matters are fast coming to a critical point here!! & if this unfortunate inexcusable war breaks out, how much the interests of the Great Powers, & England's in particular, will have to suffer.'[44]

Queen Victoria replied that England could never promise assistance without knowing the ultimate objective, and would certainly not be party to any attack on France 'unless she quarrelled with or threatened us.' She was particularly fearful of conflict breaking out at the Emperor's age; it 'would be madness' and a war would probably kill him.[45] Vicky was alarmed by what she heard from St Petersburg, and Tsar Alexander's contemptuous comments about England, which he said 'had already quite withdrawn from European politics and was too weak to take any part in them, and was not to be feared in any way.'[46] When Crown Prince Rudolf of Austria visited Berlin a few weeks later he told Vicky and Fritz of his fears of the inevitability of war, and 'spoke of the intense desirability of a close understanding between England, Germany, Austria and Italy.' Russia, he told them, was undoubtedly the strongest power in Europe 'and imposed her will on the rest', so the only way of keeping the Franco-Russian alliance in check was an alliance between the other four nations.[47]

By the beginning of 1887, with the Emperor's ninetieth birthday approaching, the *Reichstag* was increasingly preoccupied with whatever changes the next reign would bring. Whether Kaiser Friedrich would retain Bismarck was questionable. Though there were signs of a rapprochement, particularly where foreign policy and the possibility of an Anglo-German alliance were concerned, would Bismarck want to retain office under the Anglophile, liberal Kaiser, and would he be able to develop a good working relationship with the Empress? Who would lead the government should Bismarck, father and son, both resign; would an incoming government be fully supported by the political parties and people, or would there be opposition from court and the army? Among the right-wing deputies there was a feeling that the elderly Emperor was holding the fragile fabric of Germany together simply by being alive, and that it would be of benefit to the state and to continuity if Friedrich was excluded from the succession so that the throne would pass to his son Wilhelm instead. Moreover the view was widespread throughout Europe that war might break out soon, and a firm hand was needed.

On New Year's day 1887, Vicky acknowledged a letter of good wishes from a distant friend, writing prophetically that she had reached an age when she no longer thought herself secure from the blows of fate.[48] She could not have foreseen the heaviest one of all.

During the previous autumn she, Fritz and the three younger girls had spent a few weeks in Italy, staying at the village of Portofino near Genoa. One evening they went for a drive with King Umberto and Queen Margharita, and the coachman lost his way. There was a chill in the air, and Fritz had not brought his greatcoat; when they arrived back late he was shivering, and that winter he suffered from persistent colds and catarrh. Ominously, at a court ball in Berlin on 31 January hosted by General Bronsart von Schellendorff, Prussian minister for war, Kaiser Wilhelm stood around in the ballroom until 11 p.m., chatting with several of the guests and looking astonishingly spry for his eighty-nine years. Admittedly he had been showing his age for some time. It was often difficult to understand what he was saying; he had become very deaf, and shuffled his feet to such an extent when he walked that his attendants watched anxiously for any creases in the palace carpets which might trip him up. He suffered from intermittent kidney and bladder trouble, for which strong doses of morphine were prescribed. Nevertheless he seemed to have aged remarkably well.

By contrast his eldest son, also present, looked increasingly pale and in low spirits. On this occasion, a few of those around him noticed with some concern, he was so hoarse that he could hardly speak a word.

EIGHT

'The fear of what might happen'

By the end of February 1887 Fritz's voice was still little more than a hoarse whisper, and Dr Wegner decided to seek specialist advice. A few days later Professor Karl Gerhardt, lecturer in medicine at Berlin University, examined him and found a small swelling on the lower portion of the left vocal cord, a matter which he said could soon be cured with a little painful but simple treatment. After a fortnight of daily attempts to remove the swelling with a wire snare and then a circular knife failed, he resorted to cauterising it with red-hot platinum wire, but every time the swelling was removed it reappeared the next day.

Kaiser Wilhelm's ninetieth birthday fell on 22 March. Celebrations were kept to a minimum to spare him fatigue, but a large gathering of royalties, among them the Prince of Wales and Crown Prince Rudolf of Austria, joined him at a special dinner at Berlin. When Fritz made a speech congratulating him, it was evident that the effort taxed what little voice he still had. After his address he announced Henry's engagement. Their second son, Vicky noted, was 'always nice when he has been with us for some time, but not when he has been set up by others, and his head stuffed full of rubbish at Berlin.'[1] Significantly Henry had braved opposition at Berlin and gone to Osborne in July 1885 with his cousin Irene of Hesse for the wedding of their aunt Beatrice, and twenty months later, the cousins were betrothed. Though Vicky may have had reservations about the threat of haemophilia in such a union as she had in the case of Willy and Ella,* she and Fritz hoped that wedlock might have the effect on

---

* Fears of the taint of haemophilia were to be proved sadly justified. Henry and Irene had three sons of whom two were haemophiliac, one dying in infancy and one surviving to his fifties. Ella's marriage to Grand Duke Serge of Russia was childless.

Henry that had been lost on Willy, especially as Alice's daughters possessed a strength of character lacking in Dona.

Meanwhile Gerhardt suspected that the swelling on the Crown Prince's throat was not a simple tumour, but a cancerous growth. In April he sent him for a cure at Ems where a change of air with regular inhalations and douches for nose and throat ought to prove beneficial. Accompanied by Vicky, the three younger girls, and Dr Wegner he left Berlin for a few weeks, and on return in May he felt so much better, apart from continual hoarseness, that he thought he was cured. Only on medical diagnosis did Gerhardt discover that the swelling was still there, and larger than before. For a second opinion he consulted his university colleague Professor Ernst Bergmann, who recommended an immediate external operation on the growth, which he believed was malignant. To accomplish this successfully he would need to split the larynx in order to remove the swelling properly. He made light of the seriousness of such treatment, saying it was no more dangerous than an ordinary tracheotomy, or excision in the windpipe. By now Fritz feared that something was seriously wrong with him, and Vicky was desperately worried, 'more dead than alive with horror and distress'.[2] That her beloved husband should fall ill on the threshold of his accession, for which they had waited and been prepared for so many years, seemed too bitter an irony to be true. Bravely she feigned an optimism at odds with what she felt deep inside, in order to try and lift his spirits.

When Bismarck first heard that the Crown Prince was unwell he remarked cynically that the heir was simply out of sorts because of his father's longevity, and impatient for him to die. When it became obvious that he was about to undergo a serious operation the Chancellor intervened to insist that it could not be undertaken without the patient's consent and, as he was next in line to the throne, the Kaiser's permission would also be required. He summoned three more doctors: Dr Max Schrader, Fritz's own Surgeon-in-Ordinary; Professor Adalbert Tobold, an experienced, semi-retired Berlin laryngologist; and the Kaiser's physician Dr Gustav von Lauer. On 18 May all five, and Dr Wegner, held a consultation and agreed that he had cancer; four were in favour of operating immediately.

Gerhardt and Schrader objected as they thought it would probably prove fatal, and that even if the Crown Prince survived he would certainly lose his voice altogether. They reported to Bismarck, who agreed that no operation should take place without the consultation of another specialist.

When the Chancellor came to tell Vicky personally, she found him unusually pleasant. She did not appreciate at first that they were united in their apprehension of Willy. Should he get the idea that he might become Emperor before his time, the consequences would be equally unpalatable for parents and statesman alike. The word cancer was already being mentioned in Berlin, and some of Bismarck's disciples were saying among themselves that the Prussian constitution forbade the reign or accession of a sovereign who was mortally ill. An indignant Bismarck had to tell him this was nonsense; the Crown Prince was not allowed to withdraw from the succession, even if he wished to himself. Willy no longer worshipped the Chancellor so fervently and the old man suspected that, once the young Prince ascended the throne, his dismissal from office would be only a matter of time. It was imperative that Crown Prince Friedrich Wilhelm should follow his father as Kaiser. For all their differences, Vicky realized that Bismarck was more of an ally than she and Fritz had supposed. She admitted he was a 'great man, *but* his *system* is a *pernicious one*'.[3] Though his reasons were dictated by reasons of state rather than personal sympathy, she was touched by his anxiety. It was nothing to do with kind-heartedness that made him feel for them, she wrote to Queen Victoria; 'it is his reason, & his Patriotism that make him dread as an irreparable catastrophe to Germany anything happening to my beloved Fritz.'[4]

For 'the other specialist', the doctors suggested several names from outside Germany, and after Bismarck had stipulated for obvious reasons that he should not be French or Austrian, the London-based Scotsman Morell Mackenzie seemed the best choice. His qualifications were sound, and he was the author of a textbook on nose and throat diseases which had been translated into several different languages and was used in German medical schools. Gerhardt already knew him, and he spoke fluent German.

But there were more sinister reasons for his selection. The German doctors were puzzled by their heir's illness, and while they assured her that the operation they proposed was almost harmless, being undertaken without hesitation in the case of children and old people, they were privately far from confident. Their decision to consult a foreign specialist was a deliberate example of handing on the torch. Should the disease prove fatal – and they had no reason to suppose otherwise, particularly in view of the Crown Prince's rather weak constitution – it would suit them if a foreigner was left to shoulder the blame. What a triumph it would be for the anti-English faction court if a British doctor could be charged with killing their heir to the throne, and it would be easy for them to assert that their English Crown Princess was responsible for summoning him in the first place! Moreover Mackenzie was well-known for his skill, but had enemies at home. Vicky telegraphed to her mother on 19 May for her mother to send him at once, at the other doctors' request. The Queen did but, aware of her daughter's instincts of loyalty, added a caveat from her physician Sir William Jenner, that the Scot was clever but 'greedy and grasping about money and tries to make a profit out of his attendance'.[5]

On the afternoon of 20 May Mackenzie arrived in Berlin, and after consulting the other doctors he examined Fritz's throat, which he noted gave the patient no pain when breathing or swallowing. An operation, he said, would almost certainly prove fatal, and a thorough analysis should be made first to establish whether the growth was cancerous or not. He removed a small portion of the swelling and passed it to Professor Rudolf Virchow at the Berlin Institute of Pathology for examination, but Virchow could not make a conclusive diagnosis from such a small amount, so Mackenzie removed a larger sample two days later.

According to Gerhardt, in doing so Mackenzie injured the healthy right vocal cord and made it bleed. The new portion still did not prove that the growth was malignant, but Gerhardt was suspicious. Not having Mackenzie's experience or skill, he was in no position to know better, but he probably mistook the appearance of the right vocal cord and an excited imagination did the rest.[6] Mackenzie later felt that his own success on the first occasion 'had mortified him, and he was glad to find fault'.[7] At any rate, it was the first of several bitter clashes which overshadowed the rest of the patient's life. The German doctors maintained that they had to operate at once, while Mackenzie insisted that if they did the Crown Prince would die.

Bismarck reminded the doctors that they were dealing with no ordinary patient; the Crown Prince's life was too precious to be considered like that of an ordinary man.[8] Though Vicky hardly knew who or what to believe, her determination to look on the bright side was no weak-kneed attempt to avoid facing up to the worst that could happen. Fritz was already weakened by years of bitterness and frustration, and she knew she owed it to him to maintain a façade of optimism. If he believed his illness was fatal, he would turn his face to the wall. As long as she showed him there was still hope, he might recover.

From the start she unequivocally championed Mackenzie, but she overlooked his faults. He had left Harley Street in such a hurry that he did not bring his own surgical instruments and had to have them sent to Potsdam later; before examining his patient for the first time he had to buy a pair of forceps made to an unfamiliar French pattern. Moreover he was too sanguine; when the German doctors told the Crown Princess the disease was in its early stages and little harm had been done, Mackenzie promised a complete cure within weeks, subject to favourable conditions. It was imprudent to offer such a hostage to fortune. At the same time he did not inspire trust in others. Few went as far as Willy and Herbert Bismarck, who both called him a deliberate fraud, but some of the leading liberals had their doubts. Roggenbach declared he was a shrewd Englishman merely out to advertise himself by having the Crown Prince as his patient.

That summer Queen Victoria was to celebrate her Jubilee in London, and to Vicky it was unthinkable that she and Fritz should not be there to take part. As the Queen's eldest grandchild, Willy assumed he would also be invited, and if his father was unwell then he would undoubtedly be the Kaiser's representative. In fact he did not receive an invitation until April, two months before the festivities, and the Queen had seriously considered not sending him one at all as she had been so angered by his recent attitude, particularly with regard to the Battenbergs. It took all Vicky's powers of persuasion to rectify this situation, for while she admitted that he had behaved badly to them all, for him to be passed over would only increase his sense of grievance, as well as give his toadies in Berlin with another reason to 'use' him against them. Moreover a few days in England might help to counteract some of the harm that his Russian visit had caused. Whether he really wished to go for reasons of prestige or family devotion was debatable. On a hunting expedition with his friend Eulenburg early in June, he said bitterly that it was 'high time the old woman [Queen Victoria] died', and that she caused trouble, 'more than one would think.'[9]

Part of the persistent anti-Battenberg feud was the doing of Fritz's sister the Grand Duchess of Baden. She had come to Berlin in mid-March to help with their father's birthday festivities and stayed afterwards, partly to take care of him after Empress Augusta's departure for Baden, partly as she wanted to consult with her brother's doctors and act as unofficial press agent for the court. Vicky was angry that so many details about her husband's illness were appearing in the papers, and annoyed with her sister-in-law for telling reporters and journalists without asking or consulting them.

The Grand Duchess also sided with her parents in their fears that Moretta might still disgrace the Hohenzollerns by marrying Sandro. Empress Augusta had prepared a codicil to the Emperor's will stating he would disown his granddaughter and his daughter-in-law if she did, and when she left for Baden she asked Louise to get his signature on the document. Vicky had learnt of these plans from Albedyll, and realized that she had to safeguard her financial position should the worst come to the worst. After the Prince Consort's death she had asked Queen Victoria not to include her in her will, because she would be well provided for as the future Queen of Prussia. Now it seemed she might be left a disinherited widow at the mercy of an all-powerful son, and perhaps an elderly father-in-law, both of whom despised her. Queen Victoria appreciated the danger and immediately set up a small fund for Vicky and Moretta just in case.

Mackenzie suggested that the Crown Prince should come to England and be treated as a private patient in his London surgery. This suited the German doctors, as their patient's absence would relieve them for a while of their responsibility for a valuable life, and place the burden more squarely on Mackenzie's shoulders. Bismarck stood by the Kaiser who declared that he could not prevent his son, a grown man, from making such decisions. The only condition was that at least one German doctor, and preferably two, should accompany them and have a say as to how far the Crown Prince could be allowed to exert himself in the celebrations. Dr Wegner, the physician who had known him the longest, and Gerhardt's assistant Dr Landgraf, were chosen. Wilhelm's pride took a blow when he found he would be travelling to London as a mere guest among many other royalties and not as the sole Hohenzollern representative.

The news that they were going to England was greeted with indignation in Berlin. Few expected the ailing Kaiser to live another year; what if he should die while his heir was abroad – and in England of all places? What if the Crown Prince was to have a relapse and be too ill to return home? According to Gerhardt there were reasons to believe that either was probable. At the beginning of June the only symptoms of illness Fritz displayed were a sore throat, which was attributed to the constant removal of portions from the swelling, and almost total loss of voice. Already he was writing everything he wished to say on a pad of paper he carried everywhere, in the hope that his gruff whisper would improve with rest. Yet Vicky was so uneasy that on 1 June she spoke privately to Gerhardt, who warned her pessimistically that every time a part of the growth was removed it grew again; the tumour was suppurating, and the right vocal cord was starting to deteriorate. If this was the case, and if Mackenzie could not cure it, the only hope of saving the Crown Prince's life lay in an operation, without the same chance of success that it would have had a fortnight before. He could only hope that Mackenzie was right and that his treatment would work, for they had 'nothing else to suggest'.[10] Torn between so many conflicting opinions, Vicky found it hard to suppress her anxiety and keep calm in front of her husband, but she was sure they were right to go to the Jubilee; 'one cannot be kept a prisoner here, or be prevented from following a useful course by the fear of what might happen.'[11]

Vicky, Fritz and their three younger daughters left Berlin on 13 June, accompanied by the doctors, crossing the North Sea on the yacht *Victoria & Albert* and arriving at Sheerness two days later. With them they secretly took a collection of private papers for safe keeping at Buckingham Palace. At London they made for the Queen's Hotel, Norwood, a better place to stay than the centre of the city where they would be in the thick of dust and heat. After a couple of quiet days there so Fritz could attend Mackenzie's consulting-rooms for daily treatment, they moved to Buckingham Palace on 18 June for him to have two more days' complete rest before the procession to Westminster Abbey.

Though he was spared the ordeals of state banquets and receptions, he had the chance to meet various fellow guests, among them Constantine, Crown Prince of Greece, who was to marry their daughter Sophie two years later, and their friend Crown Prince Rudolf of Austria. They had much in common, as imperial heirs to two of the most reactionary powers in Europe, sharing liberal convictions that had brought them some degree of political isolation from their fathers' governments. Rudolf had visited Berlin in March for the Emperor's birthday festivities, to be entertained at the Neue Palais where he had spoken to his hosts on his distrust of Russian policies, particularly regarding Tsar Alexander III's behaviour over Bulgaria. His fears of Russia's expansionist ambitions and a desire to see the rest of Europe in strong mutual alliance impressed Fritz greatly, particularly as the Austrian ministers told him nothing and he too had to learn from secret meetings with his liberal allies. Rudolf's distrust of Bismarck and Willy, five months his junior, bound the Crown Princes closer together.

Fritz awoke feeling reasonably fit and well on the morning of 21 June. Soon after 11 a.m. the procession began through London's richly decorated streets, resplendent with triumphal arches, evergreens, flags and brightly-coloured drapery from Buckingham

Palace to Westminster Abbey. Six cream-coloured horses pulled an open landau containing the Queen, accompanied by Vicky and Alix. Behind the coach and its escort of Indian cavalry came the Queen's three surviving sons, five sons-in-law and nine grandsons. Mounted on a white charger, Fritz in his uniform of the Pomeranian Cuirassiers, his eagle-crested helmet, silver breastplate and Garter star glinting in the sunshine, towered above them all. The Londoners' cheering broke into a deafening roar as he saluted, but the more keen-eyed among them noticed how thin he had become. After the service at the abbey, all the princes and princesses moved forward to the Queen to pay her homage. When she stepped down from the coronation chair at the end, Fritz happened to be standing near her and she embraced him impulsively, lingering on his arm in a moment of deep emotion.

His throat was still congested, and he had to continue daily treatment at Mackenzie's surgery. On 28 June the doctor removed most of the growth, Wegner placed it in spirit in a sealed flask and sent it to Virchow at Berlin for examination. Nothing further could be proved about the disease, and the professor's report could advance no new information. But away from the stifling atmosphere of Berlin, and surrounded by the reserved optimism of Vicky and the care of Mackenzie, Fritz felt he was on the way to recovery. Count Seckendorff reported that the Crown Prince was 'doing well, and we all hope that Dr Mackenzie's treatment will cure him entirely.'[12]

From the Norwood hotel they went to Osborne, where the weather was so fine that they spent most of the daylight hours outside. Fritz could relax in the shade of a cedar tree beside the tennis court, watching Vicky and Moretta play with Seckendorff and Rowland Prothero, son of the local rector. On hot days they went to the beach, where Fritz sat on the sand while Vicky bathed in the sea. Some forty years later their niece Marie of Edinburgh, by then Queen Dowager of Roumania, recalled her uncle and aunt as she saw them at Osborne when a girl of eleven. Pretending to bombard her and her sisters with sand and dry seaweed, Fritz 'was jolly and yet one somehow felt he was condescending', while Vicky's forced gaiety was apparent; 'her smile had something in it of sunshine when the weather is not really warm.'[13] With hindsight Marie should have known what an anxious time it was for them.

Later that summer they moved to Scotland, staying in the Fife Arms at Braemar, and driving daily the few miles east to Balmoral. In the pure Scottish Highlands air Fritz became stronger and his voice steadily improved. He saw the Queen regularly and she was relieved to see how much better he looked. She did not know that Dr Mark Hovell, a senior surgeon at the throat hospital who was in attendance at Braemar, had examined him and was convinced the growth was malignant. While not so highly qualified or internationally famous as Mackenzie, Hovell was possibly the most skilled of all the doctors who attended the royal patient, but was brought in so late that Mackenzie was completely in command, in Britain at least, by the time he arrived. Lacking the self-assertive qualities and unguarded conviction that he was right, he said nothing for the time being.

However Mackenzie was still confident, and in August Fritz wrote that the doctor 'considered my sufferings at an end even though I undoubtedly required special care with rest and silence for a long time in order to avoid a relapse.'[14] At his request, on 7 September Queen Victoria invited Mackenzie to lunch at Balmoral, and knighted him afterwards in the drawing-room. After laying down the sword she asked Mackenzie searching questions about the case, and was disturbed that he could tell her so little, apart from his theory that the illness 'had been long coming on and had been entirely neglected.'[15]

Meanwhile at Berlin the court, which had reluctantly allowed its heir to go to England for the Jubilee, was impatient for his return home, as the Kaiser was so weak that any mild infection or sudden heart attack could prove fatal. In liberal circles there were fears that Prince Wilhelm was gaining too much influence in state affairs during his father's absence – not that the Crown Prince's presence at Berlin had made much difference before – and wanted their champion to come back and take his rightful place in the capital. Vicky retorted that 'it would be madness to spoil Fritz's cure while he is in a fair way to recovery, but not well yet!'[16]

German opinion was the least of their troubles. On one of the last days in Scotland a row broke out between Seckendorff and the Chamberlain Count Radolinski. Like most other servants in the Crown Prince's household, with the notable exception of Seckendorff, Radolinski's attention came not from a desire to serve the Crown Prince and Princess, so much as to send Bismarck a secret weekly report on the activities of the household, and of the Crown Princess's conversation in particular. In her anxiety she was completely deceived by his devoted manner, as was Fritz to some extent, until Seckendorff warned her to be on her guard. At the same time, he warned her that Radolinski was doing his best to get rid of him.

For some weeks it had been rumoured that the Crown Princess was accepting her husband's imminent demise philosophically if not with impatience, seeing it as 'the gateway to freedom',[17] so she could spend the rest of her life with Seckendorff. Bismarck, Holstein, even Fritz's loyal confidant Friedberg and others, were said to be convinced that she would regard her widowhood as a kind of deliverance. During their sojourn in the Highlands Radolinski told Sir Henry Ponsonby, Queen Victoria's secretary, that the Crown Princess and her chamberlain were having an affair, and that she had prevented the operation on her husband so she could keep him alive just long enough to sample the privileges of being Empress. Ponsonby knew better than to fall for such stories and cold-shouldered him after that but other tales, though equally false, were far more easily believed. Even the Queen, who had evidently forgotten the 'Empress Brown' tittle-tattle, was moved to ask her secretary why her daughter found it necessary to take Seckendorff everywhere with her.

By this time the Scottish weather was too damp and cold. Mackenzie advised them to avoid Berlin over winter, and in September Fritz said farewell to Britain for ever. News arrived from Germany that Kaiser Wilhelm was seriously ill, with a number of official functions being performed by the ageing wheelchair-bound Empress with her grandson Wilhelm's assistance. Fritz was ready to leave for Berlin if his father was to die suddenly, as he would have to in the event of his accession, after which spending the autumn in a different, more temperate climate would be considered, though whether he would be permitted to go outside the German empire was doubtful. He considered returning to Babelsberg briefly to see his father again, but Vicky and Mackenzie persuaded him that to return to Germany while he was still convalescent would delay his recovery.

They left for Toblach in the Austrian Tyrol, arriving on 7 September, the same day that Mackenzie was knighted. Already exhausted by the journey, Fritz found the air too cold and he was coughing badly, looked pale and suffered from insomnia. After one particularly bad night when he choked so much that Vicky dreaded he was in imminent danger of suffocation, a telegram to London brought Mackenzie and Hovell out at once. They moved south to Venice and later Baveno, on the shores of Lake Maggiore, and Fritz appeared better by the time of his fifty-sixth birthday. All the children except Willy and Ditta joined them, acting a short play and playing the piano, just as they had done in happier days at Potsdam. He was so heartened at this demonstration of affection towards him that Vicky had to force herself to remain cheerful while keeping secret a most unwelcome piece of news. That morning she had received a letter from a friend asking her to bring the Crown Prince back to Germany at once; there was talk of a plot to defy the law, exclude him from the succession, and put Wilhelm in his place.

Undoubtedly part of the concern, sometimes bordering on anger, of the Berliners for their beloved heir, stemmed from the lack of public relations. Catherine Radziwill thought the greatest mistake Vicky ever made was to keep genuine knowledge of his condition from the public; the people would have pitied her and admired her courage if only they could have shared her trials with her instead of being left to guess and listen to idle rumour.[18] Unfortunately she had to choose between either being completely open, or else keeping her agonies to herself so that her husband should not suffer unnecessarily from seeing negative reports in the press. Already there were too many of these, and she tried to check the papers before he received them, in order to help him avoid the prophecies of gloom which would depress him and therefore undo weeks of effort on her part. Sooner or later the public would be bound to know what danger he was in, but she was hardly to be blamed for drawing a veil of secrecy over his progress for as long as she did.

Already the papers were arguing between themselves. On Fritz's birthday the *Reichs-Anzeiger* issued a statement that he was better, though it was necessary for him to spare his voice as much as possible and spend the winter in a warm climate so that, he could avoid catching cold as far as possible. Some of the other papers promptly contradicted the news of his improvement and announced that he was suffering from cancer, amounting to little more than vague confirmation of the widespread rumour, and some right-wing journals promptly revived the fictitious law which forbade an incurably sick man to wear the Prussian crown. Despite Vicky's vigilant censorship Fritz's eyes naturally strayed, and he was profoundly depressed at all the misinformed, speculative articles about himself.

Within weeks there was a further setback. He did not improve at Baveno, and Vicky put it down to the humidity. At the beginning of November they moved further south to San Remo, on the Italian coast and close to the French border. The Villa Zirio stood on a mountain slope above the Riviera road, in an idyllic setting of palms and fruit trees, of roses and other flowers which bloomed all winter. Fritz's apartments were a suite of rooms facing east and west to catch the sun. Above all it belonged to an Italian; the Berlin press had made much of the fact that their house at Baveno was leased by an Englishman.

But Fritz was no better here either; he lost colour and appetite, and the heat irritated him. Vicky had to have his bed placed in a warm but sheltered area of the terrace and sit by his side fanning him, horrified to see how little interest he suddenly had in anything or anyone, even her. Then one morning, within a week of their arrival, she discovered new swellings on his throat, and he found it a strain to sit up. Panic-stricken, she summoned Mackenzie who examined Fritz the morning after his arrival at the villa, and discovered a new growth on the larynx larger than the previous swellings, with a distinctly malignant appearance. He told Fritz that the disease was more serious than he had thought; half-expecting it, Fritz wrote on his pad – his voice having gone for good – to ask if it was cancer. Mackenzie gravely replied: 'it looks very much like it, but it is impossible to be certain.'[19] Fritz thanked him for being so honest, but when he and Vicky were alone, his self-control went and he broke down. 'To think that I should have a horrid, disgusting illness! that I shall be an object of disgust to everyone, and a burden of you all!'[20]

This was the catalyst for the anti-English factions in Germany. For over twenty years aristocratic circles at court and arch-conservatives alike had waited for the chance to get even with the Crown Princess, for what they considered to be her unwarranted interference in their politics and their country. Now they asserted that she had so set her heart on becoming Empress that she had kept the gravity of her husband's illness a secret, afraid of their both being passed over in favour of their eldest son. She had refused to listen to German doctors, they said, preferring to summon an Englishman; she and Mackenzie had given him falsely optimistic hopes about his condition and, to satisfy her own whim, she had dragged him to London where he had exhausted himself in her mother's Jubilee procession. Furthermore she and 'her' doctor had conspired to distrust the German physicians, thus preventing an operation on the sick man which might have saved his life.

Almost without exception these allegations were totally without foundation. It was true that the Crown Prince and Princess had eagerly awaited their accession to the throne in order to help inaugurate a more democratic and cultural regime, but she had been assured that they could not be set aside in the succession, no matter what his physical condition. From that point of view, therefore, there was nothing to be gained by shielding the truth. On the other hand it was a deliberate falsehood to suggest that Vicky had called Mackenzie of her own accord; she had not even heard of him before the German doctors mentioned his name, but Bergmann and Gerhardt did not intend to lose face by admitting their responsibility for his appearance in the first place. Unfortunately Mackenzie's own attitude did nothing to help her; he probably preferred to believe that he had been summoned to Germany by the Crown Princess, not by mere fellow-doctors; far from trying to dispel this impression, he told this to others, including his official biographer H.R. Haweis. As for giving Fritz false hopes, her answer was mere commonsense, as she had told Queen Victoria; 'you know how sensitive and apprehensive, how suspicious and despondent Fritz is by nature! All the more wrong and positively dangerous (let alone the cruelty of it) to wish him to think the worst! We should not keep him going at all, if this were the case.'[21] Finally, the allegation that she had conspired with Mackenzie to the detriment of German medical knowledge was disproved by a letter the doctor published in *Allgemeine Zeitung* on 31 October, affirming that he had never been opposed to entering into consultation with his German colleagues; 'should any unfavourable symptoms unfortunately develop, I should be the first to ask for the cooperation of one of your countrymen.'[22]

But the most articulate of Vicky's enemies slandered her with little restraint and a good deal of imagination. While Bismarck was uncharacteristically silent, Waldersee declared that she 'scarcely seems a responsible being, so fanatically does she uphold the idea that her husband is not seriously ill'.[23] Lucius von Balhausen, Minister of Agriculture, later remarked in his memoirs with spite and total disregard for the truth that she resembled her mother, who had refused almost to the end to believe that the Prince Consort was sinking in 1861, declared he was only malingering, went for a drive and came back to find him dead.[24] Herbert Bismarck wrote that the Crown Prince had to remain in Italy because his wife feared she would be pelted with rotten eggs if she returned to Berlin.[25]

Fritz had always been popular in Prussia. The only circle who hated him as much as they loathed Vicky were the representatives of the Christian Socialist Movement, led by the notoriously anti-Semitic court chaplain Adolf von Stöcker. At a court ball some years earlier Fritz had met a young Jewess who dreaded the prospect of being ignored. He detailed his friend Count Bernstorff to dance with her, while Vicky had shown her lack of prejudice by accepting the honorary chairmanship of a newly-founded orphanage for Jewish girls in Berlin. Willy eagerly identified himself with the anti-Semitic movement, and in December 1887 he attended a meeting of Stöcker's mission at the Waldersees' house which planned to extend the movement throughout Germany. There he made a speech declaring that Christian Socialism was needed to bring people back to Christianity who had lost their faith, and to get them to recognize the absolute authority of the monarchy. Bismarck attacked him for this ludicrous address, and was coldly reminded that in Germany the Kaiser, not the Chancellor, was master.

Some took the view that Willy accepted too unquestioningly the verdict of his flatterers that his father was being mishandled by Mackenzie and, excited by the prospect of premature power, tried to exert some influence out of a sense of duty.[26] Nevertheless his next intervention at San Remo was thoroughly ill-timed. After the public criticism of Mackenzie two more doctors, Professor von Schrotter from Vienna and Dr Krause from Berlin, were sent to replace Gerhardt and Bergmann, to whom it was made clear that their services were not required any longer. They examined Fritz, and after all doctors present – Mackenzie included – had held a consultation agreeing that the disease was cancer, they declared that two alternatives were possible: either tracheotomy, an incision in the windpipe, which would avoid danger of suffocation, or total removal of the larynx, which would result in permanent loss of voice at the very least. Whatever course was taken, it would only prolong the patient's life for months rather than years.

As they were ushered into the sitting-room to break the news to the Crown Prince he stood with composed dignity, giving a nod and a gentle smile that betrayed no emotion. Vicky was beside him, white as a sheet but determined for his sake not to give way. Schrotter, acting as the doctors' spokesman, told him of their conclusion, without mentioning the word cancer but leaving them in no doubt as to what was inferred, and then gave him a choice of tracheotomy or removal. Calmly he wrote on his pad that he and Vicky wished to be alone for a while to decide. Together they selected tracheotomy, should it become necessary; Fritz felt that an Emperor mutilated by the removal of his larynx would be incapable of carrying out his duties. His resigned attitude made it clear that he knew he was doomed, but only if threatened with suffocation would he submit to a splitting of the larynx. Now that he knew the truth, he seemed a little less depressed than before. Later in front of the servants and doctors, he apologized for feeling so well under the circumstances.

At this stage Willy reappeared with yet another doctor, Schmidt, who was to examine Fritz and take a report back to Berlin with him. Whoever sent them is purely speculative; whether one, encouraged by public opinion and spurred on privately by the other, decided to take matters into his own hands, or whether the Bismarcks sent them, is not known. Whatever the circumstances, Willy was too full of his own importance when he arrived to make allowance for his mother's frantic state of mind, telling her to get his father up and dressed so that he could take him back to Berlin for an operation. She would not hear of it, and struggling to restrain her temper she suggested that they should go for a walk together. He retorted that he had no time, as he would be too busy speaking to the doctors. When she answered that they had instructions to report to her and not to him, he insisted he was acting on the orders of his grandfather, and to see that the doctors were not interfered with in any way.

The sight of her son impudently standing with his back half turned to her, as good as telling her what to do in the presence of her household, was more than she could stand. In her own words she 'pitched into him with considerable violence', declaring that she would report his behaviour to his father and see that he was forbidden the villa in future;[27] with that she swept regally out of the room. Rather taken aback, he sent Radolinski after her to tell her that he had not meant to be so rude, but he had come as the Emperor's representative, and was only doing his duty. The air cleared, she answered that she bore him no grudge, but would not put up with any interference; the head on her shoulders was just as good as his. However it was obviously only a truce, and on his return to Berlin he complained that his mother had treated him like a dog. Forty years later, chastened by abdication and a decade of exile, he recalled benignly that 'she saw everything in shadows, everything hostile, saw want of sympathy and coolness where there was only a helpless silence.'[28]

After Fritz was told the doctors' diagnosis at San Remo, correspondents were asked by Dr Schrader and Radolinski not to divulge the news. They intended to prepare the German public gradually by a series of cautiously-worded bulletins which would make the patient's state generally known without shocking his own feelings. This plan, however, was frustrated by the immediate publication of a private bulletin to the Emperor in the *Reichs-Anzeiger* which Fritz saw, much to his distress.*

When Vicky was not sitting talking with him or renewing ice bandages around his throat she forced herself to read the papers, having made him promise that he would not look at them first. Almost without exception they made unpleasant reading, and in particular the attacks on Mackenzie made her seethe with anger. Whatever his faults, notably pride which prevented him from admitting that he might have been wrong, he certainly knew how to handle them with sensitivity.

Moreover she suspected that the clique at Berlin were doing their best to see that Willy would succeed his grandfather on the throne. Wilhelm was tactless enough to raise the question of abdication to his father's face at San Remo, and Fritz was so furious that even an alarmed Vicky felt it necessary to remind them that despite everything Wilhelm was their son.[30] In a conversation with Herbert

---

* A French correspondent, Jean de Bonnefon, alleged in his book, *Drame Impérial* (1888), that the Crown Prince had become infected with and was treated for syphilis while in Egypt in 1869 (see p. 112). After Fritz's death, Mackenzie allegedly confided in a colleague in England that he was sure the Crown Prince had had syphilis of the larynx before the cancer appeared.[29] Such a hypothesis is impossible to substantiate. Mackenzie's comments are unsupported by written or printed evidence; while as a Frenchman who had no reason to admire one of the major architects of France's defeat in war less than twenty years earlier, and who was thus ready to propagate any scurrilous gossip aimed at discrediting the portrait of an unusually happy royal marriage, Bonnefon's words must be regarded with caution.

Bismarck in mid-November, General von Albedyll said the Crown Princess was responsible for giving a falsely hopeful portrait of her husband's condition as she wanted to propagate the legend that he was capable of ascending the throne and ruling, so she would be able to rule herself. The Crown Prince was at her mercy, and even if he wanted to renounce his claim to the throne she would never let him; the situation would be tantamount to takeover by a foreign power, namely Great Britain. Such arguments were rebutted by Chancellor Bismarck, who reiterated that on the death of the present Emperor his son and heir would succeed him, whether he was ill or not, and whether he would be able to perform his duties or not would be decided according to certain articles in the Prussian constitution.[31]

That the Chancellor fervently wanted the Crown Prince to succeed his father was beyond doubt, for personal as well as constitutional reasons. Prince Wilhelm, he told his associates, was a hothead incapable of holding his tongue, who let himself be swayed by flatterers, and could lead Germany into a war without realizing or wanting it.[32] It was vital that his father should have a chance to rule, so the young man would have a chance to settle down and learn. For once he and the Crown Princess were in complete agree-ment. As Chancellor he was furious with Waldersee and his obsession with a preventive war policy, in which he had influenced and was wholeheartedly supported by Wilhelm. Waldersee and his acolytes seemed convinced that Russia and France were planning a pre-emptive strike on Germany early the next year, and said it was necessary for Germany and Austria to be prepared, if not to declare war themselves first. By mid-December Bismarck was angrily threatening to resign if Waldersee continued to agitate for war.

In view of the Kaiser's increasing frailty, and in his son's absence, it was vital to appoint Wilhelm as his representative. On 15 November he was granted authority, should the Kaiser become incapable, to sign state papers on his behalf. Basically it was a reasonable idea; by now the old man was so senile that he could barely sign his own name. But it would have been only common courtesy to consult Fritz first, not to let him hear of it as a *fait accompli*. He was already convinced that Wilhelm could not wait for him to die, and was behaving as if he was

Crown Prince already. On 19 November an official document confirming Prince Wilhelm's appointment as *Stellvertreter des Kaisers* ('deputy Emperor') and duties, signed by Bismarck, had been delivered at San Remo, but Vicky hoped that by playing for time she could wait for a more opportune moment to break it to him. She asked Radolinski to put it in safe keeping, as she had nowhere secure for it, and when he begged her to inform the Crown Prince of it she refused, saying it would anger him too much.

Two days later Henry arrived with a letter from Wilhelm, triumphantly informing him of the order. Fritz was furious; he would not let them act as if he was already dead, and insisted he would go straight back to Berlin and confront his father, son and the Chancellor regardless of the consequences. When he asked Vicky about Bismarck's original letter she panicked, denying that she had ever received one. In desperation she asked Radolinski to hand it to him and take the blame. Later Radolinski told Henry of the incident, only to be told in no uncertain terms that as a senior member of the household it was his duty not to withhold any such letters to the Crown Prince, and overrule the Crown Princess if necessary.

Now that all hope of peace and quiet had gone for good, they could at least seek solace from a succession of family and friends who put in an appearance. Baron Roggenbach helped to keep Fritz's spirits up as he talked with reserved optimism on the future of Germany as a constitutional power while he played chess or backgammon with the heir to the throne. Much as he believed in the superiority of German medical skill and privately distrusted Mackenzie, he had to admit that the Scot had behaved honourably and straightforwardly.[32] The Grand Duke and Duchess of Baden, the Prince of Wales, the Duke of Edinburgh, and their sister Louise, Marchioness of Lorne, all visited at various times. So did Lady Ponsonby, who arrived at the villa early in December to find him up and about, with a deceptively fresh colour and good appetite. Reluctantly she asked not to be seated next to him at evening dinner, as she could not prevent him talking; 'if one tries to avoid this by talking oneself, then he will answer. If one is silent, then he will begin the conversation.' In front of others he tried and often succeeded in giving an impression of good health, but she could see that this was not the case. A few days later, he picked up a paper and read a gloomy report on his health, listlessly pointing it out to Vicky, asking why they had to take every ray of hope away. Trying to sound cheerful she told him not to take any notice, then she went into the adjoining room with Lady Ponsonby and broke down completely.[33]

Even Radolinski, who was not well-disposed towards the Crown Princess, found himself moved by her valiant efforts and courage, and he admitted to feeling 'terribly sorry for the poor woman,' to Baron Holstein. She kept up his morale, 'but when she is alone she gives way to tears. Only she should not smile so much in public. It does her harm and one cannot help thinking that she does not feel deeply. Which is not so. She is absolutely resolved that he will eventually ascend to the throne. After waiting so long the poor man must have this satisfaction at least, and I will do all I can in the way of nursing and care to ensure that he survives to see that day and afterwards to remain on the throne as long as possible.'[34]

Fritz was deeply touched by the sympathy shown him from the outside world. Soon after the crucial diagnosis the *Reichstag* sent him a telegram wishing him well, and Sunday 27 November was chosen as a day of prayer for him in every English chaplaincy throughout Germany. A visiting British clergyman, Bishop Wilkinson, preached a sermon at Berlin on the divine cure of the nobleman's son at Capernaum. A deaf-mute offered to have his own sound larynx removed and inserted in his Crown Prince's throat. 'Infallible remedies' were sent by well-wishers to the villa; whisky and oatmeal from the Scottish Highlands, ground oyster shells from England, a bag of live worms from the United States, and carbolic acid from France, to say nothing of medicines, ointments, and bottles of mineral water. From his letters, particularly one to Queen Victoria, it was evident that Fritz, like Vicky, placed 'unwavering trust' in Mackenzie's optimistic diagnosis, and 'more stock in his words in November than in those of the [German] doctors who had been called in for consultation'.[35] He was well aware that he would not make a full recovery, but the doctors had told him that the disease might be held at bay for a couple of years if not more. 'In no way do I despair, and hope, even if only after long and careful treatment, I shall be able to dedicate all my energies to my country as before.'[36]

In December Mackenzie was recalled from London by a telegram informing him of a sudden increase in the growth. He hurried out to San Remo, examined the throat and announced that he could discover no dangerous symptoms present, and though there was a small new growth on the left vocal cord, the general appearance of the larynx was much better than it had been the previous month. Over Christmas and the New Year Fritz appeared to rally, and under the circumstances everyone worked hard to try and create as cheerful and festive an atmosphere as possible. They had two trees, one obtained locally and the other sent by German farmers from the Black Forest to give him a breath of German air. Willy, Dona and their children stayed at Berlin, but the rest of the family joined them. Ditta, Bernhard and their eight-year-old daughter Feodora came, as did Henry, who thought his father was recovering and sent reports to Queen Victoria assuring her that he was in good spirits and looked well. Fritz wrote to Willy that if his condition continued to improve, he still hoped 'to be fit and well again.'[37]

At 8 p.m. on Christmas Eve the household gathered in the large room opening onto the balcony, to be joined by Lady Ponsonby and her daughters, and the Italian Ambassador at Berlin, Count Launay. Fritz and Vicky then appeared arm-in-arm, the folding doors opened, and the room was flooded with light as the guests gazed wide-eyed at both gaily-decorated fir trees, ingeniously placed in a setting of roses, camellias, violets, geraniums and lilies all freshly gathered from the gardens. Every guest and servant had been remembered and Fritz took his part in leading them to the tables heaped with presents in the centre of the room. No trouble was too much for those who had so loyally stood by him. In the morning they attended divine service, and in the afternoon a party of schoolchildren assembled in front of the villa to sing carols; deeply moved at the sound, he walked out onto the terrace to thank them.

Their political foes in Berlin, as well as some of the less sympathetic members of their household, maintained that the Crown

Princess clung to the hope that her husband's condition was curable as she simply could not accept that he was dying, or that she was motivated by political ambition as she still feared – despite assurances to the contrary – that an ailing Crown Prince would not be permitted to ascend the throne. Others thought she was making as light as possible of his illness in order to prevent her husband from losing heart and renouncing his place in the succession, or perhaps even contemplating suicide.[38] Such verdicts take little account of the fact that, where the argument regarding preventing him from losing heart was concerned, this was no more than commonsense in the case of a wife who was so devoted to her husband. Only their most virulent enemies could have denied that, on a personal level, their marriage had been one of the happiest in the annals of nineteenth century European royalty.

In the first week of January 1888 his condition deteriorated again; a growth formed on the right of the larynx, he became feverish, had painful spasms of coughing, and slept badly. At one point he coughed up part of the growth, which was immediately sent to Virchow for diagnosis. It contained no evidence of malignancy, but he continued to feel wretched and depressed. By the end of the month Henry felt he was making a slow but sure recovery, writing to Willy that their father was going for good walks again and 'seemed generally in good spirits.' A few days later his next report was less reassuring; their father had 'terrifying' breathing difficulties and suffered incessant headaches. 'What is astonishing is that he still eats and drinks well, and is otherwise quite interested in remaining active, though not to the same degree as before!'[39]

On the night of 8 February his condition swiftly worsened, and his breathing became so difficult that he was in danger of suffocation. An immediate tracheotomy was decided upon and performed that afternoon by Bergmann's assistant Bramann, taking about ten minutes. Henry reported that it 'afforded poor Papa great relief', though it had been 'a dreadful day, full of unrest and nervous agitation; when the operation was over we all breathed a sigh of relief!'[40] Vicky had been waiting outside the room trembling violently, with Henry, Moretta and the widowed Grand Duke of

Hesse comforting her. When it was over she was relieved to find him looking tolerably well and smiling bravely, although he could not speak, and the sound of breathing through the canula distressed her.

The doctors had predicted that he would feel much better for a while, but in vain. His condition for the next few days was miserable. He coughed persistently, had a high temperature and no appetite, could not sleep, and suffered from constant neuralgia-like pain in the face and teeth. To the doctors' dismay he continued to cough up fresh blood through the canula. Still clinging to the belief that it was not cancer, Mackenzie and Vicky accused Bergmann and Bramann of handling the laryngoscope clumsily, and Mackenzie maintained that an obsolete instrument was largely responsible for the increased bleeding. He complained that the treatment of their patient was 'entirely in the hands of the German doctors who are unwilling to receive suggestions from me. I only remain at the urgent desire of the Crown Princess.'[41] On 21 February the German doctors threatened to withdraw from the case, but Mackenzie's canula resulted in little improvement, probably as the damage had already been done.

By now with understandable if pathetic optimism, Vicky was writing to her mother that Fritz was 'turning the corner and beginning to mend'.[42] Determined to vindicate their national honour, the German doctors could not resist the temptation to drag another colleague into the case, and on 26 February Professor Kussmaul arrived. He was not a laryngeal specialist and made an unconvincing attempt to examine Fritz's throat, declared that the lungs were quite sound, and needed no other proof that cancer was present. When Vicky told Bergmann sharply that they just needed Mackenzie to adjust the tubes and treat the throat, he told her brutally that Fritz would never recover and could only rapidly worsen. To her request that he should wait a fortnight before returning, he agreed with 'a pitying incredulous smile'.[43]

At the end of February Vicky learnt from the papers that Willy was returning to San Remo, travelling from Karlsruhe where he had just attended the funeral of his cousin Louis of Baden. As she firmly believed that he was responsible for making life difficult for her by preventing Bergmann from leaving San Remo and stirring up other members of the household against her, she felt more than usually hostile to the idea of his presence and asked him to postpone his visit. Expecting something of the sort, he telegraphed to his father that as he was already halfway there, he would come to see how he was and bring the Emperor's good wishes. An attempt to obtain official sanction for Wilhelm to go instead to the Royal and Papal Courts at Rome to thank them in person for the messages of concern they had sent the Crown Prince failed, and he reached San Remo on 2 March. Shortly after arriving, he was sent a letter from his father welcoming him but making it clear that as Crown Prince he would 'under no circumstances tolerate the slightest interference in my affairs.'[44] Wilhelm was careful to heed these instructions, and Vicky reported that 'his visit did not do any harm, and he did not meddle this time.' But 'not one word of sympathy or affection did he utter, and I was distressed to see how very haughty he has become, and what tremendous airs he gives himself!'[45]

On 6 March news arrived at San Remo that the Kaiser's strength was declining fast. Now within less than three weeks of his ninety-first birthday, he was increasingly enfeebled by a series of strokes and the end was expected at any time. Even before they had given up any hope for his recovery, the doctors had urged that the Crown Prince, soon to be Emperor, ought to spend his last days at home, and Radolinski agreed that it would be undignified for their Crown Prince to die 'like a homeless wanderer in some hotel abroad'.[46] Initially the Crown Princess insisted that it was more important for the worst of his symptoms to improve first, and that the cold of Germany would only cause a relapse; he needed another few weeks in the Italian sun to recover his strength. To Lady Ponsonby, she wrote that he had not 'sufficiently recovered to be able to bear the strain of all the business and responsibility which would suddenly fall upon him'.[47] But it was impossible to postpone the inevitable. She suggested a compromise by which they would travel to Wiesbaden in April and Potsdam in May, but after urgent warnings from Bismarck and the ministry, under the circumstances they could no longer refuse to go to Berlin.

At the Berlin Schloss the Kaiser lay on his back in a narrow camp-bed, wearing his beloved white jacket and old red scarf that had seen almost as many winter campaigns on the battlefield as he had himself. Empress Augusta, confined to a wheelchair, sat beside the husband she had never loved, while their daughter Louise and grandson Willy, soon to be Crown Prince, took their places with other members of the family as the old man breathed his last. Shortly before the end, at a signal from her mother, the Grand Duchess went to his desk and fetched the miniature that had stood there for so long, a portrait of Elise Radziwill. Placing it in his feeble hands, she watched his fingers close gently round it as a look of peace came to his face.

At 8.30 on the morning of 9 March, the bells tolled and flags were lowered to half-mast to announce that Germany had a new Kaiser.

NINE

'A mere passing shadow'

Fritz was returning from a walk in the grounds of San Remo on the morning of 9 March when he was handed a telegram from Berlin addressed to His Majesty the German Emperor and King Friedrich Wilhelm. It was from Wilhelm, to tell him that his 'adored grandfather' had just passed peacefully away. Within minutes, all the household were gathered in the drawing-room. Wearing his General's uniform and accompanied by a tense Vicky, the new Emperor entered the company, seated himself at the table, and wrote out the announcement of his accession as Friedrich III, following in the Prussian tradition. He had wanted to call himself Friedrich III, King of Prussia, and Friedrich IV, German Emperor, but Bismarck would not allow this as the other German princes might be offended by the assumption of continuity with the old Holy Roman Empire and the medieval Hohenstaufen Emperors of Germany.*

Next he removed from his jacket the ribbon and star from his Order of the Black Eagle, and pinned it onto Vicky's dress. Unable to control her feelings any longer, she fell into his arms and wept unashamedly. When she had regained her composure, he took his pad and wrote for Mackenzie to read: 'I thank you for having made me live long enough to recompense the valiant courage of my wife.'[1] Later that morning he sent Queen Victoria a telegram to express his desire for 'a close and lasting relationship between our two nations.'[2]

To his eldest son, now Crown Prince, he wrote: 'In my profound grief for my father, at whose death it was granted not to me, but to you, to be present, I make known on my accession my absolute

---

* Friedrich III of Hohenstaufen had reigned as Emperor of Germany, 1440–93; Friedrich II (the Great) was King of Prussia, 1740–86.

206

reliance on your being a pattern to all others in loyalty and obedience.'[3] Though it was a perfectly dignified, civil message as befitting a sovereign to his son and heir, Waldersee thought it went beyond 'the bounds of coldness' and indicated an unpleasant 'thoughtlessness and antipathy'.[4]

One of Vicky's first thoughts as Empress was the pathos of Fritz succeeding to the long-awaited throne 'as a sick and stricken man'.[5] Nevertheless their return could no longer be postponed, and Mackenzie warned the journey could be dangerous for his health, but Fritz replied that there were occasions when it was a man's duty to take risks. Early next day they left by train, all in mourning, and Fritz with a brown woollen scarf around his neck. They broke their journey at Leipzig for Bismarck to join them, and on the evening of 11 March they reached Berlin in heavy snow. Despite the contrast between the moderate climate of San Remo, and freezing winter conditions at the capital, Fritz had stood the journey better than expected.

He and Vicky took up residence in Charlotte's and Bernhard's apartments at Charlottenburg, which had more of a country setting than the Schloss at Berlin and was considered better for an invalid. As it was relatively secluded, people could not peer in through the windows. One of his first duties was to confirm Bismarck in his position as Chancellor. On 12 March he issued two manifestos, one addressed to his people, the other to his Chancellor. The latter, published in the *Reichsanzeiger*, summarized his aims in respect of the maintenance of peace and religious toleration, education and economic prosperity, and his resolution 'to govern in the Empire and in Prussia with a conscientious observation of the provisions of their respective constitutions.'[6] Written by Fritz himself, they were carefully worded so they would not give offence to Bismarck nor the liberals. It was proof, if any was needed, that he and Bismarck admired each others' abilities, and Vicky would have been the first to agree that neither they as individuals, nor the German empire, could do without the Chancellor.

The new Kaiser's demeanour as he received official deputations and guests who had come for his father's funeral pleasantly surprised some of those who had believed the worst they heard or read about his condition. From a distance, Prince Hohenlohe thought him looking not so much ill as thin and rather sallow, and his eyes unduly prominent; only on closer observation could one notice his suffering expression.[7] Although he was obviously very sick, and had to write on his pad instead of speaking, the sight of him as he stood before them so upright in his uniform inspired hope that he might recover after all. Yet others, shocked by his appearance, were angry with the Empress and Mackenzie for disguising the gravity of the situation by giving what they felt were falsely optimistic reports of his condition.

Increasingly impatient for the next reign, Waldersee declared that as Kaiser Friedrich was incapable of uttering a single word, and physically so weak, he would never be able to cope with the work and should abdicate. The only other alternative was for him to appoint Crown Prince Wilhelm as his deputy, which was unlikely in view of the Empress's attitude. In Waldersee Vicky had an implacable enemy, perhaps her greatest foe. To him she was the German Empire's mortal enemy, an agent of the West, democracy and the Jews, spurred on by hatred of her son; 'she wishes to create ruins before retiring from the stage and to make things difficult for the Crown Prince & inflict damage on Germany.'[8] Her husband, he was convinced, had no will of his own, and as she controlled everyone who had access to him and could be at his side at a moment's notice, she was therefore running the country. Only her fear of the Chancellor, he believed, had prevented anything 'dreadful' from happening to Germany.

Vicky was under no illusions as to their transient position, writing to Queen Victoria that she thought 'people in general consider us a mere passing shadow, soon to be replaced by reality in the shape of William.'[9] To Lord Napier she wrote, 'The trial laid upon us is a very heavy one, and it is not easy to meet it with all the courage and energy necessary. One tries to keep a stout heart, and hopes on, that things may improve! The Emperor is able to attend to his business, and do a great deal, but not being able to speak is, of course, most trying.'[10]

On 14 March Fritz saw his mother for the first time since he had left Berlin in May 1887 for London. The Dowager Empress Augusta was pushed in her wheelchair as he crossed the room to greet her, went on his knees and placed his sobbing head in her lap. When she spoke to him he tried by scribbling on bits of paper to say what he wanted, but he was dissatisfied with what he had written, and simply tore up one sheet after another in frustration.

Kaiser Wilhelm was buried on 16 March. The Prince of Wales, Crown Prince Rudolf of Austria and Tsarevich Nicholas were among foreign royalties following the hearse, drawn by six black-plumed horses to the sound of muffled drums, through the crisp snow and frost on the road to the family mausoleum. Fritz had wanted to attend, but Vicky and Mackenzie had to persuade him to stay indoors and watch the procession from the palace window. Seeing the new Crown Prince as chief mourner, he wrote on his pad, 'that is where I ought to be.' As the hearse passed beneath the window he broke down completely. Next day he attended a short funeral service in Charlottenburg chapel.

For the first few weeks his routine was arranged for him to perform a monarch's duties as far as possible without over-exerting himself. Every morning he breakfasted in bed, dressed and went downstairs about 9.30 a.m. to his study or the palace orangerie to work on state business, reading the papers, and writing letters till lunch. After eating he rested for an hour or so and then received visitors, the most regular being Bismarck. When they had gone he finished any outstanding paperwork and wrote his diary, dined at 8 p.m., and went to bed between 9.30 and 10.00. Either Mackenzie or Hovell was in constant attendance by day and within call at night if needed. Sometimes the battle against his condition proved too much, and overcome by exhaustion he would drop what he was doing, lie down on his couch and close his eyes for a few moments. But in view of his appalling headaches, fits of coughing, and the morphia he needed to sleep, his devotion to duty was outstanding. Mackenzie noticed that when he felt worse than usual he worked harder than ever; having 'an almost overwhelming sense of the duties of his position', he seemed resolved literally to die at his post. The doctor never discouraged him from working, as he knew what disappointment such a suggestion would cause, and also because he realized that mental effort sustained him and diverted his thoughts from his condition.[11] As Seckendorff wrote to Lord Napier, 'May God spare the Emperor's life! We are still very, very anxious about the state of his health, and we are most uncertain about the future; yet we must say, hope for the best and prepare for the worst'.[12]

Among the new Kaiser's first official actions was the decoration of those whom he considered had served him and Prussia loyally. Nobody objected to his making his former Chief of Staff Count von Blumenthal a Field-Marshal, but his award of the Black Eagle to Friedberg, and to Dr Simson, President of the Supreme Court of Justice, caused an outcry in Berlin, especially among the anti-Semites. Both men were of Jewish descent and it was said, especially by those who recalled Kaiser Wilhelm's anti-Semitism, that Germany was now ruled by 'Cohen I, King of the Jews'.[13] A few weeks later Fritz wanted to bestow honours on some of the more moderate Liberals in the *Reichstag*, and when Radolinski asked Bismarck whether he had any objection, Bismarck replied that it was all the same to him. Awarding honours was the monarch's prerogative and not subject to ministerial approval. However when a written application was submitted to him, he consulted the ministry of state and then said he could only agree to decorations being awarded to two of the nominees, Forckenbeck, mayor of Berlin, and Virchow. He informed the Kaiser that it had unfortunately not been possible to push the decorations through against the opposition of the ministers. Even Holstein was shocked at seeing how powerless the Kaiser was, and thought it was wrong of the Chancellor not to defer to him in minor matters under such circumstances. 'What harm would a few minor decorations have done?'[14]

At the same time Fritz wanted to leave the mark of a new era in some way by granting a general reprieve for certain political refugees and offenders, but Bismarck and the ministers brushed this aside on the grounds that it would be harmful for Germany's reputation. Fritz could hardly force his wishes through against a mass of threatened resignations, but in the end they conceded by allowing him to grant a much-curtailed amnesty.

However such threats of clashes were nothing to Vicky's trials. There were many Liberals and close friends who understood and sympathized with her, but they were in almost as precarious a position as she was. Some were guided less by loyalty than by the instinct of self-preservation, such as General Hugo von Winterfeld, formerly a trusted friend; their closest allies were watched carefully and had to be extremely circumspect in their contacts with the Emperor and Empress. Dr Ludwig Bamberger, Deputy Leader of the *Freisinnige*, was one of the most reliable of their advisers, but such was the state of intrigue in which they were surrounded that he and his sovereigns could only communicate by means of letters discreetly delivered to each other by the widowed Baroness Stockmar.

Vicky's devotion to Fritz was mercilessly attacked. Because he could not speak she had to be with him almost constantly, especially when receiving visitors, and as she always pointed out to them how well he was looking, it was asserted that she wished to convey the impression his life and therefore his reign under her influence would be a long one. Herbert Bismarck maintained that the Kaiser was a mere living vegetable, his mind completely gone, while others whispered that he was dead and the Empress was concealing the fact in a bid for power. Prince Hohenlohe remarked that if every rumour he heard was true, it would take a royal commission to protect the Emperor against the Empress.[15]

If official government circles scorned Fritz and hated Vicky, their attempts to poison the peoples' minds bore little fruit. At the end of March the weather was fine enough for him to go outside, and the heartfelt reception which greeted them as they drove from Charlottenburg to Berlin in an open carriage one sunny day was reminiscent of that which had been accorded them on their arrival in the city after their wedding thirty years earlier.

Bismarck was quick to endeavour to secure his position by means of two bills that had been passed by the *Reichstag* but were not ready for the dying Kaiser Wilhelm's signature and thus kept in abeyance for his successor. One was an extension of the anti-socialist law, aimed at expelling the Social Democrats; the second was a constitutional amendment changing the period between elections from three years to five, thus retaining the current pro-Bismarck coalition in the Reichstag for two more years. Most of the liberals thought these had been drafted with the express intention of forestalling the Emperor's liberalizing intentions and passed with undue haste. Bismarck had been used to Kaiser Wilhelm rubber-stamping bills with barely a glance, and when Emperor Friedrich requested time to consider them properly before committing himself he threatened to resign if His Majesty withheld his signature. He told the Empress that her husband had no right to refuse to sign, and was exceeding his prerogatives. If he relinquished office it would create a constitutional crisis, and he could not answer for the consequences for Germany in the next reign. No further warning was necessary. An unfettered Kaiser Wilhelm II was the last thing any of them wanted, and Vicky gave in; if her husband's signature was required according to the constitution, she conceded, it would be given immediately.

That same day Bismarck obtained the sovereign's signature to an order authorizing Crown Prince Wilhelm to sign certain bills of less importance for his father. Since Kaiser Wilhelm's death over five hundred documents had accumulated, many of them for small matters such as army promotions and appointments. Vicky offered to do these herself, but while Bismarck raised no objection to her face he disparaged the idea behind her back, saying that Hohenzollern Prussia and the German Empire could not allow themselves to be led by a woman. To him it was one step away from her trying to have herself appointed Regent, which court gossips suggested was her intention. Only when Bertie, in Berlin for the funeral, advised her that it would be unwise to press the issue, did she acquiesce in favour of her son.

There were signs of a new bond between father and son at the start of the reign. Though Fritz had been so depressed by their increasing estrangement during the previous ten years or so, in these last weeks he held out an olive branch. He showed Willy plans and elevations for a projected rebuilding of Berlin Cathedral, drawn up by the architect Herr Raschdorff, and asked him to see that these were carried out after his death.

However Willy felt that attempts were being made to prevent him from trying to visit his father, and in his memoirs years later claimed that spies were posted to give notice of his arrival at the palace, so he would be greeted with the news that His Majesty was asleep and the Empress had gone out for a walk. It was clear, he maintained, that he was being prevented from talking to his father without witnesses being present. One day he successfully slipped in by the back stairs into his father's bedroom with the connivance of a sympathetic valet, and his father said he ought to visit him more often. When Willy explained why he had not, Fritz 'was greatly astonished and described this barring-out as senseless; he said that my presence was welcome to him at any time.' On his next visit he saw various unknown faces watching from the doctors' room, and he locked the door. On leaving he expressed his indignation to his father's gentlemen, and was told that they were in no position to get rid of journalists under Dr Mackenzie's protection.[16] While Willy had every sympathy for his father, he made no secret of his bitterness towards his mother at this time. He told Bismarck, and others, that she hated him more than anything else on earth.

At Bismarck's birthday dinner on 1 April Willy made a speech comparing the state of Germany to a regiment whose general had been killed and whose second-in-command lay badly wounded, therefore the soldiers should flock to the standard of their junior lieutenant. When Fritz read a report in the papers the following day, he wrote to his son expressing sorrow that his first public speech as Crown Prince showed unequivocally 'that you regard my state of health as a hindrance to the exercise of my duties', and asking him to 'avoid making any similar speeches in the future.'[17] Willy claimed that the newspapers had misrepresented his speech and a corrected version was duly published. Fritz sent him a note stating that as he had been falsely reported, his own remarks no longer applied and he was happy to regard the matter as closed.

In another matter the Empress was determined to have her way, though the odds were against her. Shortly before Christmas 1887 Sandro, now living in Austria, had written to her that, in view of the

213

unfavourable circumstances surrounding the 'attempted betrothal' between him and her daughter Victoria, he must ask her 'to help to bring this situation to an end'.[18] Yet she thought he feared the reactions of Kaiser Wilhelm and Bismarck, and was prepared to wait.

Now that Fritz was Emperor, she still hoped that Moretta and Sandro would soon be married. Sandro wrote to his brother Henry in England, asking him to make the situation clear to Queen Victoria so she could prevail on Vicky to face the facts. The Queen duly warned her daughter not to contemplate such a match without Wilhelm's acquiescence, as it would bring misery on the young couple and place Moretta in 'an impossible and humiliating position'.[19] Bismarck warned the Empress that Prince Alexander had fallen in love with Johanna Loisinger, an opera singer at Darmstadt where he had been living as a private citizen since leaving Bulgaria, but as it was the first she had heard of it she dismissed it as malicious gossip. If only Queen Victoria, who had almost certainly known about the affair from Henry for some time, had told Vicky at once, the issue might have passed into history there and then – and all of them would have been spared much bitterness. But Vicky, worn out by the strain of the last few months, seeing her plans frustrated and persecuted at every turn, had become obsessed with the idea that Moretta would he heartbroken if she did not have her Sandro. Unwisely she tried to expedite the betrothal, even if it meant a secret marriage, flight from Germany for her daughter and new son-in-law, and a commission for him in the Austro-Hungarian army. She asked Radolinski to make the necessary arrangements, but as he considered his loyalties were first and foremost to the Prussian state he promptly informed Crown Prince Wilhelm, whose loathing for Sandro still knew no bounds, and all plans were immediately halted.

Fritz still opposed the marriage of his daughter to an ex-sovereign prince. He knew that after his death, Kaiser Wilhelm and Bismarck would exact revenge on them both, and on his wife for promoting it. Moreover with no money, no country, and no future, Alexander would not be able to keep a wife brought up in an imperial family, and he himself did not have the funds to provide a settlement for them. That there was a difference of opinion between the desperate Empress and the dying Emperor there can be little doubt, though Waldersee's allusion to 'a frightful scene between the Emperor and Empress'[20] and colourful descriptions by Radolinski and Crown Prince Wilhelm of the Emperor rending his clothes, tearing his hair, ripping the bandages from his throat, stamping his foot, pointing at the door and trying to shout 'Leave me alone!' in his hollow whisper,[21] must be regarded with scepticism.* For Fritz and Vicky to indulge in such histrionics in private, let alone in front of a third party, sounds too much like court gossip to be credible.

After consulting Vicky, Fritz invited Sandro to Berlin with the intention of discussing the marriage and bestowing on him some military command, probably that of the Brigade of Guards. According to Moretta, her father gave her his consent personally; 'I believe he planned to bring about the marriage then and there'.[22] At this point Bismarck told the Kaiser firmly that such a move would embitter Russo-German relations, and if the invitation went ahead then he would resign at once. Fritz therefore had no option but to cancel Sandro's visit.

As a private citizen Alexander of Battenberg had no direct political standing, save as a possible future threat to the Tsar's peace of mind. He was still popular in Bulgaria, where an active group of Russophobe politicians, as well as those who disliked his effeminate successor Prince Ferdinand of Coburg, wanted him back. If Alexander did marry his Hohenzollern princess, his position would be firmer and subsequent demands for his reinstatement would grow louder. Outside the family few people knew about Johanna Loisinger, and those who had heard him voice his intention of never

---

* Holstein, from whose account this report is taken, did not witness any such scene himself but based it on gossip from Radolinski and others when writing his memoirs twenty years later, by which time his memory was failing, he was seriously ill and within a few months of dying. This often-repeated tale is probably false.

returning to Bulgaria shrugged it off as the wild talk of a man who would soon forget, unaware how much his ordeals had permanently undermined his health.

Whatever Sandro's future, Bismarck protested that Tsar Alexander III of Russia would lose all confidence in his relations with Germany if the marriage went through, and even a visit by Prince Alexander of Battenberg to Berlin would be interpreted as a hostile demonstration. However when Lothar von Schweinitz, German Ambassador in St Petersburg, tried to ascertain the Tsar's feelings on the issue, a message came back that the latter said he had never been so satisfied with Russo-German relations as he was at Emperor Friedrich III's accession and proclamation. Nikolai Giers, the Russian Minister, added that if Alexander did come to Berlin, they would regret it but 'we would be convinced that neither the Emperor nor the Chancellor would change their policy of friendship towards Russia.' Taken aback, Bismarck consoled himself by muttering to the press about threats of a war with Russia that could only be to Britain's advantage. His final objection was an extraordinary belief that the Battenberg marriage was part of a plot by the Empress to make Prince Alexander German Chancellor. Though he would have been well suited to a position in the army, nobody would have thought of promoting him to the Chancellorship, an office for which he was certainly not qualified. Somehow Bismarck fancied his personal power to be in danger, and saw ghosts.[23] A suggestion that Alexander might have been considered as *Statthalter* of Alsace-Lorraine was never taken seriously.

Once Bismarck had won his victory by insisting on the cancellation of Sandro's visit, he told Vicky that the marriage might be possible one day; all he required at this stage was a postponement. Aware of her financial worries, he offered to obtain the release of nine million marks from Kaiser Wilhelm's estate for her husband to dispose of as he wished; it would give him a chance to provide for his wife and daughters, and for their dowries on marriage. The parsimonious late Kaiser had kept his son and daughter-in-law in a position of complete financial dependence throughout his reign and refused to provide for his three younger granddaughters, threatening to disinherit Moretta completely if she married Sandro. In his will he had left his widow three million marks, his son one million, a similar amount to Wilhelm and Dona, a considerable amount of landed property and all his silver to Henry, and the rest to the Crown Treasury. To his daughter-in-law and her daughters he had given nothing.

That Fritz might die before he had a chance to settle his father's inheritance and make provision properly weighed heavily on his mind. In a later audience, the Chancellor advised the Empress to invest her share of the money abroad on receipt. On 12 April the Kaiser presented her with a certificate for one million marks and their four daughters certificates for two million marks each. Having disposed of one pressing problem, she decided she would ask Fritz to insert a clause in his will instructing Wilhelm II to acquiesce in the marriage of Moretta and Sandro after his death. It was a forlorn hope.

Meanwhile Bismarck told Vicky that he must continue to give the impression he was opposing the Battenberg marriage, in order to try and keep Crown Prince Wilhelm on his side. Any disagreement between the Chancellor and the heir would result in the latter going over to the far right, and looking to pious, warmongering friends like Waldersee and Stöcker for support. This must be avoided at all costs if possible. As usual the Chancellor was playing a devious game, at the same time telling his confidantes that the Empress was a 'wild woman' who was in love with 'the Battenberger' herself, and wanted to have him around her, like her mother did with his brothers. On the same day he had an item inserted in the Berlin press that he was about to hand in his resignation over a 'secret conflict', and the next editions of the papers narrowed it down to questions of 'a family nature'. A subsequent article stated that there was some consternation in diplomatic circles over his intention of resigning because of a possibility of the Battenberg marriage taking place; as Queen Victoria and Prince Alexander were due to come to Berlin, the Queen intent on acting as matchmaker and thus taking it upon herself to interfere in the Reich's foreign policy. Germany had to preserve her disinterest regarding Bulgaria and thus the trust of

Russia and Austria, a confidence which would be destroyed at once if the Tsar's most hated personal enemy was to become the son-in-law of the German Emperor.

On 12 April Fritz had a severe attack of coughing. Mackenzie was called, and after consulting Krause and Wegner he decided to try a shorter tube. When this failed to bring more than momentary relief, he chose a different canula altogether and out of professional courtesy sent a note inviting Bergmann to come to Charlottenburg as soon as possible, to see him insert it. Bergmann arrived late in the afternoon, wildly excited and thinking from the message that an emergency had arisen. According to Hovell, who was by no means uncritical of Mackenzie, the German doctor's breath smelt heavily of alcohol, and he was swaying from side to side.

On being led into the Kaiser's room where he was writing at his desk, his breathing audible but laboured, Bergmann removed the shorter canula from his throat and replaced it with a new one. It went into the patient's neck, but no breathing came out; instead he had a sudden violent fit of coughing. The doctor tried again, in the same rough and ready manner, and with a similar result. Instead of going into the windpipe as it should have done, the canula was forced in front of it, into the neck tissues, causing heavy coughing and haemorrhage. At this second failure, just as a grim-faced Mackenzie was about to insist on taking over, Bergmann (who had been invited to watch, rather than help) conceded defeat and sent for his more capable assistant Bramann, who had been outside in the carriage waiting to be called if necessary. He replaced the canula properly, but the damage had been done; Fritz continued to cough and bleed for several hours, and Bergmann's clumsiness left him weaker than before.

That evening he asked Mackenzie to prevent Bergmann from carrying out any further operations on him. Bergmann proceeded to write to Vicky asking her rather unnecessarily to relieve him of the duty of working as Mackenzie's adviser, to which the latter's answer was equally to the point; after what he had witnessed, he respectfully warned that he would withdraw from the case altogether if Bergmann was allowed as much as to touch Fritz's throat again.[24]

Since the previous autumn Queen Victoria had been determined to visit her stricken son-in-law again. If Kaiser Wilhelm had lived a few weeks longer they might have met at San Remo, for she had arrived at Florence within a fortnight of Fritz's accession. When she publicly announced her intention of coming to Berlin, the Bismarcks were convinced this could only mean one thing. Sir Edward Malet, British Ambassador in Berlin, anxious to preserve good Anglo-German relations even if it meant appeasing Bismarck and Crown Prince Wilhelm, asked Lord Salisbury, British Prime Minister, to persuade the Queen to postpone her plans for visiting the city. With some indignation she pointed out that her journey was to have no political significance. She had come north with the sole intention of seeing her gravely ill son-in-law, probably for the last time, even before the Battenberg controversy flickered into life again.

Bismarck, the ministers, and the Emperor's household did not realize that Queen Victoria was resolutely opposed to the match. Her main objection was her grandson's attitude; Sir Henry Ponsonby reported to his wife that the Queen would only accept the marriage if the new Crown Prince would welcome Sandro as a brother-in-law. Wilhelm's recent letter to the unhappy suitor, telling him that if he married Moretta then he would consider him the enemy of his family and country,[25] made it clear that he would accord him no such welcome. The Queen was aware of Sandro's feelings about this, for on 12 March he had made it clear to Vicky that only if he succeeded in winning Crown Prince Wilhelm's approval could he foresee a happy solution.[26] His brother Henry recognised that Sandro could not possibly afford to keep a wife comfortably in his present state, let alone an imperial princess; if he tried, he would surely be expelled from Germany and ruined.

On the morning of 24 April, with Beatrice and Henry, the Queen arrived at Berlin and went straight to Charlottenburg and the sickbed. Vicky ruefully observed that it was the first time she and Fritz had had her under their own roof as a guest. Though he was rather the worse for recent sleepless nights, the sight of his beloved mother-in-law cheered him as he sat up in bed, propped up on his pillows, his weary eyes lighting up with joy as his trembling hands held out a bouquet of forget-me-nots and French fern from their garden. She sat beside the bed, holding his hand and talking about the family, while he wrote at intervals on his pad and passed it to her. Not until she was able to speak to Vicky alone did she tell her about Sandro and Johanna Loisinger, and Vicky was bitterly upset at having given her daughter false hopes. With his will, Fritz left a letter to Wilhelm dated 12 April, stating that in the event of his death, he gave his consent to Moretta's marriage and charged him as Emperor to see that it took place. In order to 'obviate any political difficulties', he renounced his wish to give Sandro an army commission or decoration.

Despite Lord Salisbury's fears that his sovereign would be exposed to fierce anti-English demonstrations in the street, Victoria was enthusiastically received every time she was seen in public. The crowds cheered her and showered the carriage with bouquets, and whenever Vicky took the seat beside her mother, shouts of 'Long live the Empress!' were evident too. The Queen's greatest success in Berlin, however, was her meeting with Bismarck, which took place at his request the day after her arrival. Malet had advised that the Chancellor would be 'greatly pleased at such attention from the Queen.'[27] While waiting for her, the mere thought of coming face to face with her made him quite ill at ease, as he fussed over little details of etiquette. Where exactly would she be in the audience chamber, and would she be sitting or standing? He was quite relieved when Ponsonby finally led him to Vicky, who escorted him to her mother a little after midday.

No reference to the Battenbergs is to be found in the published extracts from her journal.* Apart from a brief discussion of inter-

---

* It is probable that the Battenberg marriage was discussed between them. Queen Victoria's journals were transcribed for posterity after her death by Princess Beatrice, and the originals destroyed. Beatrice was Alexander's sister-in-law, and she was a particularly private person who felt strongly that such personal matters should not be handed down from generation to generation. Any discussion between Queen Victoria and Bismarck of the matter would certainly never have survived what Sir Henry Ponsonby's son and biographer Arthur called 'the blue pencil or even the scissors'.

national affairs and the possibility of war with a Franco-Russian alliance if Austria should be attacked with Germany being bound by treaty to defend her, the time they spent in conversation, a little over half an hour, was kept to relatively uncontroversial matters. Bismarck alluded to their only other meeting, at Versailles in 1855. Queen Victoria mentioned her grandson Wilhelm's inexperience, to which he replied that the Crown Prince knew nothing about civil affairs, but 'should he be thrown into the water, he would be able to swim'. She asked him to stand by her daughter and he promised he would, agreeing that 'hers was a hard fate.' Most important of all he assured her that he was not contemplating any form of Regency, as he knew it would upset the Emperor.[28] At the end the 'Iron Chancellor' walked out of the room, smiling with admiration and mopping his brow: 'What a woman! One could do business with her!'[29]

On the last day of her visit the Queen saw Fritz again as she told him that he must repay the visit as soon as he felt better. With a ready smile and a wave of her hand, she took her leave for the last time of the son-in-law on whom such a bright future had depended. She also warned her daughter that she had to reconcile herself to the fact that 'this unfortunate project', the Moretta-Sandro marriage, would never come to pass. That the Queen returned to England unsure of whether her warning had been taken to heart was evident from one of her letters four weeks later. 'I only hope you will see your way to put an end to a state of things which is quite ruinous', she advised Vicky, adding that the betrothal scheme had 'been the indirect cause of all his misfortunes', and that if Vicky and Moretta really loved him, 'you ought to set him free and spare his honourable name being assailed as it is now being'.[30]

A few days after the Queen's departure from Berlin, Bismarck publicly denounced the 'notorious' article which had attacked Queen Victoria's 'interference' *vis-à-vis* her support of the Battenberg marriage. It had been written by Moritz von Busch on Bismarck's orders, and when both men discussed this denunciation, the Chancellor smiled cynically. The article, he said, 'was really quite first rate.'[31]

During her husband's reign Vicky's own health was far from good. Under constant stress, rheumatism and headaches gave her constant trouble, and while friends were sympathetic, her enemies thought or professed to think that she was on the edge of hysteria if not madness. By April she could only sleep fitfully when exhaustion overtook her, and every morning at 6.30 she was by Fritz's side before he awoke. On stirring he mouthed the words 'tell me', and she told him 'every tiny little thing I had done, seen and heard the day before, what I had thought, hoped and imagined'.[32] At times he would feel slightly better and his temperature would subside; if the weather was warm enough, they would have a tent erected in the garden and a seat on the lawn screened by shrubs and trees, so he could lie outside and enjoy the fresh air.

Occasionally the Dowager Empress would be brought along in her wheelchair to sit by her son and talk to him in her shaking voice. Neither of them now had much in common, Augusta's interests extending little beyond court functions and the gossip which she had always loved, but Fritz was grateful for her company.

When he felt strong enough to drive into Berlin with Vicky and the girls, he had only to show himself at the railings of the palace for the crowds, anxiously awaiting each bulletin on his health, to cheer; when he ventured through the streets, his subjects would wave their handkerchiefs and raise their hats in the air in their enthusiasm for the Emperor whose life was hanging by a thread. Women threw flowers into the carriage, and mothers lifted babies or small children to catch a glimpse of his face. In recognition he raised his cap as often as his energy would permit, until a sudden coughing fit necessitated them turning off briefly into one of the city palaces for the bandage to be renewed. The widespread sympathy and admiration were testified to by the bouquets delivered daily to Charlottenburg, from expensive blooms from Berlin's most exclusive florists, to humble bunches of primroses and violets from less wealthy but equally devoted well-wishers. One morning a lady bought up the entire contents of a basket of fresh violets from a street vendor and sent them to her sovereign, and a footman came out to give her his thanks.

His mind remained clear, and he always studied the newspapers and state documents passed to him with the keen interest of a ruler determined to do his duty. He was distressed by the news of floods in East Prussia after a period of torrential rain, and though he had to send Vicky to represent him on a visit to the affected areas – the only occasion during his reign on which she left him for any length of time – he made a personal gift of 50,000 marks to help the victims. One of his plans was to alleviate slum areas in the cities by more state expenditure on housing for the poor; 'in this way part of the so-called social question would be solved'.[33] Bismarck had not neglected the lower classes either, but his own tentative steps towards socialism were motivated by absolutist principles; he rejected the idea of factory inspection and statutory limitation of working hours, preferring to establish employee insurance against accidents, sickness, redundancy and old age. This philosophy was too revolutionary for some of his contemporaries, though some of it anticipated the twentieth century welfare state, yet it was too transparent for the more discerning liberals. They saw that the Chancellor's real aim was to make workers feel more dependent on the state, and therefore on him. Fritz's honest intentions of improving social conditions had no such motives. Since his first years as Crown Prince he had discussed the socialist movement with his mother and wife, and they agreed that self-help was the best means of combating distress; one would have less to fear from the fanaticism of early socialists if one made good some of the grievances of these would-be revolutionaries. With a more liberal ministry such ideas would have been put into practice.

It grieved him to think that so much would be left undone at his death. When asked about rebuilding the Berlin cathedral, a scheme with which he and Vicky had been concerned during a previous visit to Italy, he wrote sadly on his pad that it was 'all over and done with'. At a ministerial meeting he asked the Finance Minister Adolf Scholz how long it would take the mint to produce new coins bearing his likeness. When told that they would not be ready for two or three months, he raised his hands and the look of despair on his face revealed that he knew he would not live to see them.[34]

223

Nevertheless a few of his ideas still bore fruit. He appointed an army commission to devise new rules for drill and training regulations, part of the military reforms he had planned, in time for him to give his assent, and he entrusted Henry with responsibility for choosing designs submitted for a new uniform for the imperial navy.

Bismarck's own description of his dealings with his new sovereign and consort was a masterpiece of courtliness. To Fritz's biographer Margaretha von Poschinger, he recalled in his last years that they were 'always on the best of terms', and that 'any differences of opinion between us were discussed with Their Majesties in the most friendly way.' The Empress was 'very clever and decided', while the Emperor was 'a very remarkable and estimable man, extremely amiable and friendly, yet none the less far-sighted, intelligent and decided.' The Chancellor was impressed with his monarch's kindly bearing and courage under such difficult circumstances, especially with the way Fritz always accompanied him to the door of the room after their audiences and opened it himself to let him out on taking his departure. 'One day, as he was walking with me through the room, I noticed that he was shaking with pain and weakness, and had already stretched out my arm, as I thought he was about to fall, when he managed to seize the door-knob and steadied himself. Yet he uttered no complaint and bore his pains in manly silence.'[35] He gave the impression of a man who would do what his sovereign wanted if only the ministers would let him, and though Fritz was not deceived he was too weak to argue.

In matters of foreign policy, Bismarck and Crown Prince Wilhelm were poles apart. The former was in despair over the heir's 'lust for war' and evident obsession with declaring or participating in war against Russia, convinced that he would draw his sword at once if he could.[36] Like the Emperor and Empress he was exasperated by the hawkish Waldersee and his influence on Crown Prince Wilhelm, and tried to separate the two men by finding the General a command in Hanover where he could do less mischief, but he had too many powerful allies. Vicky complained to Bismarck that nobody could approach Waldersee, as he, Moltke and Albedyll were 'sticking together like a nest of rats.'[37]

While hardly the devoted son he made himself out to be in later years, Willy had some sympathy for his parents, and one incident during his father's reign does him credit. Waldersee scoffed at the 'petticoat rule which is being exercised indirectly through the sick Emperor', and told him that it was unnecessary 'to carry out the commands sent from Charlottenburg on the part of His Majesty the Emperor . . . considering that it is well known what is the true source which inspires them'. The Crown Prince reminded him that, like all other German officers, he had sworn the military oath of loyalty to the Kaiser, which implied 'strict execution of every command' from the sovereign. If one of them was to charge Count Waldersee with attempting to seduce the brigade commander of the 2nd Infantry Brigade of Guards (the Crown Prince) into disobedience and breach of his military oath, and sentencing him to be placed in front of a sandheap and shot, he would 'execute the command to the letter – with pleasure.'[38] At last Waldersee saw he had overstepped the bounds of propriety.

However if Kaiser Friedrich was generally an object of compassion, there was little for the Empress. As Colonel Swaine, the British military attaché in Berlin, observed with sadness, it was 'as if a curse had come over this country, leaving but one bright spot and that is where stands a solitary woman doing her duty faithfully and tenderly by her sick husband against all odds.'[39] Fortunately political allies were aware of her plight, and the *Freisinnige* party member Eugen Richter gallantly came to her defence whenever the *Reichstag* was in session. On 26 May he accused the government and nationalist parties of offending the Empress in every way possible, in speech and in print. They shouted him down and tried to stop him from speaking, but he would not be deterred, and he concluded by asking Bismarck what he would do if taunted with just one-hundredth part of the calumnies she had to bear.[40] After he sat down, several of them mounted the rostrum in turn to declare that they never had the slightest desire to offend Her Majesty. When she read an account in the papers the next day, Vicky was alarmed that it might galvanize her political enemies into a new campaign of persecution against her.

She was distressed that Willy seemed to be doing everything he could to irritate them. After Bergmann stormed out of the case, the Crown Prince asked him to dinner 'as demonstratively as possible, which considering his strange behaviour, is, to say the least, not very good taste.' Their eldest son was 'in a "ring", a *côterie*, whose main endeavour is as it were to paralyse Fritz in every way.'[41]

On 24 May, Queen Victoria's birthday, Henry and Irene were married at Charlottenburg chapel. Among the guests were the Prince of Wales in his Prussian regimental uniform, the Grand Duke and Duchess Serge of Russia, and Prince and Princess Louis of Battenberg. Fritz had enjoyed helping to make arrangements and seeing to the invitations as far as his ebbing strength allowed, and welcoming the bride with her father and family the morning before, but on the day itself he was not so strong. While he waited for a signal that the family had assembled and were ready for him, the officiating clergy thought he was staying away in order to avoid overtiring himself. The court chaplain Dr Kogel was about to begin his address when the door opened and Fritz entered, wearing his general's uniform with the Hessian Order and the Star of the Garter, his collar open to facilitate breathing through the canula, and a stick in his hand for support. He took his seat quietly on the right of the altar, between his mother and Vicky. When the bridal couple exchanged rings he stood up, and as the organist played the closing voluntary he walked out unaided.

While Field-Marshal von Moltke, now a sprightly eighty-seven, paid tribute to his bravery, Herbert Bismarck told the Prince of Wales afterwards that a sovereign who could not take part in debates should not be allowed to reign. When he returned to England Bertie told the Queen angrily that he had felt like throwing the insolent young man out of the room. Official reports in government-controlled newspapers mentioned eagerly how the Empress had forced her husband to attend the ceremony, having built up his strength with wine and stimulants, and that those sitting near him in the chapel could hear his piteous gasps for breath; a quarter of an hour later they saw him in his invalid chair in plain dress, utterly exhausted.[42] Such accounts were grossly exaggerated, but the day had obviously taken its toll of his remaining strength. He had stood the occasion without so much as coughing, and afterwards he drove around the park in his pony carriage for an hour and a half, but that evening his temperature rose and he spent the following day in bed.

On 29 May Willy led his Guards Infantry Brigade in a march past his father in the Charlottenburg Palace grounds. Fritz sat watching from his open carriage in full uniform, but huddled up in his overcoat. This may have been a gesture by Willy to atone for his previous misdemeanours, but his father found it a trial to be seen in such a pitiful state by his troops, as well as a brutal reminder that he was unable to take part in this or any similar functions as a reigning Emperor. Willy later maintained that his father had requested it, while according to Vicky it was their son's idea and he 'meant well, but it was most unfortunate, for Fritz only agreed with the utmost reluctance'.[43]

On 1 June the court moved from Charlottenburg to the Neue Palais, Potsdam. Here Fritz had been born, and here he had spent nearly every summer of his married life. More than anywhere else in Germany, except perhaps for the little cottage and farm at Bornstädt, this was his home. As they travelled there on the royal steamer *Alexandria*, he lying on a couch on deck with Vicky sitting beside him, the sun shone brightly and the banks were lined by cheering crowds. It was as if the well-wishers, waving and throwing flowers, had a premonition that this would be their last sight of him. As Moretta, Sophie and Mossy welcomed them on landing and helped their father into the carriage which was to drive them to the palace, he was evidently very happy to be home at last. Just before he and Vicky walked inside, he wrote on his pad that he wanted it to be known as Friedrichskron.

Their old home had never looked more lovely to them than it did in the days following, all the more so as they knew that they had so little time left together on earth; 'the sun is always said to shine more beautifully just before setting.'[44] Fritz's sleep and appetite were poor, and meals were 'a torment'. It had been arranged that they would go to Homburg in July, but with each passing day it was increasingly evident that he would not last that long.

Yet this slow death did not put an immediate end to everything Fritz enjoyed. On warmer days he would sit or lie on the balcony and admire the view, and sometimes they would go driving around the estate to see once again the trees and flowers which they had carefully tended for nearly thirty precious years during which only their love and devotion to each other had remained the same. Indoors he continued with his work of signing documents, writing letters, and reading the papers from beginning to end, showing Vicky with his finger or pencil anything that particularly impressed him. 'What will become of me?' he asked her on 11 June, four days before the end. 'Do I seem to improve? When shall I be well again? What do you think? Shall I be ill long? I must get well, I have so much to do.'[45]

A week after their arrival at Friedrichskron he carried out the only important political act of his reign. The Minister of the Interior, the anti-Semite Robert von Puttkamer, one of the most reactionary members of the government, had been responsible for the official proclamation of Kaiser Wilhelm's death in March without any allusion to his successor, and had been implicated in a case of corruption, namely thwarting electoral reform in order to save his brother's seat in the *Reichstag*. To dismiss a colleague of Bismarck's, and a closely related one at that – Puttkamer was a cousin of Princess Bismarck – was easier said than done, but when the Chancellor asked the Emperor to sign a bill prolonging the life of the *Reichstag* from three to five years in order to maintain a recently-gained conservative majority, the latter made assent conditional on Puttkamer's departure. Fritz had won, but Bismarck held an ostentatious banquet two days later at which the ex-Minister was guest of honour. Privately the two men were too alike to be really friendly, and Puttkamer was an uncomfortable colleague whom the Chancellor suspected was waiting to step into his place, but the dinner party was little more than a deliberate act of defiance to get even with his dying master.

On the following Sunday, the choir of the Twelve Apostles Church in Berlin asked if they could sing their Emperor some choral music. It was arranged that they would stand outside his sitting-room, where he could sit and listen. When they began their performance Vicky was standing with them, but as they began an anthem Mackenzie beckoned her back, as Fritz was in tears; hearing it for the first time as Emperor had affected him deeply. When the choir had finished he wiped his eyes and, unaided except for his stick, got up and walked towards them to offer his thanks.

Even at this final stage, he could still make a physical effort when duty demanded. On 12 June his old friend King Oskar of Sweden arrived unexpectedly at Potsdam. Vicky begged him not to tire himself, but he wanted to receive his fellow sovereign properly. Putting on his uniform, which literally hung on him, carrying his helmet in one hand and leaning on his stick, he walked slowly into the sitting-room and listened for a few minutes to his guest's conversation about his recent Spanish travels. However the King did not stay long; he was appalled at his host's wasted appearance, haunted expression and greying, thinning hair. It was the last time Fritz was ever on his feet, and from then on he was confined to bed.

By now Vicky was all but overwhelmed by the change in her husband, hardly sleeping and rarely leaving his room except to hide the tears she could not hold back. On the next morning some food went down the wrong way in Fritz's throat and eventually through the canula. Mackenzie obtained a tube through which to feed him milk, but it was too late to do anything about the food which had gone into the lung, causing an inflammation and sending his temperature soaring. 'I feel so like a wreck, a sinking ship,' she wrote to Queen Victoria, 'so wounded and struck down, so sore of heart, as if I were bleeding from a thousand wounds.'[46]

One important action was not beyond him. In the afternoon he removed a key from the chain he always wore around his neck and pushed it down the front of Vicky's dress. He made his meaning clear by pointing to a small black cashbox which contained family papers. She promised to look after it, and he smiled; now all his private papers were safe. The rest had gone to London with them before the Jubilee, except for a few in a parcel which was handed by Mackenzie the next day to an American correspondent who was invited to Potsdam to collect and deliver it to the British Embassy in

Berlin. There it was passed by the Ambassador to the British Attaché, who was to ensure that it reached Windsor. It arrived there within a week, by which time these elaborate precautions were proved to have been justified.

That same day, Fritz received Bismarck for the final time. The Chancellor said he had come to discuss the matter of Puttkamer's successor, and Vicky asked him to write everything down on paper so the Emperor could read it first. After he had talked to the Emperor and was about to leave, Vicky returned to the latter's room and he beckoned them both to his bedside. Taking his wife's hand and placing it in that of their inveterate foe, he gave them an appealing look which no words could express. 'Your Majesty may rest assured,' said Bismarck, looking into his eyes, 'that I shall never forget that Her Majesty is my Queen'. But Vicky had seen too much of the man to believe she could trust him; words were only words and not promises. As she led him stiffly out of the room she saw no sorrow or sympathy in his face, instead a look of ill-concealed triumph. 'Fritz after all was finished, so why waste time in sentimental lamentations!'[47]

At 3 a.m. next day she was woken from a troubled sleep by a gentle sound in her room. Mackenzie had come to say that the Emperor's pulse had become weaker and faster, his breathing was rapid and though suffering no apparent pain or discomfort, he was in a feverish state. Going downstairs quietly so as not to wake anyone, she stood outside his door; to go in at such an unusual hour would alarm him. He was tossing about restlessly from side to side, coughing every quarter of an hour, and the air went loudly through the canula. By dawn he had improved a little, but she hardly left his bedside all day.

At 9 a.m. the three younger girls came to say good morning. It was Sophie's eighteenth birthday, and with a supreme effort her father placed into her hands the bouquet he had ordered as her present. He looked so cheerful for a moment that she thought he must be getting better. Later that day telegrams were sent to the honeymooning Henry and Irene in Silesia, and to Charlotte and Bernhard, to warn them that the worst was expected before long.

Willy and Dona came too, followed by a vast suite; they bullied Fritz's servants and chose their rooms as if they owned the place already, but Vicky was too distraught to pay them much attention. From the Berlin Embassy Malet telegraphed to Queen Victoria at Balmoral that the worst was expected within the next twenty-four hours, but reassured her that 'His Majesty's head is quite clear and he is suffering no pain.'[48]

During the night Vicky fetched a chaise-longue and placed it by his open door in the passage. There she lay during the hours of darkness, getting up from time to time to see how he was as he tossed about, coughing and struggling for breath.

On the morning of 15 June the family gathered with a sense of grim foreboding in the sickroom with the servants, some of whom never left their master's side. The appearance of Werner, who had been asked to sketch Kaiser Wilhelm's features immediately after death, was to the newspaper correspondents 'a sign more eloquent than bulletins'.[49] The German doctors showed little emotion as they waited for their master's imminent demise. Only Mackenzie, weary from working long hours and wheezing with his recurrent asthma, looked unhappy. Ironically Hovell had been called back to England a week earlier to his own father's deathbed. Fritz was not blind to the suffering of this most faithful of servants. As Mackenzie stooped over him to change the canula Fritz laid his hand gently on the doctor's chest, and though too weak to utter the words he longed to say, looked up into his face with a mute glance of tender sympathy, as if to apologise for causing him physical suffering as well.

Vicky would have given anything to spend these last moments alone with her beloved husband, but it was a privilege not granted to a reigning Emperor and Empress. He dozed for short periods, and when he regained consciousness it was usually to write with faltering hand a question on his pad, or with difficulty to mouth a few words; there was still so much he wanted to know. How was his pulse? Were the doctors satisfied with his condition? Vicky asked if he was thirsty, and when he nodded she gave him some white wine on a sponge. Then she asked if he was tired, and he nodded again.

Towards mid-morning his strength was plainly ebbing. At about 11 a.m. his eyes glazed over, and she held a light to them but he did not blink. She took his hand, but he let it drop limply. He coughed hard, took three deep breaths, gave a jerk and closed his eyes tightly as if something was hurting him, then lay still. Mackenzie turned to her to say that his last struggle was over.[50]

Almost numb with shock, Vicky took down from the wall a withered laurel wreath she had given him in 1871 and laid it on his chest, then his cavalry sabre which she placed on his arm, kissed his hands and folded them.

'The wrench is too terrible – when two lives that are one are thus torn asunder, and I have to remain and remember how he went from me!' she wrote to Queen Victoria that evening. 'Oh, the look of his dear eyes, the mournful expression when he closed them for ever, the coldness and the silence that follow when the soul has fled. . . . Now all struggles are over! I must stumble on my way alone! I shall disappear as much from the world as possible and certainly not push myself forward anywhere!'[51]

TEN

'My life is left a blank'

When Vicky left Fritz's deathbed to go into the garden for some roses to put on his bed, she saw men suddenly appearing with rifles at the ready from behind every tree and statue. An officer took her by the arm to lead her back into the house, and she was too astonished to resist. He told her he was acting on the orders of His Majesty Kaiser Wilhelm, who had to prevent important papers from leaving the house.

During the previous twenty-four hours, while his father lay dying, Crown Prince Wilhelm had filled the grounds and corridors of Friedrichskron with officers preparing for a virtual state of siege. The palace was to be sealed off from the outside world by armed guards, establishing divisions at every gate of the park. Orders were issued that not even doctors or members of the imperial family could leave without a signed permit. All outgoing letters, telegrams and parcels were to be checked and censored. The new sovereign had to be dissuaded from issuing an order for the immediate arrest of Dr Mackenzie. He had anticipated the removal of some of his parents' private correspondence, knowing that it was bound to show him in an unfavourable light, but though his soldiers ransacked every desk they could, they found nothing. Fearing something of the kind, Vicky and Fritz had ensured that everything was or would soon be safely at Windsor. General Winterfeld, formerly their devoted servant and now equally loyal to the new regime, searched his late master's desk thoroughly for written evidence of 'liberal plots' while Wilhelm likewise went through his mother's room, feverishly checking every drawer in her desk. Frustrated by his failure to find anything, he turned his attention to settling other scores. Contrary to normal practice, neither members of the clergy nor his father's family were summoned for prayers or any form of service inside the death chamber.

'Why does such pain not kill immediately?' a distraught Vicky wrote in Fritz's diary that evening.[1]

In defiance of his father's instructions and his grief-stricken mother's pleas, Emperor Wilhelm permitted an autopsy to be conducted on his father's body. He was determined to uphold the name of German medicine by proving that the diagnosis of the German doctors had always been right, and that Mackenzie was at fault. According to a hasty post-mortem, conducted with a verdict pronounced on the evidence of the naked eye, the whole of the larynx apart from the epiglottis had been destroyed and it consisted of one large, flat, gangrenous ulcer, with patches of septic broncho-pneumonia present in the lungs.[2]

General Waldersee remained graceless to the last. On the day after Kaiser Friedrich's death he wrote in his diary of the late sovereign's 'weakness' towards his wife, 'his complete submersion in her being, his absolute subjugation to her will', concluding that during his reign the Empress 'ruled over us and was quite capable of destroying Germany & Prussia.'[3] He overlooked the fact that almost everything the Emperor had tried to do, even the awarding of decorations, had been thwarted by the official world.

Whereas the funeral of Kaiser Wilhelm I had been held a week after his death in order to give everybody adequate time for preparation, the obsequies for his successor and son were hurried through three days later, on 18 June, at the Friedenskirche. Kaiser Wilhelm II sent out no invitations to other European sovereigns or princes, though as the sad event had been anticipated for several weeks, some had been chosen by their heads of state to attend and were ready to travel to Berlin at once. Among them were Bertie and Alix and their elder son Eddy, Vicky's brother-in-law Lord Lorne, her uncle, the Duke of Saxe-Coburg, and Grand Duke Vladimir of Russia, brother of Tsar Alexander III. To discourage spectators, Kaiser Wilhelm had the route of his father's funeral procession cordoned off by soldiers. Before the obsequies began, clergymen waiting for the coffin to arrive stood around talking and laughing with Herbert Bismarck. His father had returned to his estates at Varzin, too busy to pay any last respects to his late master. Vicky and her daughters wisely absented themselves from this insulting display, and held a private service of their own at Bornstädt.

Soon after the funeral the Kaiser curtly informed his mother that she would have to leave Friedrichskron, the palace she and Fritz had looked upon as home throughout their marriage. She asked if she could move to Sans Souci, a small villa in the park at Potsdam where Charlotte and Bernhard had lived, but this was refused. The Kaiser and his camarilla wanted her to go far away, she felt bitterly, in case she might try and gain some influence over him, or continually remind the public of what they had lost in his father. She was convinced that Fritz was missed less in Germany than in England. 'My beloved husband was cheered and gratified beyond measure by the affectionate sympathy shown him from England during his illness', she wrote to Lord Napier two months after his death. 'Now he is taken from us, and my life is left a blank, but I feel gratefully that he is mourned and appreciated in my own dear Home he loved so well!'[4]

Their son, she realized, was anxious to stamp his own personality on the era and ensure that his father was forgotten as soon as possible. When Queen Victoria wrote to remind her grandson that his mother was 'the first after you' as well as the first Princess after his Aunt Alix in Britain, he replied defensively that he was doing his utmost to fulfil his mother's desire for a country home, but he needed Sans Souci to offer his visitors hospitality. The other palaces in Potsdam belonged to Empress Augusta, and only reluctantly did he concede that his mother could stay at Friedrichskron as a temporary measure.

His attitude regarding the provision of a roof over her head was remarkably mean. If his treatment was calculated to make her so uncomfortable that she might even consider leaving Germany, he was going the right way about it, and in her darkest moments she suspected he would like to drive her away. His father had ensured that Empress Augusta would never need for anything; she had palaces in Berlin, Potsdam, and Koblenz, with their upkeep paid for by the crown, and an annual revenue of four million marks. Vicky was given her own palace in Berlin, and the Villa Liegnitz, the latter only temporarily, until he told her it must be vacated as his gentlemen-in-waiting would need it as a place to stay when they were in attendance on him. She was expected to maintain them herself out of an inheritance less than one-sixth of that provided for her mother-in-law, and had to fall back on her English dowry, which had helped to cover household expenses during her marriage, as Fritz was never well provided for until his accession. Though the income from the crown estates had been paid to him as Kaiser, his three months' reign had given him no chance to build up any substantial capital to bequeath her. After his accession in March he had signed an order specifying that the living allowance for his mother and Vicky after his death should be increased, but when this mandate was published after his death, the normal proviso stating that the salaries of Vicky's entourage should be paid by the crown was missing.

Baron Reischach, head of her household, asked the head of the Privy Council to suggest to Kaiser Wilhelm that he should provide a living allowance for his mother proportionate to that granted to his grandmother. This was declined with the excuse that His Majesty was incurring considerable expenditure on his visits to European courts and on his forty-eight castles, and he could not be expected to increase his mother's allowance as well. He also required a large amount to refurbish Friedrichskron, his father's old home, which on his orders reverted to its old name of Neue Palais. Any reminders of the brief reign of Kaiser Friedrich III had to be ruthlessly swept aside.

On 24 September she wrote to Queen Victoria that she was 'sadder than ever, worn, worried & badgered. The sum that Fritz wanted me to have, to buy myself a place – and which they had as good as *promised* me in June – I am not going to have. The Hausministerium say the crown cannot afford it. Wilhelm did not even say he regretted it, & seemed to think it quite natural! I am glad in one way, as the less I am under obligations to the present system the better pleased I am, independence is a grand thing. How I shall get the place now, I do not yet know, but I think the Hausministerium will lend money at a low rate of interest &c.'[5]

A few days later she was almost at her wits' end. On the anniversary of her engagement, 29 September, she was particularly depressed, feeling she had nothing to hope for, except a chance that one day the truth about her and her husband and all they tried to do for Germany would come out. 'This is our dear "Verlobungstag" – 32 [*sic*] years ago! Oh how it wrings my heart! How I pine & long for him, & for his kind words & looks, & for a kiss! It is all gone – & over. Day by day I feel more lonely & *unprotected*. No one to lean on, and the difficulties I have to face alone are really too terrible. Yesterday I felt very *near putting an end* to myself!'[6]

Not before time, she had one stroke of good luck in her first few months as a widow. During the Franco-Prussian war she had spent some time at Homburg, the former home of her great-aunt Elizabeth, Landgravine of Hesse-Homburg, near the Taunus mountains in an area famed for its considerable natural beauty. A villa that had belonged to a wealthy wholesale tea-merchant came up for sale, and she was also left a substantial legacy by her friend the Duchess of Galliera. With this she bought the villa and 250 acres of land surrounding it, had it demolished and commissioned the building of a new Schloss on the site, under the supervision of the architect Ernst Eberhard von Ihne. All this happened just in time, for a few days after the purchase was completed Wilhelm ordered her out of the Villa Liegnitz.

While her new home was being built, she had to live in the old palace at Potsdam during the winter (though she had to ask special permission each time), her dower house in the Schloss at Bad Homburg during summer, or her little farmhouse at Bornstädt. Permission was denied her for any modernization of the house at Homburg, surrounded by rubbish and weeds growing up to the front door, with no heating, drainage or indoor plumbing. She asked for these to be installed, only to be told that His Majesty could not afford to do so as he still needed to refurbish his palaces. Within five months of his accession he had demanded and received an increase to his annual income of six million marks, part of which was required to convert a warship into an imperial yacht, *Hohenzollern*. If his mother was not satisfied with her house, she was informed, she could remain in the palace at Berlin.

Though she and Fritz had sent over most of his papers to England in the last twelve months and burnt others, she was advised to ask Queen Victoria to return everything only a month after Fritz's death. Friedberg, one of the few men still loyal to her, convinced her that it was essential to prove to the government that in doing so she had not removed German state property. Back came the numerous boxes from England to Berlin, but Fritz had left them all to Vicky in his will. When Friedberg was obliged to inspect them, he confirmed that they were not state documents but personal papers for her to do with as she liked.

Her wish to have documentary evidence to put the record straight was prompted by a pamphlet war which soon broke out. Less than a month after Fritz's death, a broadside was written by Bergmann and Gerhardt (but significantly excluding the more politically liberal Virchow), defending themselves and attacking Mackenzie for not consenting to an immediate operation on the then Crown Prince Friedrich Wilhelm's throat. Two weeks later an article appeared in a government paper stating that Kaiser Friedrich had declared he would not ascend the throne if it could be proved that he was suffering from an incurable illness, and claiming that those close to him, namely his wife and Dr Mackenzie, had tried to deceive him as to his real condition.

Rather against his better judgement, Mackenzie was persuaded to answer it with his angry book *The Fatal Illness of Frederick the Noble*. On publication in October 1888 it was an instant success in terms of sales; 100,000 copies were bought in Britain within a few days, and a similar print run was commissioned by the German publisher who outbid more than thirty rival firms to issue a German translation, but his entire stocks were confiscated by the imperial police. To Vicky this was 'a perfectly despotic proceeding worthy of St Petersburg'.[7] Its popularity cost the author dearly, for in London he was censured by the Royal College of Physicians and the Royal College of Surgeons for airing sickroom secrets in public. Most of his detractors were jealous or resentful fellow physicians who thought him too keen to advertise himself, and few if any of them had made an effort to read the German pamphlets against which he was attempting to vindicate himself.

The medical controversy was nothing to the affair of Fritz's war diary. After the Franco-Prussian campaign he had showed some of his writings to Heinrich Geffcken, a friend from university days and now Professor of Political Science at Strasbourg. With his approval Geffcken had copied extracts for his personal use, and by September 1888 he was so angered by the continued posthumous attacks on his late sovereign and friend that he published them in the *Deutsche Rundschau*. At last the public were made aware of their late Emperor's nationalist beliefs, his passionate desire for German unification, and his role in the founding of the German Empire, especially in the face of Bismarck's hesitation. Geffcken was arrested and charged with treason, but no case could be brought against him and he was released from prison three months later. Nevertheless it marked the beginning of a savage witch-hunt against the late Emperor's partisans, derided as conspirators against the welfare of Germany. Roggenbach, Morier and others suffered similar persecution, their houses were broken into, and their private correspondence seized. Morier, now ambassador to St Petersburg, was accused of having betrayed military secrets from the then Crown Princess of Prussia to one of the French commanders in 1870, thus enabling the French to inflict heavy losses on the German forces in a surprise attack during the Franco-Prussian war. Sadly he received no support in defending himself against this libel from Sir Edward Malet, the British ambassador in Berlin, who in his eagerness to prove accommodating to the new regime was evidently prepared to sacrifice Morier's reputation on the altar of Anglo-German relations.

With a few notable exceptions, most of Vicky's relatives in Germany had unhesitatingly thrown in their lot with Kaiser Wilhelm and Bismarck. Though she still cordially disliked the new Empress, her sister-in-law, the wayward Ditta fawned on her elder brother; she and her husband Bernhard told others it was their mother's fault that Wilhelm and Dona had not been permitted to take their rightful places at Queen Victoria's Jubilee, as she had prevented Wilhelm from representing his grandfather. The Duke of Saxe-Coburg, a fervent disciple of Bismarck, sanctioned (if he did not actually write) a couple of anonymous pamphlets accusing her, Fritz and Queen Victoria, as well as Morier, of treason against Germany and colluding with France during the Franco-Prussian war.

Dowager Empress Augusta gave the impression of being quite unaffected by her son's death, and did not allow mourning to interfere with her social programme. Though wheelchair-bound, she still ruled her attendants with a rod of iron and her sharp tongue, keeping up appearances and attending all receptions and parties given in her name as far as possible. She had always spoilt her eldest grandson, and made a point of asking his permission every time she intended to go from one residence to another. In turn Wilhelm and Dona made a great show of asking her opinion on various domestic and procedural matters, making it obvious that to them Vicky's opinions were not worth knowing. She lamented bitterly that as far as the three of them were concerned she might as well not exist.

Thankfully there were exceptions to this roll of dishonour. Her widowed brother-in-law Louis, Grand Duke of Hesse, had been deeply saddened at the 'quite incomprehensible' way the political establishment of Prussia had moved so quickly to efface any memory of Fritz, and assured her that he for one had not altered his political principles; 'when I can do anything to propagate Fritz's views I will do so', adding that he had to take care not to do anything that would bring down reprisals on his duchy.[8] His third daughter Irene, now Vicky's daughter-in-law, had done much to make Henry more amenable to his mother, and he no longer felt obliged to side with his brother against her, against his better judgment.

Queen Victoria had urged her daughter to come back to England for a visit ever since Fritz's death. The British Prime Minister Lord Salisbury cravenly suggested it was too soon, and that it would undermine Anglo-German relations, but the Queen retorted that it would be 'impossible, heartless and cruel' to prevent her daughter from coming back, and only encourage the Bismarcks and the Emperor in their disgraceful behaviour towards her.[9] On 19 November Vicky and her *Kleeblatt* or trio, Moretta, Sophie and Mossy, arrived in England for three months. Queen Victoria sent the royal yacht *Victoria & Albert*, with Bertie and his second son

George on board, to Flushing to meet them and accompany them on the crossing to Gravesend. Though as a matter of course the Queen normally never went further than her front door when welcoming even her most exalted guests to England, this time she made the journey to Gravesend to meet her daughter draped in crêpe, trembling with grief, a thick black veil concealing the tears running down her face. Her granddaughters on board the yacht were equally overcome when she landed. Nothing was too much trouble for the Queen's eldest daughter whose brightest hopes had been dashed so tragically, and she hoped that when he heard of this reception Kaiser Wilhelm would be shamed into treating her with more respect when she went home. Two days later there was a family gathering to observe her first birthday since being widowed, with a present table laid out with gifts, as there always had been in her childhood. The Queen's present was a generous contribution towards a mausoleum for Fritz at the Friedenskirche.

The Queen had always been ready to make allowances for her firstborn grandchild, but even her remarkable patience with him had come close to snapping after his high-handed refusal to meet the Prince of Wales at Vienna the previous month. She agreed with Lord Salisbury that Anglo-German relations should not be affected by 'miserable personal quarrels', but 'with such a hot-headed, conceited, and wrongheaded young man, devoid of all feeling, this may at ANY moment become *impossible*.'[10] However she knew that there must be no deepening of the rift between mother and son, and while Vicky was in England they had long conversations during which she tried to soften her resentment and anguish. The Queen appreciated, and Vicky realized in her heart of hearts, that Wilhelm was not fundamentally evil, so much as thoughtless, weak and easily swayed by others.

The time she and her daughters spent in England did them much good. 'It has been a great boon and blessing to me to have been allowed to spend these months here in beloved England with the Queen, whose goodness and kindness and sympathy helps me to bear the heavy burden of bitter sorrow and bereavement laid upon me!' she wrote to Lord Napier in February. 'I shall want much strength and courage to live on, now that the light and joy has passed from my life, and its object has gone, its hopes buried. But if it be God's will I should remain yet in for a while, to struggle on alone, I must try and turn my time to good account, and be what little use I can to my 3 dear girls, left without a father at this age, when they most wanted him!'[11]

Slowly but surely she began to regain her perspective, and could even make sardonic jokes about herself. To the end of her days she wore mourning for her husband, and in accordance with German custom she had a peaked cap with two long streamers hanging down the back. One day while in England she met her old friend Lord Ernle; during their meeting she accidentally sat down on one of the streamers and pulled it slightly out of shape. As she straightened it out afterwards she remarked how glad she was that she had not done so in Berlin, as otherwise 'the whole press would have shouted that I had insulted the national mourning'.[12] Nevertheless it was surely the saddest, most difficult journey of her life when she and her daughters had to return to Berlin.

Kaiser Wilhelm was desperate to be forgiven and invited to England himself, and with some misgivings the Queen asked him to come the following summer. In the process she had to receive his advisers, many of whom had behaved disgracefully to Vicky. If the widowed Empress felt bitterly hurt at what looked like a change of loyalty, or jealous of her son, she could hardly be blamed. Yet the British government felt obliged to put state expediency before the personal feelings of the royal family by building bridges between England and Germany. Her son and his entourage, who had denounced her and Fritz for being too friendly to England, were now doing exactly the same. It was a cruel reminder of what she had lost, and of what had been denied to her husband. Without him she could not even be an ambassador for the country or empire over which he had reigned so briefly. She had to accept that she was no longer of any significance in diplomatic relations between both countries, and neither Queen Victoria nor the Prince of Wales, the two closest members of her family, were officially obliged to treat her as of political importance, though in private they showed her every courtesy. As she had written on the first evening of her widowhood, 'I shall disappear as much from the world as possible and certainly not push myself forward anywhere!'[13] It was not easy for a German Dowager Empress, the eldest child of the Queen of England, to 'disappear'. Yet unlike her mother, she was no reigning monarch, but a foreigner ostracized by the political establishment of the day, reminded that she was a foreigner, and not considered an asset to Germany.

Vicky's *Kleeblatt* were an ever-present personal support during these dark days. The news that Sandro had closed an unhappy chapter for them all by his marriage to Johanna Loisinger in February 1889 came as a relief to all concerned, though he was a sick man, destined to die of peritonitis some four years later at the age of thirty-six. By this time Sophie was betrothed to Constantine, Crown Prince of Greece, and Vicky was among those who went to Athens for the wedding on 27 October 1889. The occasion brought sadness to Moretta, whom her mother feared might become an old maid after the thwarted romance with Sandro. Vicky was also deeply affected by the breaking up of the trio, and decided that returning to Berlin straightaway would be too miserable for all of them. Instead mother and spinster daughters went to Rome to spend the rest of the winter. The climate was mild, King Umberto and Queen Margharita treated them like members of their own family, and they were thoroughly enjoying themselves when sad if not unexpected news arrived from home.

On 7 January 1890 the Dowager Empress Augusta succumbed to influenza, aged seventy-eight. They returned to Berlin for the funeral at once, and Vicky went to see her mother-in-law for the last time, lying in state in the Schloss chapel, her palsied body wrapped in her ermine and gold cloak with a wedding veil on her head. She looked calm and peaceful, even young, Vicky thought; 'the eyes that used to stare so and look one through and through were closed, which gave her a gentle expression I never saw in life.'[14]

The elderly Empress had left her daughter-in-law a characteristically small-minded legacy. During her lifetime Augusta had been the nominal head of the German Red Cross, but had shown no inclination for or interest in the work unlike Vicky, who had every reason to expect Wilhelm to ask if she would take the Empress's place. It would have been a chance for Wilhelm to fulfil the promise he had made to Queen Victoria during his state visit to England – to do something to please his mama. But Augusta had already offered Dona the position, without telling Vicky. The snub rankled deeply, for Dona knew nothing at all about the work, whereas Vicky herself already had years of experience.

She consoled herself with seizing the opportunity to 'do good' and stop herself from brooding by looking after her charities, particularly the founding of a children's hospital with a sum given her in Fritz's memory by the citizens of Berlin, and lending her name and presence to fund-raising bazaars in the capital. If she gave the impression of being determined not to be consoled, it was because she intended to keep her husband's name and ideals before the nation. In a sense, she was in perpetual mourning for the Germany that was never allowed to flourish because of his untimely death, and their dreams that never came to fruition. There could have been little greater contrast than that between her mother-in-law Augusta, who was admittedly sick and disabled by the time she was widowed and had less than two years to live, yet threw off all mourning as soon as possible and conveniently put aside her liberal principles, and Vicky, who held steadfast to her values – and suffered for it. Had Kaiser Wilhelm shown or allowed some kind of respect for his father, it would have eased her path. When her old adversary Bismarck resigned the Chancellorship in anger in March 1890 after a series of disagreements with Wilhelm, she felt no sense of elation, believing he had been dismissed for the wrong reasons, at a time when he could still have been of benefit to Germany and a guarantor of peace throughout the empire.

Appearances at functions in Berlin were a painful duty. She attended family dinners at the Schloss with great reluctance, as they made her feel so miserable. 'There are so many things which make one feel so sore, that aggravate and wound one and rub one up the wrong way, that one would wish to run away and hide oneself and let one's life flow on in peace. . . . No one feels for one or grieves or understands what one is going through. So much is said and talked which one so completely disagrees with and yet it is best to keep one's opinion quite to oneself.'[15] On 21 November 1890 Vicky celebrated her fiftieth birthday, a landmark not even her son could ignore. He gave a luncheon for her at the Schloss, though it was conducted in some haste as the gentlemen in attendance were anxious to get to another Court event immediately afterwards.

Two days earlier Moretta had been married to Prince Adolf of Schaumburg-Lippe, a good-hearted if uninspiring army officer distantly related to the Württemberg royal family. The wedding was overshadowed by an argument between Sophie and her brother. As wife of the heir to the Greek throne, she had announced she would enter the Greek Orthodox Church. In his capacity as head of the family, Kaiser Wilhelm vowed to forbid her to do such a thing, and if she persisted in doing so without his permission she would be barred from setting foot in Germany ever again. He entrusted the task of telling her to Dona, who was *enceinte*, as he assumed that Sophie would not dare to argue with his wife while she was in such a condition. Sophie firmly told her sister-in-law to mind her own business and was duly banished from Germany for three years.

Early in 1891 the Kaiser decided it was time to try and improve Franco-German relations. Having alienated Russia over the Reinsurance Treaty, he was faced with the likelihood of an alliance between two powerful hostile neighbours. He had never revised his unfavourable opinion of France as a nation, and the previous year he had refused to let his mother and sisters visit Queen Victoria while she was in Aix-les-Bains, on the grounds that he was duty-bound to uphold a law passed by his grandfather in 1887 forbidding any prince or princess of the Prussian house to cross the French frontier without the Emperor's consent. However Vicky had been a regular visitor to Paris, and as a patron of the arts she would be less likely to attract hostility than him. He asked her to go and invite French artists in person to participate in an international art conference to be held in Berlin. When it was suggested by her old friend Count Münster, now German ambassador to France, she was so delighted to have a chance to be of use at last that she did not realize her son was using her to pull national chestnuts out of the fire.

Accompanied by Mossy, she arrived in Paris on 19 February 1891. A small but vociferous right-wing nationalist group in Paris, eager to make political capital out of her presence in order to discredit Germany, watched her carefully. When she paid discreet visits to Versailles and St Cloud, scenes of happier days in 1855 when she and her parents had visited the Emperor and Empress, but later of national humiliation and defeat for the French, the press claimed she had gone out of her way to insult France. The painters who had accepted invitations to exhibit in Berlin were accused of dishonouring their country, and when the German press replied in kind, feeling between both countries rose to such a pitch that Vicky and her daughter were advised to leave France at once. Though Count Münster had discussed the itinerary with her and accompanied her everywhere, he made no effort to defend her, and joined Kaiser Wilhelm in letting her take the blame for everything. She consoled herself with the reflection that 'an impertinent set of mischief-makers who do *not* represent French public opinion one bit'[16] had been responsible, but it was a sad end to what would always remain her last role in representing Germany abroad in even a semi-official capacity.

Mossy had been her mother's constant support since Moretta's marriage, but Vicky would not dream for a moment of clinging to this youngest daughter, or insisting that any man she married would have to be prepared to make a home for himself and his wife with her, as Queen Victoria had done with Beatrice and Henry of Battenberg. At one stage there had been talk of a betrothal with the Tsarevich, or with her cousin Eddy, Albert Victor of Wales, Duke of Clarence, who had succumbed to influenza in January 1892 shortly after becoming engaged to May of Teck. These schemes, and an unreciprocated passion on her part for Max of Baden came to nothing, and in the summer of 1892 she was betrothed to Friedrich Karl (Fischy), son of Friedrich Wilhelm, Landgrave of Hesse. A cultivated, serious-minded young man, he proved a perfect partner for Mossy, and they were married in the Friedenskirche, Potsdam on 25 January, Vicky's own wedding anniversary. The date brought back the saddest of memories, especially after the young couple had left on their honeymoon. Two days later she poured out her heart in a letter to Sophie, who had been unable to attend. Thinking of her own nuptials, she 'had a heart-sick longing for dear Papa, to be able to throw my arms around his neck and say, now we are alone, in the house together once more, as we were when we were bride and bridegroom. But all was silence around me.'[17]

By the spring of 1894 Vicky's home, Friedrichshof, was ready. The name had been suggested by Moretta, and the words *Frederici Memoriae* were carved over the main entrance porch. She had thoroughly enjoyed the four years during which it had been under construction as she watched her architect and workmen fashioning a country house in the way she had wanted. They soon knew better than to do anything without her approval, and regarded her with a mixture of irritation and admiration when she never hesitated to correct them, explain something or even seize a tool and show them exactly how it had to be done. Regardless of the weather she was outside, supervising and inspecting to make sure everything was or would be in the right place. She paid meticulous attention to the trees and shrubs best suited to the local soil and climate, planning carefully the locations of the rose gardens, rockeries, ponds and lawns, though she was so enthusiastic about choosing trees that there were far too many for the limited space, and several of them grew stunted.

The first day she spent at Friedrichshof, she wrote to Sophie, was extremely tiring, and there would be several more weeks of work before everything was in order. 'What will you say when you see all you used to call the 'dirty, ugly, horrid old rubbish' which I used to collect on journeys, to your utter horror and despair and contempt now placed about the house?'[18] She regretted that her daughters never appreciated her insatiable appetite for collecting paintings, autographs, coins, medallions, objets d'art and old fossils. The sheer extent of her collections was not the least of her problems. When she began arranging her personal library formed since childhood, including many books personally dedicated to her, there were barely enough shelves to place a third of them properly, though the plans had looked adequate on paper. Her photographs alone, all carefully annotated, took up about 300 albums.

Later that summer she was writing with enthusiasm to Sophie of the horses in the stables, the cows and new-born calves in the fields, and the meadows filled with wild flowers. Every afternoon she came home with an armful of heather and flowers from the hedges and sides of the ditches, baskets and pocket handkerchiefs filled with blackberries and mushrooms; 'you see your Mama is still like a baby over these things!'[19] When she had to leave Kronberg every autumn she found the departure sad, and when she was travelling she felt 'like a mussel without its shell.'[20]

Now she had a home of her own in Germany purchased with her personal funds, her sense of martyrdom lessened. Nevertheless her experiences had undoubtedly aged her, and photographs taken during the last years show a woman who looked rather older than her mid-to-late fifties. As a small girl Meriel Buchanan, daughter of Vicky's friends Sir George Buchanan and his wife, recalled 'a very old lady, always dressed in the deepest black, bearing a strong resemblance to Queen Victoria, her hair, which had lost its former bright colour, parted in the middle and brushed plainly back from her face.'[21] Unlike Queen Victoria, Vicky did not suffer from lameness, remained an indefatigable walker until her last illness, and though she had inherited the family tendency to run to fat, never became as large around the waistline as her mother.

Under her own roof, she seemed much younger in spirit. One friend recalled her regularly going upstairs and downstairs more like a young girl than a woman of her age, and when she greeted the company assembled at table, 'every compulsion of etiquette seemed to be instantly removed.'[22] Dressing for dinner one night, Lady Georgina Buchanan was startled to be interrupted by her hostess who walked in unannounced. Vicky explained that she had come to make sure that everything was in order in her room, and then roared with laughter as she saw she had not chosen her moment too well. 'Don't be so shy, Lady Georgina,' she reassured her. 'What does it matter if you are only half-dressed?'[23]

At the same time the tone of her letters improved. She was no longer at the whim of a son who could eject her from 'his' residences, and slowly but surely old wounds were healing. By 1896 she could write to the Queen that her personal relations with Willy were good; 'he is quite nice to me, and I have forgiven him with all my heart the cruel wrong he did me'.[24] She was almost pathetically grateful for the small things that he did to give her pleasure, and such consideration as he showed her from time to time. Yet she had to admit that they seldom met and she still felt a complete outsider, unable to do any good (she was always modest about her charity work) and anxious about the future. His blundering follies and inane behaviour made her fear for the consequences for Germany, if not for Europe, under his rule. It was impossible not to think, if not to dwell, on what might have been.

Like his doctors and a few of his close friends, she dreaded the threat to Willy's mental stability. The last years of her great-grandfather, King George III, had been blighted by porphyria or, as everyone believed then, madness; in the first few weeks of widowhood her mother had feared losing her reason; and her second cousin Charlotte, widowed Empress of Mexico, had been confined for nearly thirty years bereft of her reason. In March 1888, the month of Fritz's accession, the British surgeon John Erichsen had seen confidential notes from the then Crown Prince Wilhelm's surgeon, expressing grave fears about his mental balance. While it was unlikely that he would become insane, he would always be subject to 'sudden accesses of anger', incapable at times of 'reasonable or temperate judgment', 'some of his actions would probably be those of a man not wholly sane', and his accession might be a danger to Europe.[25]

Vicky had few illusions about the course on which her son was set. With remarkable foresight, she confided her fears to Frau von Stockmar in 1892. The sovereign, she said, 'should help in building up a strong, firm and sound edifice on a broad foundation, if Germany is not to slip down the steep path which leads to a Republic or even a Socialist state. The latter could never last, there would be chaos, then reaction, dictatorship and God knows what further damage.'[26] On a visit to Palermo at around this time, Donna Laura Minghetti, stepmother of the future German Chancellor Bernhard von Bülow, was struck by her look of intense sadness. She explained that she mourned not only for her dear husband, but also for Germany. With a fixed stare, she went on to tell her firmly, 'Mon *fils sera la ruine de l'Allemagne.'* ('My son will be the ruin of Germany.')[27]

Even after settling at Friedrichshof, Vicky continued to spend part of the winter at Berlin, more out of duty than inclination. She liked to keep an eye on her various charities, notably the Victoria Haus for retired British and American governesses, and children's hospitals, and at the same time she found it easier to see her professor, politician, writer and artist friends in the capital. However she disliked the city and never felt really well or comfortable there; 'I shrink so from all that is show and ostentation and which forces one into public when one's feelings seem so sacred that one cannot bear to be amongst a quantity of people, some most well-meaning and others who have behaved so ill and now make a show of loyalty, the hypocrisy of which makes me sick'.[28]

As ever she found solace in visits to Britain, and her informality sometimes led to anxious moments for the family and court. At Osborne in 1896 the Queen's equerry Frederick Ponsonby was awaiting her arrival when told that a German gentleman was anxious to see him. A man was ushered in and explained in broken English that he had to see the Empress immediately on her arrival. As soon as Her Majesty arrived, Ponsonby said, he would give his card to Count Seckendorff, who would arrange an interview. The man insisted he must see the Empress the moment she stepped ashore. Fearing he was either an anarchist or an escaped lunatic, Ponsonby sent a message to the detective at the gate, telling him that a German passing by in a few minutes had to be watched. A plain-clothes policeman who followed him reported that he was staying at the Medina Hotel, and seemed quiet and respectable if eccentric in his habits, but surveillance was maintained. The next day Vicky arrived, and when she got into a carriage with Princess Beatrice and drove off Ponsonby was astonished to see her wave and kiss her hand to the man as she passed. He was an eminent sculptor from Berlin and an intimate friend of hers, she had told him she would see him the instant she set foot in England and he had taken it literally.[29]

Her literary tastes and passion for books never ceased to amaze the family and court, as well as provoke arguments. On another visit to Osborne, Lady Ponsonby wrote to her husband of the Empress carrying off six books at a time and finishing them off in a couple of days. Both women regularly discussed their reading matter, and both were forthright personalities who might accept each others' views with some reluctance. When Lady Ponsonby defended a book she had just read, the Empress 'listened now and then, but puts on a second-century look which rather prevents one going on.'[30] A discussion at dinner between Queen Victoria and her eldest daughter at Balmoral on the subject of novelist Marie Corelli proved an even more lively occasion. The Queen thought she was one of the greatest writers of the day, while the Empress called her work 'trash'. To support her argument she asked Frederick Ponsonby for his opinion. Unaware that his sovereign was such an admirer, he said that notwithstanding the popularity of Corelli's books, he thought the secret of her success was that her writings appealed to the semi-educated. The Empress clapped her hands and the subject was instantly dropped.[31]

Count Seckendorff had remained at the head of her household, as devoted as ever. As a gifted draughtsman who shared her love of art, he particularly enjoyed their expeditions abroad when both would sketch or paint side by side in the open air. A belief persisted in certain sections of Berlin society until his death in 1910 that he and the Empress Frederick had shared much more together, that they had been lovers or even secretly married. The liberal journalist Maximilian Harden published a tribute after her death in which he referred to her resting in the Friedenskirche, Potsdam, beside her *first* husband; and 'a celebrated old general', who had been a friend of Fritz, once remarked that he was convinced that the widowed Empress had married Seckendorff, as he was 'a very charming gentleman and their tastes harmonise in everything.'[32]* Yet Vicky had loved Fritz passionately, and the possibility that she could have

---

* That the general is not named, and that the memoirs in which this story was quoted were based on the diary of a 'German court official' who died in 1914 and published anonymously in 1929, suggest that the story lacks authenticity.

secretly taken a second husband cannot be taken seriously. When discussing similar gossip with her maid of honour Marie de Bunsen, regarding a theory that Baron Roggenbach and a princess of Wied were husband and wife, she dismissed it at once. To her it was merely 'an unusually beautiful friendship, but of course people can't be induced to believe it.'³³

In 1897 Vicky returned to England for her mother's Diamond Jubilee festivities. She was saddened by the absences of those who had attended the Jubilee celebrations of ten years previously; Fritz, the Duke of Clarence, Grand Duke Louis of Hesse and Henry, Beatrice's husband, were all sorely missed. Nevertheless she wrote excitedly to Sophie of the celebrations, London streets beautifully decorated, immense crowds and tremendous enthusiasm, and the impressive scene in front of St Paul's. It was good to be among family once again, though Buckingham Palace was 'like a beehive, the place is so crammed we do not see very much of one another.'³⁴

In September 1898 she was riding with Mossy when her horse took fright at a threshing machine and threw her off. Her coat caught in the pommel as she fell, and though her head and shoulders were on the ground, she was badly shaken but otherwise only bruised by the horse treading on her hand. She made light of the accident, and the doctors confirmed that her injuries were only superficial. For a few days she was confined to her room with a temperature and a swollen arm, restlessly moving from bed to sofa to keep the aches and pains at bay.

A few days later she went to Breslau for the wedding of her granddaughter Feodora to Prince Henry XXX of Reuss. Horrified by the recent assassination of her friend Elizabeth, Empress of Austria, stabbed by an anarchist in Geneva, she was already in low spirits. On the way she was unwell with severe lumbago, and the ceremony was further overshadowed by the absence of the Kaiser. His presence at manoeuvres nearby did nothing to dispel the impression that a rift between himself and Ditta had never healed, following a scandal at court some six years previously in which an indiscreet diary of hers containing 'secrets' about her brother and the Empress had been lost or stolen and fallen into his hands.

Later that month she went to Balmoral for what proved to be her last visit to Britain, but she was in such pain that she could only find relief in long walks which exhausted her ladies-in-waiting. While there she received confirmation from the doctor that she had cancer, which was too advanced to be operable. As Fritz had done eleven years earlier, she received the verdict with courage. She had survived a desperately unhappy period of widowhood, calumniated and ostracized beyond measure; she had built her own home in Germany, and found some peace of mind with family and friends; she had had the time to enjoy her collections of books and arts, to look after her charities, to see all her surviving children married, and welcome several grandchildren into the world. Yet the Germany of the day was not, and never would be, the empire that it might have been had it not been for her husband's untimely death. At first she told nobody of her illness but her mother, Bertie, and Beatrice. An attack of dizziness alarmed her while she was visiting friends near Edinburgh, but otherwise she had no premonition of anything being seriously wrong with her. From England she went to Bordighera, on the Italian Riviera, and after staying at Florence and Venice she returned to Friedrichshof in May 1899.

Soon afterwards she told her Lord Chamberlain, the faithful Baron Reischach, in confidence. He could not believe her at first as she still looked so healthy, 'sunburned and robust',[35] and when he realized she was telling the truth he broke down and wept. She assured him that she felt she would be able to resist the illness for another ten years, and that by the time she was seventy she would be ready to enter eternal rest.

From this time onwards her health began to deteriorate, and she was too ill to go to England for Queen Victoria's eightieth birthday celebrations on 24 May. As her sufferings steadily increased, the doctors advised her to go abroad to a warmer climate. She chose her beloved Italy, but by the time she reached Trento the pain was so severe that she could get up and down the hotel stairs only with difficulty. It hurt her to lie down at night, and when she tried to sit up in a chair; walking was easier. Professor Renvers wanted her to be out of doors and have as much sun and fresh air as possible. By

December her doctors realized that the persistent denial that she was suffering from anything worse than lumbago was beginning to sound hollow, and they thought it was essential that her family should be warned that the problem was more serious. She was also experiencing acute discomfort, it was announced, from neuralgia in the region of the spine and hips.

Returning to Germany in spring 1900 and temporarily improving, she celebrated her mother's eighty-first birthday by inviting all her children, their spouses and several of their small children to Friedrichshof for luncheon. A few group photographs were taken to mark the occasion and to be sent to England. Vicky appeared in the centre of them all, a small white-haired figure clad in black, dwarfed by the imposing figures of her eldest son and Moretta, the tallest of her daughters.

In July she was horrified to hear that her brother Affie, who had succeeded their uncle Ernest as Duke of Saxe-Coburg Gotha in 1893, had cancer of the throat, and a few days later she was told of his death. It was a severe shock to mother and daughter, especially as by this time Queen Victoria's former remarkably good health was beginning to give cause for concern. By the autumn Vicky was rarely free from pain, which frequent morphia injections, sometimes as frequently as every two hours throughout the night, did not always alleviate. 'Never have the spasms been so frightfully violent as these last days,' she wrote to Sophie. 'If somebody had put me out of my misery I should have felt intensely thankful.' Sleep was almost impossible, with frequent pain, 'too violent, like ever so many razors driven into my back.' By the time of her sixtieth birthday in November, it was clear that this would be her last. Her hands were so swollen that she had to dictate most of her letters to her daughters, who took turns to come to Friedrichshof and help look after her, while her legs were 'shrunken and fallen away to nothing, a mere skeleton.'[36]

Her brothers and sisters felt she might not outlive her mother, but it was not to be the case. On 22 January 1901 Queen Victoria died at Osborne. Overwhelmed with grief when Mossy broke the news to her, Vicky was too helpless to leave Friedrichshof, let alone travel to England for the funeral. Kaiser Wilhelm had joined the family at his grandmother's deathbed, helped to support her with his good right arm as she passed away, and stayed in England for the funeral. On returning to Germany he came to see his mother for the first time in three months, and the family felt his solicitude for his 'unparalleled grandmama' contrasted with the less than eager devotion he showed his dying mother. But he was deeply moved by her sufferings, reporting to his uncle Bertie, now King Edward VII, that she was in such a terrible state of suffering 'that one really sometimes is at a loss as to think whether she could not be spared the worst.'[37]

A week later she had the consolation of seeing Bertie again. The court was still in mourning, and the King was anxious to emphasize that he was paying a private visit to see his favourite sister for what he knew would surely be the last time. Among the entourage was his physician-in-ordinary, Sir Francis Laking, whom the King hoped might be able to ease Vicky's sufferings by persuading the German doctors to give her larger doses of morphia, but they viewed his presence with hostility. The previous autumn, Queen Victoria had begged the Kaiser to receive Laking, but he refused, on the grounds that he was not going to 'have a repetition of the confounded Mackenzie business, as public feeling would be seriously affected here.'[38] Cheered by his visit, Vicky ventured into the fresh air for the first time for several weeks, as her attendants wrapped her in shawls and rugs and wheeled her in her bath-chair along sheltered paths in the castle park while she and her daughters talked to him.

One evening Sir Frederick Ponsonby was asked to go and see Vicky in her sitting room, and she asked him to take her letters back to England; nobody, least of all the Emperor, must know where they were. She would have them sent to his room at 1 a.m. that night. When the appointed hour came, Ponsonby was aghast to find that she had not meant a small packet of letters which could easily be slipped into a case, but instead two enormous trunks wrapped in oilcloth and firmly fastened with cord, brought by four stablemen who were evidently unaware of their cargo's contents. Marking them 'China with care' and 'Books with care', he had them placed in the passage with his luggage later that morning, and they were safely returned to Windsor.

Numerous relations and friends came to see her during the last few months. Henry, Irene and their three children came in the spring, though the baby screamed and cried loudly every time he saw his invalid grandmother. Queen Alexandra she found 'so kind and dear and gentle and quite touching in her goodness to me, and admirable in the way she fills her new position, with such true tact and good sense.'[39] Special family occasions were always remembered, and on her sister Louise's birthday in March Vicky pencilled a short letter in her own hand expressing 'every manner of *good wish*. . . . What *I* wish for you most ardently is that you may ever be spared sufferings such as mine – the untold misery of a long lingering illness, bearing only the name of Life – but cutting one off from all and everything!'[40]

She lingered throughout the spring and early summer months. In May her old friends the Bishop of Ripon and his wife came to visit her, and found her lying on a couch in the garden. They were impressed by her resemblance to her mother, and by the practical interest she still took in everything concerning her home. The face of the clock tower needed repainting, and she asked for slips of paper with different shades of blue to be held up against it so she could choose the one she liked best. She pointed out the beauty of the trees most recently planted, telling them sadly that she felt like Moses on Pisgah, 'looking at the land of promise which I must not enter.'[41]

Two months later the Kaiser noted she was still taking an interest 'in everything that is going on in the world, politics as well as literature & art', and in the furnishing of some of her rooms at Friedrichshof. Nevertheless she was in frightful pain for much of the time, except when allowed relief through injections of morphia which were eventually given in larger doses. Sentries on duty outside Friedrichshof asked to be moved further away, so they could not hear her screams of agony. After her last visit, Beatrice sent a harrowing description of her sister's plight to Lady Mallet; 'every feature and every limb distorted and that charming countenance quite unrecognizable, her mouth drawn up, her teeth project, her nostrils are dilated by her terrible struggle for breath which makes her nose bleed constantly and the whole face yellow.'[42] It was difficult to understand what she said, but she enjoyed being read aloud to much of the day. She was unable to eat properly, and the doctors expected her to get weaker for lack of food. Despite this the Kaiser reported optimistically to King Edward VII in July that 'the vital organs' were not yet attacked by the disease, 'so that there is nothing to inspire any momentary anxiety; if things go on like this at present the doctors think that it may go on for months even into the winter possibly.'[43]

Mercifully for her this verdict was soon proved wrong. On 4 August an official bulletin announced that her strength was 'fading fast', and the rest of her children were summoned. The Kaiser had been cruising on his yacht in the North Sea when he was summoned back by telegram. Dona met him at Kiel, and he scolded her in front of his entourage for not having remained at his mother's bedside, though Vicky had personally not wanted her daughter-in-law to stay. Henry, Ditta, Moretta, Sophie, and Mossy, who had all known for weeks that release from her sufferings could come to their mother at any time, had been there a while, and their eldest brother joined the vigil.

Canon T. Teignmouth-Shore, a long-standing friend of the British royal family, was visiting Germany at the time, and next morning a telegram from the Emperor invited him to Friedrichshof. On arrival he was shown up to her bedroom on the first floor, where the family were gathered around her in reverential silence. He knelt down to join them in prayers for the Visitation of the Sick, and they could see the lips of the semi-conscious Empress moving faintly as she tried to join in the Lord's Prayer. Withdrawing respectfully afterwards he was shown into the library, to wait until called again. Taking a book from the shelves at random to pass the time, which happened to be Lady Bloomfield's *Diary*, by coincidence he opened it to find a glowing account of the Princess Royal in early youth just before her marriage, some forty years earlier, speaking of 'the bright, intelligent face, flushed with the joy of life.' 'What a contrast to that face upstairs, so aged with suffering, on which I had looked a few moments before,' he noted. 'The expression on that face, so awfully and sadly changed from what it was even in recent years, was sanctified with the sacrament of pain and sorrow.'[44]

By now she had slipped into unconsciousness. Maybe she was dreaming of happier times, of her first meeting with Fritz just half a century before; of their ride along Deeside that never-to-be-forgotten September day more than forty years earlier, when he had handed her a sprig of heather and asked her to be his wife; of the January morning when they had knelt together at the altar and been united as one. If so, she was happy in the knowledge that soon they would be reunited for ever.

Towards 6 p.m. the Canon was called back to say a few more prayers, as the end was near. Ironically Sophie and Mossy, who had rarely left their mother's side, had just gone out to the garden for a breath of fresh air. While they were there, a white butterfly – the symbol of the resurrection – flew in through the window, fluttered around over her, and out again, just as she breathed her last.

Earlier that summer she had left instructions with her nearest surviving sister Helena for her wishes after death. There was to be no post mortem, no embalming, no photographs, no lying in state, and her body was to be covered with the Prussian royal standard. Her coffin was to be closed at once, taken to the town church at Kronberg and kept there until the funeral after which she was to be buried in the Friedenskirche mausoleum beside her husband and their two youngest sons. The court chaplain was to say a short prayer at the ceremony but not to make a speech.

Unlike Fritz's funeral, hers was conducted with dignity, taking place at Potsdam on 13 August. Whether Vicky would have wanted her son to take the opportunity to make a great military display out of her death and burial was debatable, but perhaps he was making amends for his callous behaviour by burying her like an Empress. He and Bertie were united in their grief for the sorely-tried mother and sister, and for once nobody could doubt the depth of his feeling as he arranged the wreath on her coffin at the altar and fell to his knees, placing his face in the folds of the pall as he silently broke down.

History is full of 'what ifs'. It is impossible to resist asking what might have happened if a fit and well Kaiser Friedrich III had ascended the throne in March 1888? Even Emil Ludwig, one of whose main claims to fame was publishing a biography of ex-Kaiser Wilhelm II in 1926 with a highly damaging portrait of his mother, which led directly to Sir Frederick Ponsonby setting the record straight with *Letters of the Empress Frederick* two years later, allowed himself the luxury of such speculation. A few years later he wrote an essay, 'If the Emperor Frederick had not had Cancer', published in *If it Had Happened Otherwise*, edited by J.C. Squire. In it he took as his fantasy the scenario that Frederick had recovered from what proved to be a minor throat ailment in 1887, succeeded his father and reigned until August 1914, having maintained peace with Russia, held a formal reconciliation with France, and introduced parliamentary government into Germany.

All this was not only feasible, but very likely. By the mid-1880s both Fritz and Vicky were despondent and embittered to some extent by the years of waiting, by the direction of political affairs under Bismarck, and by the constant humiliations inflicted on them with the preferential treatment shown by the military and political establishment, to say nothing of Kaiser Wilhelm I, to their eldest son. Nevertheless it would not have been beyond them and their political allies – the hypothetical 'Gladstone ministry' of Richter, Virchow, Bamberger, and Miquel – to oversee a turning of the tide. It is unarguable that their respect for Bismarck and all that he had done for Germany, despite their disapproval of his methods, would have precluded any sudden break. It is equally beyond doubt that in Bismarck they would have had an ally if necessary against their son Wilhelm and the pernicious influence of Waldersee and his ilk. Bismarck himself observed that, had he lived longer, the 'Extreme Liberals would have been greatly surprised and disillusioned by the energy and indignation with which the Emperor and King would have met their plan of a "truly constitutional government", i.e. the diminution of his prerogative rights and the conduct of his

government under the tutelage of Liberalism.'[45] As his writings from
the 1860s showed, in his adherence to the power of the crown – a
modified variation on the divine right of Kings, perhaps – Fritz was
less radical than his wife and father-in-law. Nevertheless a more
liberal climate would certainly have prevailed in Germany.

One of Wilhelm II's more sympathetic modern biographers has
suggested that forces at work throughout Germany were strong
enough to have frustrated even a healthy Friedrich, and doubts that
he had either the inclination or stamina to dominate.[46] Fritz was
certainly not one of nature's 'dominators', but he did not need to be
in order to appoint the men who would have presided over a change
in political direction. Kaiser Wilhelm I did not need to dominate
Prussia in 1862; all he had to do, as events proved, was appoint one
particular man.

Wilhelm certainly did have the inclination and stamina; he was
clearly intent on imposing his personality on the German Empire
from the moment he ascended the throne. The results, as his mother
and uncle had foreseen, were bound to lead to disaster. Vicky's
predictions of doom and gloom to Frau von Stockmar and Donna
Laura Minghetti* about Germany's future and that of her son were
realized all too soon. Four or five years after her death King Edward
VII, who saw clearly that Kaiser Wilhelm was at the mercy of his
hawks and sycophants, noted that it would be 'not by his will that
he will unleash a war, but by his weakness.'[47] About two or three
weeks before his death in 1910, he remarked to a friend in Paris that
he did not have long to live. 'And then my nephew will make war.'[48]

When Wilhelm II is taken out of the picture and Friedrich III put
in his place, the European scene is transformed. There would almost
certainly have been a reconciliation between Germany and France;
fragile Russo-German relations, notwithstanding the Battenberg
crisis, would have healed and been placed on a firmer footing;
and the naval arms race, presided over by Admiral Tirpitz and
Wilhelm II with such devastating effect, would surely never have
happened.

* See above, p. 249.

A few weeks after her husband's death, Vicky had written to Bamberger of her certainty that one day there would be a reaction among the German people. While they would still praise the national virtues such as the readiness to sacrifice, the capacity for work, and the heroic deeds of their army, they would 'revolt against the poisonous spirit which is now spreading so widely – against the confusion of ideals and the ignoble sense, against idol worshipping, against blindness and delusion which seems to prevent any un-prejudiced local judgment!' By then, she knew she would be resting in her grave and reunited in the world hereafter with her husband, 'and they will hardly know what we wanted, and how much we loved our fatherland for which we were permitted to do so little.'[49]

Notes

Abbreviations used: A – Albert, Prince Consort; E – Prince of Wales/King Edward VII; F – Prince Friedrich Wilhelm/Kaiser Friedrich III; LN – Lord Napier; QV – Queen Victoria; u/d – undated (letter); S – Princess Sophie; V – Princess/Empress Victoria/Empress Frederick; W – Prince/Kaiser Wilhelm II

Chapter One

1. Wilhelm II, *My Ancestors*, 129.
2. Bülow, I, 1897–1903, 17.
3. Tschudi, 63.
4. Radziwill, 34–5.
5. Roberts, 14.
6. Longford, *Victoria R.I.*, 153 (all Longford references are to this title unless noted otherwise).
7. Royal Archives, RA VIC/Y/37/4, Princess Feodora of Hohenlohe-Langenburg to QV, 19.11.1843.
8. Lyttelton, 310.
9. Victoria, *Letters 1837–1861*, II, 3, QV to King Leopold, 9.1.1844.
10. Lyttelton, 344–5.
11. Poschinger, 16.
12. ibid, 18.
13. ibid, 19.
14. Kollander, 3.
15. Simon, I, 34.
16. Albert, 136, A to King Leopold, 28.3.1848.
17. Kollander, 4.
18. Poschinger, 21, Gerlach diary, 3.5.1849.
19. Kollander, 5.
20. Poschinger, 28.
21. Kollander, 18.
22. Rodd, 38. Though the date of this passage is not quoted, most biographers have assumed that the description refers to a period of study prior to F's first visit to England in 1851.
23. Kollander, 6.
24. Radziwill, 46.
25. Victoria, *Letters 1837–1861*, II, 106, QV to King Leopold, 29.9.1846.
26. Royal Archives, RA VIC/QVJ/29 April 1851.
27. Bennett, *King Without a Crown*, 207.
28. Radziwill, 47.
29. Royal Archives, RA VIC/QVJ/8 May 1851.
30. Victoria, *Further Letters*, 25, QV to Princess Augusta, 19.6.1851.
31. Poschinger, 39–40.
32. Victoria, *Further Letters*, 39, QV to Princess Augusta, 28.3.1853.
33. Longford, 258–9.
34. Rowell, 82, QV journal, 10.2.1852.
35. ibid, 82–3, QV journal, 11,13.1.53.
36. Victoria, *Further Letters*, 44, u/d, probably April 1854, QV to Princess Augusta.
37. Woodham-Smith, 364–5.
38. Simon, I, 69.
39. Martin, III, 240.
40. Epton, 62.

Chapter Two

1. Barkeley, 30, quoting Helmuth von Moltke, *Briefe an seine Braut und Frau* (1894).
2. Victoria, *Letters 1837–1861*, III, 147, QV to King Leopold, 22.9.1855.
3. Albert, 236, A to Baron Stockmar, 20.9.1855.
4. Longford, 260.
5. Victoria, *Leaves...Highlands*, 154, 29.9.1855.
6. Corti, *English Empress*, 24, A to F, 15.10.1855 (all Corti references are to this title unless noted otherwise).
7. Royal Archives, RA I/29/86, F to A, 22.10.1855.
8. *The Times*, 3.10.1855.
9. Corti, 24, A to F, 1.11.1855.
10. Victoria, *Further Letters*, 58–9, QV to Princess Augusta, 22.10.55.
11. Longford, 260, QV journal, 21.11.1855.
12. Rodd, 46–47.
13. Royal Archives, RA I/29/86, F to A, 22.10.1855.
14. as 13.
15. Poschinger, 67.
16. Bennett, *Vicky*, 47 (all Bennett references are to this title unless noted otherwise).
17. *Empress Frederick: a Memoir*, 41–42, Otto von Bismarck to Leopold von Gerlach, 8.4.1856.
18. Lowe, 83.
19. Victoria, *Letters 1837–1861*, III, 182, Cobden to 'a friend', 20.3.1856.
20. Corti, 29.
21. Bloomfield, II, 63.
22. Longford, 262, QV journal, 7.1.1856.
23. Poschinger, 79.
24. Ponsonby, M., 241.
25. Poschinger, 79.
26. *Illustrated Times*, 4.7.1857.
27. Bennett, *King Without a Crown*, 300, A to F, 24.2.1857.
28. Victoria, *Letters 1837–1861*, III 253, QV to Earl of Clarendon, 25.10.1857.
29. Corti 36, F to V, 3.12.1857.
30. Paget, 62.
31. *Empress Frederick: a Memoir*, 68.
32. Greville, II, 583, 26.1.1858.
33. Woodham-Smith, 390, Duchess of Kent journal, 3.2.1858.
34. Albert, 288 A to V, 3.2,1858.
35. Radziwill, 55–6.
36. Albert, 290, A to V, 11.2.1858.
37. Victoria, *Dearest Child*, 205, V to QV, 4.8.1859.
38. ibid, 60, V to QV, 26.2.1858.
39. Martin, IV, 176, A to V, 17.2.1858.
40. Pakula, 106, QV to V, 6.6.1858.
41. Albert, 296, A to Princess Augusta, 9.3.1858.
42. Martin, IV, 242, A to Baron Stockmar, 5.6.1858.
43. Victoria, *Dearest Child*, 108, QV to V, 26.5.1858.
44. Corti, 47, V to F, 16.7.1858.
45. Martin, IV, 287.
46. Poschinger, 115.
47. Pakula, 119, V to PA, 6.11.1858.
48. Victoria, *Dearest Child*, 136, QV to V, 4.10.1858.
49. Pakula, 107, V to QV, 9.10.1858.
50. Victoria, *Dearest Child*, 137, V to QV, 9.10.1858.
51. Greville, II, 584, Baron Stockmar to Lord Clarendon, 12.12.1858.
52. Victoria, *Dearest Child*, QV to V, 15.6.1858.

Chapter Three

1. Bennett, 84.
2. Kohut, 32.
3. Sinclair, 45, Dr Clark to QV, 31.1.1859.

4. Pakula, 127, V to QV, 6.3.1859.
5. ibid, 127, V to QV, 11.12.1875.
6. Victoria, *Letters . . . Empress Frederick* 20, V to QV, 28.2.1859.
7. Victoria, *Dearest Child*, 190, V to QV, 30.4.1859.
8. Röhl, *Young Wilhelm*, V to F, 25.5.1859.
9. Corti 55, V to F, 26.5.1859.
10. Bennett, 92.
11. McClintock, 35, Elphinstone diary, 26.11.1859.
12. Victoria, *Letters . . . Empress Frederick*, 29, V to QV, 2.1.1861.
13. Corti, 65, A to Ernest Stockmar, 16.1.1861
14. ibid, 66, A to V, 17.1.1861.
15. Kollander, 15, A to F, 1.5.1861.
16. Victoria, *Dearest Child*, 357, 15.11.1861.
17. Röhl, *Young Wilhelm*, 61, V to F, 2.9.1861.
18. Victoria, *Letters 1837–1861*, III, 457, V to QV, 19.10.1861.
19. Wiegler, 203.
20. Röhl, *Young Wilhelm*, 101, 29/30/31.10, 10.11.1861.
21. Roberts, 125, A to V, probably 20.11.1861.
22. Victoria, *Dearest Child*, 375, V to QV, 16.12.1861.
23. Pakula, 160, QV to V, 15.1.1862.
24. Ponsonby, M., 242.
25. Paget, 64–5.
26. Bülow, I, 1897–1903, 529.
27. Corti, 82, V to F, 26.2.1862.
28. ibid, 85, V to F, 15.3.1862.
29. ibid, 86, F to V, 18.3.1862.
30. ibid, 89–90, F to V, 15.7.1862.
31. *Empress Frederick: a Memoir*, 156, Queen Augusta to F, u/d, probably August 1862.
32. Pakula, 168, V to F, 20.9.1862.
33. Kollander, 33, V to F, 20.9.1862.
34. Taylor, A.J.P., 51.

Chapter Four

1. Corti, 95, F's diary, u/d.
2. Taylor, A.J.P., 56.
3. Lee, I, 147.
4. Kollander, 49–50.
5. ibid, 38, V to F, 1.6.1863.
6. Poschinger, 140.
7. ibid, 142.
8. Victoria, *Letters . . . Empress Frederick*, 41, V to QV, 8.6.1863.
9. ibid, 42, V to QV, 8.6.1863
10. *The Times*, 16.6.1863.
11. Sinclair, 81, QV to V, 13.6.1863.
12. Victoria, *Letters . . . Empress Frederick*, V to QV, 21.6.1863.
13. Victoria, *Dearest Mama*, 225, QV to V, 8.6.1863
14. Victoria, *Letters . . . Empress Frederick*, 46–7, F to Otto von Bismarck, 30.6.1863.
15. Victoria, *Dearest Mama*, 242–3, V to QV, 3.7.1863.
16. Kollander, 43, F to V, 3.9.1863.
17. Corti, 112, F to V, 3.9.1863.
18. Busch, III, 238.
19. Victoria, *Dearest Mama*, 243, V to QV, 3.7.1863.
20. Corti, 115.
21. ibid, 118.
22. Victoria, *Letters 1862–1885*, I, 117, QV to King Leopold, 19.11.1863.
23. Busch, II, 127.
24. Corti, 123, F diary, 9.2.1864.
25. Poschinger, 186, F to Max Duncker, u/d, c.22.2.1864.
26. Corti, 121, QV to V, 3.2.1864
27. Lee, I, 250, E to Mrs Bruce, 17.2.1864.
28. *The Times*, 6.5.1864.
29. Victoria, *Letters . . . Empress Frederick*, 53–4, V to QV, 13.4.1864.
30. Corti, 133, V to QV, 5.5.1864.
31. Pakula, 214, V to F, 31.3.1864.

32. Lee, I, 256, E to Lord Spencer, 7.11.1864.
33. Rodd, 63.
34. Taylor, L, 509.
35. Poschinger 201–2, 209, Gustav zu Putlitz to his wife 26/27.6, 7.7.1864.
36. *Empress Frederick: a Memoir*, 200.
37. Pakula, 221, V to QV, 1.8.1865.
38. Battiscombe, 76.
39. Longford, 350.
40. Corti, 144.

Chapter Five

1. Royal Archives, RA Z/18/32, V to QV, 9.3.1866.
2. Victoria, *Your Dear Letter*, 61, V to QV, 16.3.1866.
3. Poschinger, 240, F to EDC, 26.3.1866.
4. Victoria, *Letters 1862–1885*, I, 311, QV to F, 28.3.1866.
5. Victoria, *Letters . . . Empress Frederick*, 61, V to QV, 26.6.1866.
6. Kollander, 100, F diary, u/d.
7. ibid, 79.
8. Pakula, 239, V to QV, 23.7.1866.
9. Frederick III, *Diaries*, 48, 3.7.1866.
10. Poschinger, 279.
11. Taylor, L., 171.
12. Pakula, 245, V to QV, 3.11.1866.
13. Corti, 158, F to V, 13.11.1866.
14. Victoria, *Your Dear Letter*, 127, V to QV, 2.4.1867.
15. ibid, 129, V to QV, 20.4.1867.
16. Corti, 161 V to QV, 17.8.1867.
17. Röhl, *Young Wilhelm*, 97, V to F, 4.7.1868.
18. Poschinger, 309.
19. Röhl, *Purple Secret*, 123, V to F, 27/ 29.4.1868.
20. Royal Archives, RA Z/18/76, V to QV, 10.8.1866.
21. Reid, 261; Stevenson, 166.
22. Frederick III, *Diaries*, 195, 18.7.1870.

23. Victoria, *Letters . . . Empress Frederick*, 80, V to QV, 25.7.1870.
24. Corti, 171, V to QV, 1.8.70.
25. Victoria, *Letters . . . Empress Frederick*, 80, V to QV, 25.7.1870.
26. Poschinger, 321.
27. Pakula, 277, V to QV, 6.9.1870.
28. ibid, 277, QV to V, 26.8.1870.
29. ibid, 278, V to QV, 6.9.1870.
30. Victoria, *Letters . . . Empress Frederick*, 94, V to QV, 17.9.1870.
31. Lee, I, 304–5.
32. Friedrich III, *War diary*, 202–3, 28.11.1870.
33. ibid, 203, 28.11.1870.
34. ibid, 168, 24.10.1870.
35. ibid, 241, 31.12.1870.
36. ibid, 267, 17.1.1871.
37. Pakula, 287, F to V, 28.7.1872.
38. Röhl, *Young Wilhelm*, 174, V to F, 27.1.1871.
39. Friedrich III, *War diary*, 328–9, 7.3.1871.
40. Victoria, *Your Dear Letter*, 322, Lord Granville to QV, 2.3.1871.
41. Kollander, 99, V to F, 6.1.1871.

Chapter Six

1. Sinclair, 165, V to QV, 9.9.1871.
2. Pakula, 297, QV to V, 10.4.1872.
3. Röhl, *Young Wilhelm*, V to F, 8.11.1872.
4. Victoria, *Darling Child*, 157, V to QV, 15.10.1874.
5. Poschinger, 362.
6. Victoria, *Darling Child*, 248, V to QV, 14.4.1877.
7. Poschinger, 363.
8. Royal Archives RA Z/28/8, V to QV, 10.2.1874.
9. Radziwill, 127.
10. Ponsonby, A., 251, QV to Sir Henry Ponsonby, 18.11.1874.
11. Hough, 56, QV to Princess Victoria of Hesse, 21.9.1883.
12. Kohut, 43.

13. Victoria of Prussia, *Memoirs*, 4.
14. Bigelow, 46.
15. Victoria, *Letters . . . Empress Frederick*, 123, QV to V 11.2.1871.
16. ibid, 138, V to QV, 5.6.1875.
17. Poschinger, 375–6, F to Prince Carol of Roumania, Oct. 1875.
18. Wilhelm II, *My Early Life*, 5.
19. Röhl, *Young Wilhelm*, 267, V to W, 16.7.1878.
20. Longford, 386.
21. Radziwill, 144.
22. Victoria, Darling Child, 215, V to QV, 20.6.1876.
23. Napier Letters, 16/85, V to LN, 30.12.1876.
24. Lee, I, 432.
25. Pakula, 351, V to QV, 4.6.1878.
26. McClintock, 192.
27. *The Times*, 16.8.1878.
28. Radziwill, 150.
29. ibid, 153.
30. Corti, 207.
31. Radziwill, 96–7.
32. Röhl, *Young Wilhelm*, 388, W to George II, Duke of Saxe-Meiningen, 30.3.1879.
33. Napier Letters, 16/93, V to LN, 14.4.1879.
34. Poschinger, 417.
35. Kollander, 121, F to V, 27.5.1879.
36. Röhl, *Young Wilhelm*, 552, F to V, 5.12.1879.
37. *Empress Frederick: a Memoir*, 279.
38. Röhl, *Young Wilhelm*, 370, V to F, 18.9.1879.
39. Victoria, *Beloved Mama*, 53, V to QV, 11.9.1879.
40. Röhl, *Young Wilhelm*, 375, V to F, 12.9.1879.
41. ibid, 376, 6/7.11.1879.
42. Victoria, *Beloved Mama*, 79, V to QV, 24.5.1880.
43. Cecil, 45, V to Countess Dönhoff, 24.12.1880.

Chapter Seven

1. Sinclair, 184 ,V to QV, 13.2.1880.
2. Victoria, *Letters . . . Empress Frederick*, 179, V to QV, 26.3.1880.
3. Victoria, *Beloved Mama*, 96, V to QV, 28.8.1881.
4. Victoria, *Letters. . . Empress Frederick*, 183, V to QV, 27.2.1881.
5. Sinclair, 186, V to QV, 28.3.1881.
6. Victoria, *Beloved Mama*, 115, V to QV, 18.1.1882.
7. ibid, 131, QV to V, 3.1.1883.
8. Victoria, *Letters . . .Empress Frederick*, 195, V to Lady Ponsonby, 17.10.1884.
9. Röhl, *Young Wilhelm*, 383, Princess Charlotte to Hermann Hohenlohe-Langenburg, 15.3.1882.
10. Corti, 219–20, F to V, 12.11.1883; Röhl, *Young Wilhelm*, 393, F to V, 12.11.1883.
11. Röhl, *Young Wilhelm*, 393, V to F, 14.11.1883.
12. Friedrich III, *Diaries*, 283, 25.11.1883.
13. ibid, 305, 30.11.1883.
14. ibid, 323, 4.12.1883.
15. Hollyday, 133.
16. Kollander, 139–40, Heinrich Geffcken to Baron Roggenbach, 23.3.1883.
17. Corti, 226, QV to V, 10.1.1885.
18. Epton, 166.
19. Röhl, *Young Wilhelm*, 524–5, V to F, 25.8.1883.
20. ibid, 525, V to F, 23.9.1885.
21. ibid, 540, Herbert von Bismarck to Otto von Bismarck, 23.9.1886.
22. Corti, 219, F to V, 26.8.1883.
23. Hough, 52, QV to Princess Victoria of Hesse, 30.8.1883.
24. Victoria of Prussia, *Memoirs*, 67.
25. Röhl, *Young Wilhelm*, 523, Princess Charlotte to V, 9.1.1885.

26. Corti, 231, V to F, 3.9.1886.
27. Napier Letters, 16/95, V to LN, 26.12.1886.
28. Cecil, 72, V to Countess Dönhoff, 21.10.1885.
29. Rich & Fisher, II, 113, 14.4.1884.
30. Kollander, 148, V to F, 7.11.1884.
31. Rich & Fisher, II, 195, 6.5.1885.
32. ibid, 99, 9.3.1884.
33. ibid, 47, 6.1.1884.
34. ibid, 155, 6.6.1884.
35. Röhl, *Young Wilhelm*, 565, Waldersee diary, 9.4.1886.
36. Radziwill, 178.
37. Bennett, 228.
38. Kollander, 151–2, V to Friedberg, 1.7.1885.
39. Busch, II, 215–6.
40. Röhl, *Young Wilhelm*, 550, F to V, 6.5.1886.
41. Ludwig, 21.
42. Salisbury Papers, Box F14, V to QV, 11.10.1886.
43. Röhl, *Young Wilhelm*, 625, F to V 14.11.1886.
44. Salisbury Papers, Box F14, F to QV, 22.1.1887.
45. Victoria, *Beloved and Darling Child*, 44, QV to V, 11.2.1887.
46. Victoria, *Letters . . . Empress Frederick*, 209, V to QV, 7.2.1887.
47. ibid, 210–1, V to QV, 17.3.1887.
48. Radziwill, 180.

Chapter Eight

1. Victoria, *Letters . . .Empress Frederick*, 266, V to Lady Ponsonby, 8.12.1887.
2. ibid, 226, V to QV, 17.5.1887.
3. Pakula, 442, V to QV, 22.4.1887.
4. Röhl, *Young Wilhelm*, 651, V to QV, 3.6.1887.
5. Corti, 242, QV to V, 20.5.1887.
6. Stevenson, 282.
7. Mackenzie, 27.
8. Corti, 243, Bismarck to Sir Edward Malet, 24.5.1887.
9. Röhl, *Young Wilhelm*, 679, memorandum by Eulenburg, 8/9.6.1887.
10. Victoria, *Letters . . . Empress Frederick*, 237, V to QV, 2.6.1887.
11. ibid, 239, V to QV, 3.6.1887.
12. Napier Letters, 16/97, Seckendorff to LN, 27.6.1887.
13. Marie, I, 36–38.
14. Corti, 246, F to QV, 25.8.1887.
15. Victoria, *Letters 1886–1901*, I, 350, QV journal, 7.9.1887.
16. Victoria, *Letters . . . Empress Frederick*, 242, V to QV, 30.8.1887.
17. Röhl, *Young Wilhelm*, 666.
18. Radziwill, 189.
19. Mackenzie, 63.
20. Victoria, *Letters . . . Empress Frederick*, 260, V to QV, 18.11.1887.
21. ibid, 260–1, V to QV, 18.11.1887.
22. Mackenzie, 63.
23. Ludwig, 46.
24. Barkeley, 213, quoting Balhausen, *Bismarck Erinnerungen* (1921).
25. Röhl, *Young Wilhelm*, 702, Herbert Bismarck to Count Rantzau, 11.11.1887.
26. Balfour, 111.
27. Victoria, *Letters . . . Empress Frederick*, 256–7, V to QV, 15.11.1887.
28. Ponsonby, F., 114–5.
29. Stevenson, 166–7.
30. Cecil, 94.
31. Röhl, *Young Wilhelm*, 703–5.
32. ibid, 741, Roggenbach to Stosch, 8.1.1888.
33. Ponsonby, M., 261, 265, Lady Ponsonby to Sir Henry Ponsonby, 3.12.1887.
34. Rich & Fisher, III, 231,

Radolinski to Holstein, 23.11.1887.
35. Röhl, *Young Wilhelm*, 700–1, F to QV, 29.12.1887.
36. Corti, 257, F to Hinzpeter, 4.12.1887.
37. Röhl, *Young Wilhelm*, 700, F to W, 29.12.1887.
38. ibid, 701.
39. ibid, 777, Prince Henry to W, 2.2.1888.
40. ibid, 779, Prince Henry to W, 9.2.1888.
41. Corti, 262, Mackenzie to Reid, 16.2.1888.
42. Victoria, *Letters . . . Empress Frederick*, 277, V to QV, 20.2.1888.
43. ibid, 277, V to QV, 26.2.1888.
44. Röhl, *Young Wilhelm*, 785, F to W, 2.3.1888.
45. Victoria, *Letters . . . Empress Frederick*, 279, V to QV, 6.3.88.
46. Holstein Papers, III, 265, Radolinski to Holstein, 28.2.1888.
47. Ponsonby, M., 268, V to Lady Ponsonby, 7.3.1888.

Chapter Nine

1. Stevenson, 110.
2. Victoria, *Letters 1886–1901*, I, 390, F to QV, 9.3.1888.
3. Ludwig, 47.
4. Röhl, *Young Wilhelm*, 788–9, Waldersee diary, 11.3.1888.
5. Victoria, *Letters . . . Empress Frederick*, 287, V to QV, 9.3.1888.
6. Rodd, 194.
7. Wiegler, 447.
8. Röhl, *Young Wilhelm*, 817–8, Waldersee diary, 2.3.1888.
9. Victoria, *Letters . . . Empress Frederick*, 293, V to QV, 16.3.1888.
10. Napier Letters, 16/99, V to LN, 31.3.1888.

11. Mackenzie, 173–4.
12. Napier Letters, 16/98, Count Seckendorff to LN, 22.3.1888.
13. Corti, 270.
14. Rich & Fisher, II, 377, 15.5.1888.
15. Ludwig, 50.
16. Wilhelm II, *My Early Life*, 291–2.
17. Corti, 271–2, F to W, 3.4.1888.
18. Corti, *Alexander von Battenberg*, 267.
19. Corti, 271, QV to V, 21.3.1888.
20. Ludwig, 49.
21. Rich, I, 141.
22. Victoria of Prussia, *Memoirs*, 74.
23. Eyck E., 302–3.
24. Mackenzie, 148–9.
25. Ponsonby, A., 293–4.
26. Corti, *Alexander von Battenberg*, 278.
27. Victoria, *Letters . . . Empress Frederick*, 302, Edward Malet to Sir Henry Ponsonby, 24.4.1888.
28. Victoria, *Letters 1886–1901*, I, 404–5, QV journal, 23.4.1888.
29. Victoria, *Further Letters*, 268.
30. Victoria, *Beloved and Darling Child*, 71–2, QV to V, 21.5.1888.
31. Nichols, 252–3.
32. Corti, 290.
33. ibid, 293.
34. Wilhelm II, *My Early Life*, 290.
35. Poschinger, 450–3.
36. Rich & Fisher, II, 374, 13.5.1888.
37. Röhl, *Young Wilhelm*, 817, Waldersee diary, 9.6.1888.
38. Nowak, 21–23.
39. Victoria, *Letters . . . Empress Frederick*, 299, Colonel Swaine to E, 13.4.1888.
40. Barkeley, 249–50.
41. Victoria, *Letters . . . Empress Frederick*, 310–1, V to QV, 18/19.5.1888.
42. Ludwig, 50.
43. Corti, 279.
44. ibid, 296.
45. ibid, 279.

46. Victoria, *Letters . . . Empress Frederick*, 315, V to QV, 13.6.1888.
47. Corti, 297–8.
48. Victoria, *Letters 1886–1901*, I, 416, QV journal, 14.6.1888.
49. *The Times*, 16.6.1888.
50. Haweis, 175; Corti, 302.
51. Victoria, *Letters . . . Empress Frederick*, 315–6, V to QV, 15.6.1888.

Chapter Ten

1. Corti, 304, diary 15.6.1888.
2. Reid, 101.
3. Röhl, *Young Wilhelm*, 821, Waldersee diary, 16.6.1888.
4. Napier Letters, 16/100, V to LN, 11.8.1888.
5. Royal Archives, VIC/Z 43/7, V to QV, 24.9.1888.
6. Royal Archives, VIC/Z 43/11, V to QV, 29.9.1888.
7. Sinclair, 225, V to QV, 18.10.1888.
8. Pakula, 512, Louis, Grand Duke of Hesse to V, 13.10.1888.
9 Victoria, *Letters 1886–1901*, I, 443, QV to Lord Salisbury, 24.10.1888.
10. ibid, I, 441, QV to Lord Salisbury, 15.10.1888.
11. Napier Letters, 16/102, V to LN, 9.2.1889.
12. Ernle, 160.
13. Victoria, *Letters . . . Empress Frederick*, 316, V to QV, 15.6.1888.
14. ibid, 399, V to QV, 11.1.1890.
15. Victoria, *Beloved and Darling Child*, 107, V to QV, 10.3.1890.
16. Victoria, *Empress Frederick . . . Sophie*, 81, V to S, Feb/Mar 1891.
17. ibid, 137, V to S, 27.1.1893.
18. ibid, 168, V to S, Apr 1894.
19. ibid, 174, V to S, u/d.
20. *Empress Frederick: a Memoir*, 353.
21. Buchanan, 19.
22. *Empress Frederick: a Memoir*, 353.
23. Buchanan, 19.
24. Pakula, 563, V to QV, 12.4.1896.
25. Röhl, *Kaiser and his Court*, 23.
26. Corti, 343, V to Frau Stockmar, 10.5.1892.
27. Bülow, I, 1897–1903, 76.
28. Victoria, *Beloved and Darling Child*, 181–2, V to QV, 16.10.1895.
29. Ponsonby, F., 21.
30. Ponsonby, M., 321, Lady Ponsonby to Arthur Ponsonby, 12.2.1893.
31. Ponsonby, F., 51–2.
32. *Recollections of Three Kaisers*, 130–31.
33. Bunsen, 214.
34. Victoria, *Empress Frederick . . . Sophie*, 253, V to S, 23.6.1897.
35. Mallet, 156, 18.3.1899.
36. Victoria, *Empress Frederick . . . Sophie*, 336, 339, V to S, u/d.
37. Pakula, 592, W to E, 9.2.1901.
38. Reid, 196.
39. Victoria, *Empress Frederick . . . Sophie*, V to S, 345, u/d.
40. Longford, *Darling Loosy*, 264, V to Duchess of Argyll, 18.3.1901.
41. *Empress Frederick: a Memoir*, 370.
42. Epton, 225.
43. Van der Kiste, *Crowns in a Changing World*, 7, W to E, 24.7.1901.
44. Teignmouth-Shore, 307.
45. Poschinger, 450–51.
46. Balfour, 62–3.
47. Brook-Shepherd, 255, E to Marquis de Soveral, c.1905.
48. Leslie, 337.
49. Barkeley, 309, quoting Bamberger, *Bismarcks grosses Spiel* (1932).

Bibliography

All titles are published in London unless stated otherwise

I MANUSCRIPTS

Royal Archives. Letters from Princess Feodore of Hohenlohe-Langenburg, and Crown Princess Frederick William, later Empress Frederick, to Queen Victoria

Napier Letters. Letters from Crown Princess Frederick William, later Empress Frederick, and Count Götz von Seckendorff to Lord Napier of Magdala. India Office Library and Records, European Manuscripts, British Museum

Salisbury Papers. Steward's Diary; letters from Crown Prince and Princess Frederick William to the Marquess of Salisbury. Hatfield House

II BOOKS

Albert, Prince Consort. *Letters of the Prince Consort*, ed. Kurt Jagow, John Murray, 1938

Anon. *The Empress Frederick: a Memoir*, James Nisbet, 1913

—— *Recollections of Three Kaisers*, Herbert Jenkins, 1929

Aronson, Theo. *The Kaisers*, Cassell, 1971

Balfour, Michael. *The Kaiser and his Times: with an afterword*, Harmondsworth, Penguin, 1975

Barkeley, Richard. *The Empress Frederick: daughter of Queen Victoria*, Macmillan, 1956

Battiscombe, Georgina. *Queen Alexandra*, Constable, 1969

Bennett, Daphne. *King without a Crown: Albert, Prince Consort of England, 1819-1861*, Heinemann, 1977

—— *Vicky, Princess Royal of England and German Empress*, Collins Harvill, 1971

Bigelow, Poultney. *Prussian Memories 1864–1914*, Putnam, 1915

Bloomfield, Georgina, Baroness. *Reminiscences of Court and Diplomatic Life*, 2 vols, Kegan, Paul, Trench, 1883

Brook-Shepherd, Gordon. *Uncle of Europe: The Social and Diplomatic Life of Edward VII*, Collins, 1975

Buchanan, Meriel. *Queen Victoria's Relations*, Cassell, 1954

Bülow, Bernhard von. *Memoirs*, 4 vols, Putnam, 1931

Bunsen, Marie von. *The World I Used to Know, 1860–1912*, Harper, 1930

Busch, Moritz. *Bismarck: some Secret Pages of his History*, 3 vols, Macmillan, 1898

Cecil, Lamar. *Wilhelm II, Vol. I, Prince and Emperor, 1859–1900*, University of North Carolina, 1989

270

Corti, Egon Caesar Conte. *Alexander von Battenberg*, Cassell, 1954

—— *The English Empress: a study in the relations between Queen Victoria and her eldest daughter, Empress Frederick of Germany*, Cassell, 1957

Epton, Nina. *Victoria and her daughters*, Weidenfeld & Nicolson, 1971

Eyck, Erich. *Bismark and the German Empire*, Allen & Unwin, 1958

Eyck, Frank. *The Prince Consort: a Political Biography*, Chatto & Windus, 1959

Frederick III, Emperor. *Diaries of the Emperor Frederick during the Campaigns of 1866 and 1870–71 as well as his Journeys to the East and to Spain*, ed. Margaretha von Poschinger, Chapman & Hall, 1902

—— *War diary of the Emperor Frederick, 1870–71*, ed. A.R. Allinson, Stanley Paul, 1927

Greville, Charles C.F. *The Greville Diary, including passages hitherto withheld from publication*, ed. Philip Whitwell Wilson, 2 vols, Heinemann, 1927

Haweis, H.R. *Sir Morell Mackenzie, Physician and Operator*, W.H. Allen, 1893

Hollyday, Frederic B.M. *Bismarck's Rival: a Political Biography of General and Admiral Albrecht von Stosch*, Durham, N.C., Duke University Press, 1960

Hough, Richard, sel. *Advice to a Grand-daughter: Letters from Queen Victoria to Princess Victoria of Hesse*, Heinemann, 1975

Kohut, Thomas. *Wilhelm II and the Germans*, Oxford University Press, 1991

Kollander, Patricia. *Frederick III: Germany's liberal Emperor*, Westport, Connecticut, Greenwood, 1995

Leslie, Anita. *Edwardians in Love*, Hutchinson, 1972

Longford, Elizabeth. *Victoria R.I.*, Weidenfeld & Nicolson, 1964

— ed. *Darling Loosy: Letters to Princess Louise 1856–1939*, Weidenfeld & Nicolson, 1991

Lowe, Charles. *The Tale of a 'Times' Correspondent* (Berlin 1878–1891), Hutchinson, 1927

Ludwig, Emil. *Kaiser Wilhelm II*, Putnam, 1926

Lyttelton, Sarah. *The Correspondence of Sarah Spencer, Lady Lyttelton*, ed. The Hon. Mrs Hugh Wyndham, John Murray, 1912

Macdonell, Anne, Lady. *Reminiscences of Diplomatic Life*, A. & C. Black, 1913

Mackenzie, Sir Morell. *The fatal illness of Frederick the Noble*, Sampson Low, 1888

McClintock, Mary Howard. *The Queen thanks Sir Howard: The life of Major-General Sir Howard Elphinstone, VC, KCB, CMG*, John Murray, 1945

Magnus, Philip. *King Edward the Seventh*, John Murray, 1964

Mallet, Victor, ed. *Life with Queen Victoria: Marie Mallet's Letters from Court 1887–1901*, John Murray, 1968

Marie, Queen of Roumania. *The Story of my Life*, 3 vols. Cassell, 1934–5

Masur, Gerhard. *Imperial Germany*, Routledge & Kegan Paul, 1971

Nichols, J. Alden. *The Year of the Three Kaisers: Bismarck and the German Succession 1887–88*, Chicago, University of Illinois Press, 1987

Nowak, Karl Friedrich. *Kaiser and Chancellor: the Opening Years of the Reign of the Emperor William II*, Putnam, 1930

Packard, Jerrold. *Victoria's daughters*, Stroud, Sutton, 1999

Paget, Walburga, Lady. *Scenes and Memories*, Smith, Elder, 1912

Pakula, Hannah. *An uncommon woman: The Empress Frederick*, Weidenfeld & Nicolson, 1996

Ponsonby, Arthur. *Henry Ponsonby, Queen Victoria's Private Secretary: His Life from His Letters*, Macmillan, 1942

Ponsonby, Sir Frederick. *Recollections of Three Reigns*, Eyre & Spottiswoode, 1951

Ponsonby, Mary. *Mary Ponsonby: a Memoir, some Letters, and a Journal*, ed. Magdalen Ponsonby, John Murray, 1927

Poschinger, Margaretha von. *Life of the Emperor Frederick*, ed. Sidney Whitman, Harper, 1901

Prothero, Rowland, Lord Ernle. *Whippingham to Westminster: reminiscences of Lord Ernle*, John Murray, 1938

Radziwill, Princess Catherine. *The Empress Frederick*, Cassell, 1934

Reid, Michaela. *Ask Sir James: Sir James Reid, personal physician to Queen Victoria and physician-in-ordinary to three monarchs*, Hodder & Stoughton, 1987

Rich, Norman. *Friedrich von Holstein: Politics and Diplomacy in the Era of Bismarck and Wilhelm II*, 2 vols, Cambridge University Press, 1965

Rich, Norman and Fisher, M.H., ed. *The Holstein Papers: The Memoirs, Diaries and Correspondence of Friedrich von Holstein*, 4 vols, Cambridge University Press, 1955–63

Roberts, Dorothea. *Two Royal Lives: Gleanings from Berlin and from the Lives of Their Imperial Highnesses the Crown Prince and Princess of Germany*, T. Fisher Unwin, 1887

Rodd, James Rennell. *Frederick, Crown Prince and Emperor: a biographical sketch dedicated to his memory*, David Stott, 1888

Röhl, John C.G. *The Kaiser and his Court: Wilhelm II and the Government of Germany*, Cambridge University Press, 1994

—— *Young Wilhelm: the Kaiser's early life, 1859–1888*, Cambridge University Press, 1998

Röhl, John C.G., Warren, Martin, and Hunt, David. *Purple Secret: Genes, 'Madness' and the Royal Houses of Europe*, Bantam, 1998

Rowell, George. *Queen Victoria Goes to the Theatre*, Elek, 1978

Simon, Edouard. *The Emperor William and his Reign*, 2 vols, Remington, 1886

Sinclair, Andrew. *The other Victoria: the Princess Royal and the Great Game of Europe*, Weidenfeld & Nicolson, 1981

Stevenson, R. Scott. *Morell Mackenzie*, Heinemann, 1946

Taylor, A.J.P. *Bismarck, the Man and the Statesman*, Hamish Hamilton, 1955

Taylor, Lucy. *'Fritz' of Prussia: Germany's Second Emperor*, Nelson, 1891

Teignmouth-Shore, T. *Some Recollections*, Hutchinson, 1911

Tschudi, Clara. *Augusta, Empress of Germany*, Swan Sonnenschein, 1900

Tisdall, E.E.P. *She Made World Chaos: the Intimate Story of the Empress Frederick of Prussia*, Stanley Paul, 1940

Van der Kiste, John. *Crowns in a changing world: The British and European Monarchies 1901–36*, Stroud, Sutton, 1993, *Frederick III: German Emperor 1888*, Gloucester, Sutton, 1981

Bibliography

—— *Kaiser Wilhelm II: Germany's last Emperor*, Stroud, Sutton, 1999

Victoria, Princess of Prussia. *My Memoirs*, Eveleigh, Nash & Grayson, 1929

Victoria, Queen. *Dearest Child: letters between Queen Victoria and the Princess Royal, 1858–61*, ed. Roger Fulford, Evans Bros, 1964

—— *Dearest Mama: letters between Queen Victoria and the Crown Princess of Prussia, 1862–64*, ed. Roger Fulford, Evans Bros, 1968

—— *Your dear letter: private correspondence between Queen Victoria and the Crown Princess of Prussia, 1865–71*, ed. Roger Fulford, Evans Bros, 1971

—— *Darling Child: private correspondence between Queen Victoria and the Crown Princess of Prussia, 1871–78*, ed. Roger Fulford, Evans Bros, 1976

—— *Beloved Mama: private correspondence between Queen Victoria and the Crown Princess of Prussia, 1879–85*, ed. Roger Fulford, Evans Bros, 1981

—— *Beloved and Darling Child: last letters between Queen Victoria and her eldest daughter, 1886–1901*, ed. Agatha Ramm, Stroud, Sutton, 1990

—— *Further Letters of Queen Victoria, from the Archives of the House of Brandenburg-Prussia*, ed. Hector Bolitho, Thornton Butterworth, 1938

—— *The Letters of Queen Victoria: a Selection from Her Majesty's Correspondence between the Years 1837 and 1861*, ed. A.C. Benson and Viscount Esher, 3 vols, John Murray, 1907

—— *Leaves from the Journal of Our Life in the Highlands, from 1848 to 1861*. Smith, Elder, 1868

—— *The Letters of Queen Victoria, Second Series: a Selection from Her Majesty's Correspondence and Journal between the Years 1862 and 1885*, ed. George Earle Buckle, 3 vols, John Murray, 1926–8

—— *The Letters of Queen Victoria, Third Series: a Selection from Her Majesty's Correspondence and Journal between the Years 1886 and 1901*, ed. George Earle Buckle, 3 vols, John Murray, 1930–2

Victoria, Consort of Frederick III, German Emperor. *Letters of the Empress Frederick*, ed. Sir Frederick Ponsonby, Macmillan, 1928

—— *The Empress Frederick writes to Sophie, her Daughter, Crown Princess and later Queen of the Hellenes: Letters 1889–1901*, ed. Arthur Gould Lee, Faber, 1955

Wiegler, Paul. *William the First, his Life and Times*, ed. Constance Vesey, Allen & Unwin, 1929

Wilhelm II, Ex-Emperor. *My Ancestors*, Heinemann, 1929

—— *My Early Life*, Methuen, 1926

—— *My Memoirs, 1878–1918*, Cassell, 1922

Woodham-Smith, Cecil. *Queen Victoria, her Life and Times, Vol. 1, 1819–1861*, Hamish Hamilton, 1972

Index

Index

Index